THE BRANDER

Marken und ihre Macher
Creators of Brands

THE BRANDER

Marken und ihre Macher
Creators of Brands

René Allemann

Eden BOOKS

Marken vermitteln Werte, sie stiften Identität und schaffen Vertrauen. Doch ab wann ist eigentlich etwas – oder jemand – eine Marke? Und wie wird aus einer Idee, egal wie klein und absurd diese anfangs schien, ein fruchtbarer Boden für ein Unternehmen? Was zeichnet die Menschen aus, die diese Ideen umsetzen – die Unternehmer, die CEOs, Designer, Erfinder, die Treiber und Macher der Marken unserer Zeit?

Als Gründer der Agentur Branders faszinieren mich diese Fragen seit jeher und mit meinem Team setze ich mich täglich damit auseinander. In unserem Alltag geht es um Strategien, Inhalte, Design, um Kommunikation. Dabei gilt unser besonderes Interesse der emotionalen Ebene von Marken. In unserem Online-Magazin thebrander.com, das wir im März 2011 lanciert haben, geht es um diese Verbindung des fachlichen und des emotionalen Aspekts von Marken. Wir porträtieren Menschen, die mit viel Herzblut eine Marke kreiert haben und diese erfolgreich führen – oder gar selbst eine sind. Dabei gilt, wie in nahezu allen Bereichen des Lebens: Es gewinnt, wer die beste Geschichte erzählt, sei dies nun ein Mensch oder eine Marke. Denn es sind Geschichten, die uns Inhalte vermitteln, die uns berühren und unseren Horizont erweitern. Wir identifizieren uns mit den Figuren, die darin vorkommen. In Geschichten dürfen wir ein paar Zeilen lang in andere Identitäten schlüpfen, mit neuen Augen sehen und in fremde Welten tauchen. Und genau in dieser Form, in der Form von Geschichten verschiedener Markenmacher, möchten wir Ihnen unser Verständnis von Branding vermitteln. Denn das Thema begeistert uns, es macht uns neugierig und fordert uns heraus.

Im Rahmen unserer Arbeit begegneten wir vielen herausragenden Menschen, die uns mit ihrer Fantasie, ihrem Mut und ihrer Begeisterung inspirierten. 29 Geschichten über solche Markenmacher haben wir für dieses Buch zusammengetragen: eine Sammlung spannender Porträts, entstanden aus vielen persönlichen Begegnungen mit anregenden Kreativen, die Einblick hinter die Kulissen gewähren. The Brander ist nicht nur ein Buch, es ist ein Abbild des Schaffens, der Leidenschaften, der Ideen und der unzähligen realisierten Träume Einzelner.

René Allemann, CEO Branders Group

Brands convey values, establish identity and foster trust. Yet at what point does something – or someone – become a brand? And how can an idea, no matter how tiny and absurd it seemed at the outset, form a fruitful basis for an enterprise? What sets the individuals apart who put their ideas into action – the entrepreneurs, CEOs, designers, inventors, the drivers and makers of brands in our day?

As founder of the agency Branders, these questions have always held a great fascination for me; and, to a large extent, they form our daily routine at the agency. Our everyday business deals with strategies, content, design, with communication, and we place a special focus on the emotional level of a brand. In our online publication, thebrander.com, launched in March of 2011, we explore the connection between the professional and emotional aspects of a brand. We portray the people who have put their heart and soul into creating a successful brand – or who have become a brand themselves. And the maxim is, as with most things in life: the winner is the one who tells the best story, be this a person or a brand. Because the stories are what touch us and broaden our horizons. We identify with the characters that appear in them. Stories which, for a brief moment, allow us to take on a different identity, to see things with fresh eyes, and to immerse ourselves in unknown worlds. It is precisely in this form, in the form of stories about distinctive brand creators, that we want to convey our understanding of branding to you. Branding: a theme that fascinates us, makes us curious – and that challenges us.

In the course of our work, we have had the pleasure of meeting many exceptional brand creators who inspired us with their vision, their courage and their passion. For this publication, we have collected 29 stories of precisely such extraordinary brand creators. A collection of fascinating portraits resulting from numerous personal encounters with creative minds who generously gave us a glimpse behind the scenes. And so, The Brander is not simply another book. It is a reflection of the creative process, the passion, the ideas and the unlimited dreams of these individuals.

René Allemann, CEO Branders Group

01

Alex Monroe
Alex Monroe

Text **Olivia El Sayed** Photos **Reto Caduff**

love
love

Sein Name ist seine Marke. Und diese wird von Hunderten von Händlern und Shops weltweit vertrieben, ziert in regelmäßigen Abständen die Covers von »Harper's Bazaar« und »Vogue« und zählt Frauen wie Sienna Miller, Emma Watson oder Carey Mulligan zu ihren bekennenden Fans. Trotzdem – oder gerade deshalb – muss man ungeachtet der knapp zwanzig Millionen Google-Einträge zu seinem Namen relativ lange suchen, bis man über den Menschen Alex Monroe etwas Persönliches findet.

His name stands for his jewelry. Jewelry that is distributed globally by hundreds of large retailers and little shops, that regularly adorns the covers of "Harper's Bazaar" and "Vogue," and that counts the likes of Sienna Miller, Emma Watson or Carey Mulligan among its devoted fans. All the same – or maybe that's why – personal information about Alex Monroe is hard to come by, despite nearly twenty million hits on Google.

Seine Karriere ist beeindruckend. Seit nunmehr 25 Jahren geht Alex Monroe unentwegt dem Beruf des Schmuckdesigners nach. Er begann mit nichts und heute wird sein Schmuck auf der ganzen Welt verkauft und fehlt bei keiner wichtigen Fashion Show. Das Geschäft läuft sogar noch besser, seit man den Schmuck auch online bekommen kann. Und was ihn besonders macht: Alles wird nach wie vor in England handgefertigt. »Anfangs machte ich sogar alles selbst«, erinnert sich Alex und streicht sich über den ungeliebten Schnurrbart, den er sich nur für »Movember« und den damit verbundenen guten Zweck hat stehen lassen, wie er in einem Nebensatz hastig erklärt. »Heute fertige ich einfach jeweils das Original«, fährt er fort. Denn außer der Fertigung gibt es auch noch den Verkauf und die Logistik, um die es sich zu kümmern gilt. Das ginge alles auch anders, aber Alex ist ein Mann mit Prinzipien: »Klar, ich könnte auch in China produzieren, das ist billig und die Leute leisten hervorragende Arbeit«, sagt er. »Aber wenn eine Bestellung mal raus ist, kann man daran nicht mehr viel ändern.«

His career is impressive, to say the least: for almost 25 years, Alex Monroe has worked as a jewelry designer. He started with nothing, yet today his creations are sold all over the world and never miss a major fashion show. And business is even better now that his jewelry is available online. One of the signature elements of Monroe's jewelry is that every piece is handmade in the United Kingdom. "At first I did it all by myself. Now I just don't have the time to do all the manufacturing, but I did use to quite enjoy that," Alex recalls and pats his unloved moustache that – he's quick to explain – he is only sprouting for "Movember" to raise awareness and funds for prostate cancer. "Today I only make the original pieces," he continues. Understandably, as next to production, matters such as sales and the international distribution have to be dealt with as well. He could most likely find an easier way, but Monroe has his principles.

AND IF A PIECE BREAKS OR NEEDS TO BE ALTERED, THE CUSTOMER CAN BRING IT BACK AND WE'LL FIX IT. WE KNOW HOW TO DO IT – AFTER ALL WE MADE IT IN THE FIRST PLACE.

Deshalb zieht Monroe es vor, alles vor Ort zu produzieren. Zusätzlich zu seinem Atelier unweit der London Bridge gibt es in Kensington eine weitere Werkstatt, wo ungefähr zehn Mitarbeitende dem delikaten Handwerk nachgehen. »›Handmade in United Kingdom‹ ist schon etwas Spezielles«, fügt er an. »Es birgt den Vorteil, dass Kunden, inklusive der Männer, die einen Tag vor ihrem Hochzeitstag panisch und schweißgebadet vor unserem Laden stehen, direkt bei uns vorbeikommen können und wir die Möglichkeit haben, vor Ort auf ihre Wünsche einzugehen. Wenn etwas kaputt geht oder geändert werden soll, kann man es direkt bei uns reparieren lassen. Wir wissen ja, wie das geht, wir haben es schließlich gemacht.«

"Obviously I could manufacture in China, it's cheaper and really good quality. And if you sell it, you can earn good money," he says. "But, what you can't do is change things once the order is out." Which is why he prefers to produce everything within a stone's throw of his business address. His offices, not far from London Bridge, include a production site and there is another workshop in Kensington, where approximately 10 employees ply their fine handicraft. "In addition, handmade in the UK has a special ring to it," Monroe points out. "And a further advantage is that clients – including the occasional panic-stricken husband who shows up on our doorstep a day before his wedding anniversary – can come directly to the workshop and we cater to their wishes right there and then.

3

Alex Monroe
BEST OF BRITISH

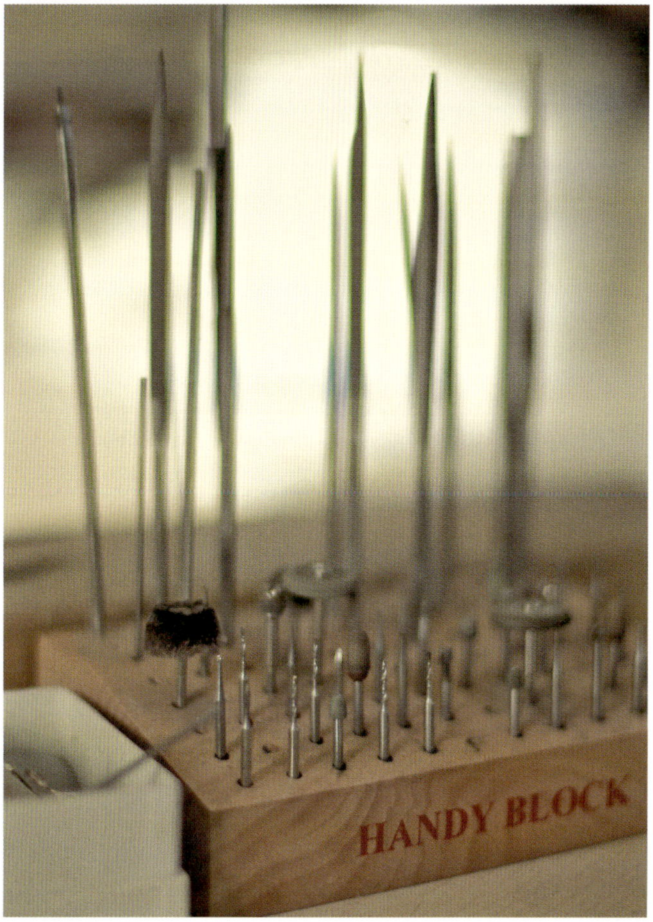
HANDY BLOCK

Alex Monroes Kollektionen sind dafür bekannt, von der Natur inspiriert zu sein. Mal ist es eine Biene, die ihm in seinem Cottage auf dem Land über den Weg summt, mal eine Feder oder aber das Fahrrad seiner kleinen Tochter, das ihn zu einer Kreation animiert. »Es gibt keinen Ort in der Ferne, der mich besonders inspiriert für meine Arbeit«, verrät Alex. »Ich käme nie auf die Idee, eine ägyptische Kollektion zu machen und dafür nach Kairo zu reisen. Ich reise nicht besonders gern. Flughäfen, Hotels und das Schlimmste: Air Condition. Hätte ich eine Woche frei, ich ginge lieber mit meiner Familie aufs Land. Es ist britisch, was ich tue, inspiriert von der Natur und der Landschaft hier, von Pflanzen und Blumen.« Bei aller Verspieltheit und Liebe zum Detail, die sein Schmuck aufweist, scheinen Alex' Gedanken dahinter meist eher rationaler Natur. Die Weiterentwicklung seiner Kollektionen beruht auf einer genauen Analyse des Vergangenen. »Ich schaue mir meine bisherigen Kollektionen an und überlege, was ich noch optimieren könnte«, sagt er. Vorbilder aus seiner Branche hat er keine. »Ich respektiere alle, die versuchen, damit ihr Geld zu verdienen, aber wirklich inspirierend finde ich wenige mit großem Namen.« Bevor ihm einer einfalle, glaube er eher, dass er auf der Suche nach Inspiration an einer Ausstellung von Studienabgängern fündig würde. »Sobald jemand mit einer Marke rauskommt, verwässert immer alles ein bisschen. Das ist vermutlich normal», sinniert er. »Aber ich finde es deshalb schwierig zu sagen, zu wem ich aufschaue. Ich lebe halt auch einfach ein wenig in meiner kleinen Welt und mache da meine kleinen Dinge.«

Auch was Alex' beruflichen Werdegang anbelangt, gab es keine wegweisenden Personen in seinem Umfeld. »Ich war nicht oft in der Schule, ich hatte weder mit Eltern noch mit Großeltern viel zu tun, ich war es einfach immer gewohnt, Dinge allein zu machen. Natürlich habe ich meinen Bruder und wir arbeiten beide hart, um etwas zu erreichen«, erzählt er. »Es war eher das Fehlen gewisser Leute, das mich inspiriert hat, meinen Weg zu gehen: Irgendwann bist du alt genug zu verstehen, dass es nur an dir liegt, was du mit deinem Leben anfängst.« Er nimmt einen großen Schluck Kaffee und schaut aus dem Fenster. »Manche Menschen sind einfach mit dem zufrieden, was sie haben.« Und er erzählt liebevoll von seinem Vater, der mit einem Bier und dem richtigen Buch in der Hand keinen einzigen Grund mehr gesehen habe, je seinen Sessel zu verlassen. Dass weder das eine noch das andere richtig oder falsch ist, steht für Alex fest: »Es geht doch nur darum, was jedem lieber ist.« Ähnlich pragmatisch beschreibt er seinen Erfolg: »Wenn man früh zu arbeiten beginnt, so wie ich, stellt sich eine gewisse Zielstrebigkeit automatisch ein.« Als Schüler war er sich dessen nicht bewusst, das Leben passierte einfach. »Wenn man weder besonders sportlich noch besonders schlau ist, landet man einfach in der Kunstklasse.« Nach der Schule wollte er eigentlich »etwas mit Mode« machen, wurde aber nirgends genommen, schlug sich daraufhin mit einem schlecht bezahlten Job herum und lebte auf dem Land. »Das war alles nicht das, was ich wollte – ich hasste es«, sagt er und rümpft dabei die Nase. Also zog er nach London und fing an, Schmuck zu machen. »Ich hatte immer schon geschickte Hände und interessierte mich für Mode, und da war das naheliegend.« Er schmunzelt. »Das war also alles kein ausgetüftelter Karriere-

Alex Monroe's collections are famous for being inspired by nature. Possibly a bee that buzzes by him at his cottage in the country or a beautiful feather found lying on the ground. Even his young daughter's bicycle has served as a model for a new design. "There is no place abroad that especially inspires me for my work," Alex reveals. "It would never occur to me to make, say, an Egyptian collection and travel to Cairo for ideas. What I make is essentially very British: it's inspired by our nature and countryside, by the plants and flowers that grow here." Despite all the playfulness and love for detail that his jewelry reveals, Alex's business strategy is consummately systematic. His collections evolve according to concise analyses of previous developments that leave no room for fantasies and daydreams. "I look at my existing collections and think about what can be improved and try to make that happen," he says. When asked if he has role models, he says he doesn't really look up to anyone in the trade. "I respect everyone who tries to earn a living in this business, but few of the big names are really inspirational." Rather than looking to a famous name for creative ideas, he would probably find visiting a degree show at an art college more inspiring. "Yet, quite often, when someone comes out with a brand, things get watered down a bit. But that's probably just the way it is," he muses. "I find it very hard to say who I really look up to. I'm kind of stuck in my own little world, doing my own little thing."

There were no role models in Alex's early career, either. Nor can he define the exact moment when he realized that jewelry making was what he wanted to do to earn his livelihood. "I wasn't at school very much, and I didn't do a lot with my parents or grandparents. I just used to do things on my own. Of course, I have my brother and we both work hard to get somewhere," he tells us. "Maybe it's the lack of people that actually influenced me to do things my way. At some point you realize you have a choice to either do something with your life, or just sit back." He takes a swallow of coffee and looks out the window before continuing, "Some people are quite happy doing nothing." And he affectionately talks about his father, who, with a bottle of beer in reaching distance and a book to read, saw no reason to get out of his armchair anymore. "I think you have a certain personality from the beginning, determining whether you choose to throw yourself into something or sit around and watch television all day." And that there's neither a right nor a wrong is a given for Alex: "In the end, everybody should just do as they like." Equally pragmatic, he goes on to describe his success: "If you have to work from an early age, as I did, you automatically develop ambition." As a student he was happy to go with the flow, life just happened. "If you were a bit rubbish at everything, you were no good at sports, you ended up in the art room. Certainly it was like that at my school." When he was finished he wanted to "do something with fashion," but wasn't accepted to any programs and instead ended up working in a badly paid job and living in the country. "That was not at all what I wanted – I hated it," he recalls, making a face. And so he went to London and started making jewelry. "I'd always been good with my hands and was interested in fashion, so this seemed quite an obvious move," he grins. "It wasn't a well-thought-out route. But I like it now." This is one of the reasons there are no plans for Alex Monroe, either man or brand, to change from the course they are on. Ideally, everything should stay as it is now because, as Monroe puts it, his work is

ICH DENKE, ES HÄNGT AB VON DER PERSÖNLICHKEIT EINES MENSCHEN, OB MAN GELEGENHEITEN BEIM SCHOPF PACKT ODER HALT LIEBER SITZEN BLEIBT UND FERNSEHEN GUCKT.

plan. Aber ich mag es, wie es jetzt ist.« Das ist auch ein Grund dafür, warum die Marke Alex Monroe nichts werden soll, was sie nicht schon ist. Seine Arbeit soll nicht Mittel zum Zweck sein, sondern der Zweck selbst. »Wenn ich etwas anderes machen wollen würde, dann würde ich das tun. Aber das hier und jetzt ist es, was ich machen, will: ein Schmuckdesigner sein. Ich finde die Herausforderung größer und wichtiger, etwas ein Leben lang gut zu machen anstatt nur für eine kurze Zeit erfolgreich zu sein, um dann zu expandieren und mehr Geld zu verdienen.« Spricht's und fährt sich schmunzelnd über den Schnurrbart.

—

not a vehicle to achieve a better life; this is his life. "If I wanted to do something else, I would just do something else. But this, here and now, is what I want to do: be a jewelry designer. In fact, I think it's more of a challenge to continue to do something well over a lifetime than to do something well for a short time and then expand to make more money." Speaks, smiles and gives his moustache another pat.

—

02

Bugaboo
Max Barenbrug & Aernout Dijkstra-Hellinga

Text **Olivia El Sayed** Photos **Cyrill Matter**

bugaboo

Schnee- und Geländeräder, Sonnendach mit Lüftungsfenstern, Mitfahrbrett und Stoßdämpfer – das klingt für Nichtfachkundige nach verspielten Elementen für einen Sportwagen. Doch Max Barenbrug, Mitbegründer und ehemaliger Design Director von Bugaboo, entwickelt all diese Sperenzchen mit seinem Team nicht etwa für große Autobegeisterte, sondern für die kleinsten Insassen. Die Marke Bugaboo hat sich als Rolls-Royce unter den Kinderwagen etabliert.

All-terrain wheels, breezy sun canopies, wheeled boards and adjustable suspension – to the uninitiated, this may sound like a catalog of sports car accessories. Yet, fact is that Max Barenbrug, founder and former Design Director of Bugaboo, and his team did not develop these nifty extras with a car in mind. Instead they were uniquely conceived for the smallest of passengers and have contributed in establishing Bugaboo as the Rolls Royce among strollers.

Seit 2002 stehen die drei ineinandergreifenden Kreise als Logo für Bugaboo. Aber die Geschichte der Marke geht zurück in die frühen Neunzigerjahre und ihren Anfang nahm sie an der Design Academy Eindhoven in Form einer Abschlussarbeit des Studenten Max Barenbrug. Der großgewachsene Niederländer verfolgte schon damals den Anspruch, einen ebenso schönen wie praktischen Kinderwagen für moderne Eltern zu entwerfen. Seine Arbeit wurde ausgezeichnet, die Idee patentiert und der Grundstein für die Marke gelegt, bevor Max Barenbrug sich dessen wirklich bewusst war. Die etablierten Kinderwagenhersteller wollten von den Plänen des motivierten Absolventen nichts wissen. So entschloss er sich kurzerhand, gemeinsam mit seinem Schwager Eduard Zanen eine eigene Firma zu gründen.

Since 2002, Bugaboo's logo has consisted of three intertwined rings, but the brand's beginnings date back to the early 1990s with designs that Max Barenbrug created for his graduate project at the Design Academy Eindhoven in the Netherlands. Already then the towering Dutchman had set his sights on designing an attractive and practical stroller for the modern parent. His work was highly commended, the idea patented and the cornerstone for the brand laid before Barenbrug was really aware of it. But despite the acclaim, established stroller manufacturers were not interested in the ambitious graduate's ideas. And so Barenbrug and his brother-in-law Eduard Zanen, decided to found their own company.

YOU DON'T HAVE TO GIVE PEOPLE WHAT THEY NEED. YOU NEED TO SHOW THEM WHAT THEY WANT.

Die drei Kreise im Logo vereinen die Kernwerte der Marke: Bewegung, Energie und Dynamik. Das Logo wurde 2002 überarbeitet, als die Marke dank eines kurzen Auftritts in der Serie »Sex and the City« einen regelrechten Boom erfuhr. »Eine Dame aus der Marketingabteilung verfolgte die Serie regelmäßig und als Miranda, eine der vier Hauptdarstellerinnen, schwanger wurde, rief sie kurzerhand bei HBO an und fragte, ob denn für das ungeborene Kind schon ein Kinderwagen in Planung sei«, verrät eine quirlige Mitarbeiterin. HBO verneinte und Bugaboo sandte Fotos eines Modells ein. Kurze Zeit später war der Deal unter Dach und Fach und Miranda rollte ihr Baby in einem Bugaboo über Millionen von Bildschirmen. Die sieben Sekunden genügten, um eine der Hauptdevisen von Max Barenbrug exemplarisch zu untermauern: »Man muss den Leuten nicht geben, was sie brauchen. Man muss ihnen zeigen, was sie wollen.« Die Folge: Modebewusste Eltern aus aller Welt wollten ihre Kleinen genauso chic und zeitgemäß herumchauffieren, wie es die Heldinnen ihrer Lieblingsserie vormachten.

The logo's three rings symbolize the brand's core values: movement, energy and dynamism. It was reworked in 2002 when, after a cameo appearance in "Sex and the City," the brand experienced a regular boom. A bubbly employee explains to us how this came about. "A lady from the marketing department watched the series regularly, and when Miranda, one of the main characters, became pregnant, this lady decided to call HBO and ask whether a stroller had already been chosen for the fictional unborn child." Upon hearing that this was not yet the case, Bugaboo immediately sent some pictures of their top-of-the-line model. In no time at all, everything had been arranged and images of Miranda taking her baby for a walk in a Bugaboo stroller flickered across millions of TV screens. Seven seconds that sufficed to corroborate one of Max Barenbrug's favorite maxims: "You don't have to give people what they need. You need to show them what they want." The consequence? Fashion-conscious parents everywhere wanted to take their babies for a stroll in the same chic and du jour vehicle that the heroine in their favorite series used.

MODE INTERESSIERT MICH NICHT. MANCHMAL IST SIE SCHÖN, ABER LEIDER NUR SELTEN PRAKTISCH. UND ICH BIN EIN PRAKTISCHER MENSCH.

Doch chic und »stylish« ist nicht das, wonach der verheiratete Familienvater Max Barenbrug strebt. Die Worte allein scheinen bei ihm direkt ans Nasenrümpfen gekoppelt. »Für mich ist ein Produkt stylisch, wenn es schön, aber nicht funktional ist. Deshalb mag ich keine stylischen Produkte.« Nur bei Kleidung macht er eine Ausnahme: »Da weiß ich, dass ich es in drei Monaten ohnehin nicht mehr anziehen werde, weil es sich bis dahin erübrigt hat. Funktionalität und Optik sollten sich immer auf gleicher Ebene begegnen. Und das ist eine stetige, iterative Suche.« Dabei bewegt er seinen schmalen Oberkörper demonstrierend hin und her, so engagiert, dass man fürchtet, er kippe gleich um. Dieser Ansatz, kombiniert mit Kampagnen, die statt Babys und hingerissenen Müttern viel mehr junge Väter, technische Vorzüge und kinderlose Wagen in urbanen Umgebungen in den Vordergrund stellen, funktioniert: Das Unternehmen wächst und wächst und Barenbrugs Bestreben setzte sich in den Köpfen fest: Bugaboo gilt als der Kinder-

Yet chic and stylish are not attributes family man Barenbrug aspires to at all. The mere words elicit a frown with every mention. "To me, stylish stands for a product that's pretty, but not functional. As a rule I don't approve of stylish products. Except for clothes. That doesn't count because I know I'll only be wearing something for about three months, and then it doesn't bother me. Fashions don't interest me. Though stunning at times, they are hardly ever practical. And basically, I'm a practical man. "Functionality and form should always be in sync. A permanent, iterative quest," Barenbrug rocks his upper body from side to side in a non verbal attempt to underscore his explanation – with such vigor that we fear he might overbalance any moment. Barenbrug's philosophy – along with Bugaboo's advertising campaigns which focus on young fathers, technical features and strollers displayed in an urban setting, instead of cute babies and delighted mothers – works extremely well. The enterprise has gone from strength to strength, and Barenbrug's intentions have been

UGABOO

wagen mit der größten Funktionalität. Je nach Lust, Laune und Möglichkeit kann man den Wagen ziehen oder schieben. Er ist modular verwendbar, zusammenklappbar, verfügt über einen wendbaren Sitz und Schiebebügel. Und das gefällt nicht nur dem stereotypen »Sex and The City«-Zuschauer. Wenn ein Mann nur den Namen eines einzigen Kinderwagens kennt, so ist es vermutlich Bugaboo (dies ist eine statistisch nicht geprüfte Behauptung). Fest aber steht: Über die Jahre bildete sich um die Marke eine eingeschworene Fangemeinde, die durch Mund-zu-Mund-Propaganda dafür sorgte, dass die Beliebtheit nie abnahm. Man munkelt sogar, dass sich Bugaboo-Schiebende per Handzeichen untereinander grüßen, ähnlich wie die Mitglieder einer Bikercrew. Dem Urheber des ganzen Zaubers ist das Drumherum aber nicht annähernd so wichtig wie das Innenleben, und dies in mehrfacher Hinsicht. Mit der Idee und der Marke verhält es sich gleich: Beides muss im Innern entstehen und dann nach außen wachsen. Nie umgekehrt.

successfully established in public awareness. Indeed, Bugaboo has become synonymous with the stroller that offers greatest functionality: a vehicle that can be pushed or pulled according to requirement, even able to cope with sandy and snowy conditions. Easily collapsible, and sporting a reversible seat along with adjustable handlebars as well as excellent suspension, it is small wonder that Bugaboo's appeal has spread to a far larger target group than just the viewers of "Sex in The City." Ask any man to name the brand of a stroller and, at a guess, nine times out of ten he will come up with the name Bugaboo. Certainly over the years a die-hard fan base has developed around the brand, and word of mouth ensures its continuing popularity. Rumor even has it that Bugaboo pilots greet each other with a discreet wave the same way some bikers do. Yet to its creator, the outer trappings are not nearly as important as the product's interior makeup. An idea and a brand are similar in certain ways. Both have to develop from the inside out. Never the other way round. Barenbrug goes on to explain: "If a company continues to grow, its administration grows with it, and more people get involved. Hiring experienced staff can, in a way, even be dangerous for a brand."

AN IDEA AND A BRAND ARE SIMILAR IN CERTAIN WAYS. BOTH HAVE TO DEVELOP FROM THE INSIDE OUT. NEVER THE OTHER WAY ROUND.

Er erklärt: »Wenn eine Firma stetig wächst, nimmt die Bürokratie zu, und je erfahrener die Leute, die man einstellt, umso gefährlicher wird das in gewisser Hinsicht für die Marke. Neue Denkweisen und Prozesse gelangen in das Unternehmen, und ehe man sichs versieht, arbeitet die einst so authentische Firma auf eine Art, die nicht ihrem Inneren entspringt, sondern unüberlegt adaptiert wird. Dem versucht Barenbrug aktiv entgegenzusteuern, indem er seinen Posten als Design Director Aernout

"New mindsets and processes are introduced and, before you know it, the once oh-so-authentic company starts working in a way that does not come from the gut, but that has come about unconsciously." In a ploy to actively prevent this from happening, Barenbrug has handed his prior position as Design Director over to Aernout Dijkstra-Hellinga. "To have more time for other things," he says with a wink. By this he means maintaining stakeholder relations and overseeing the growth of the company. Barenbrug also plans to continue

Dijkstra-Hellinga überließ. »Um mehr Zeit für anderes zu haben«, wie er augenzwinkernd sagt. Damit meint er das Betreuen von Stakeholdern und die Weiterentwicklung des Unternehmens. Vom Tüfteln und Designen wird er die Finger aber auch nicht ganz lassen. Dies betont er oft und gern, verrät aber partout nicht, in welche Richtung es denn gehen soll. Ich wünsche mir für Bugaboo, dass wir uns zu einem Consumer Brand entwickeln können und damit genauso erfolgreich sein werden, wie wir es jetzt mit den Kinderwagen sind. Gespielt tröstend fügt er an: »In zwei Jahren wird man es sehen.« Die Wartezeit bis dahin kann man sich seit Kurzem mit dem neuesten Modell aus dem Hause Bugaboo vertreiben, dem Cameleon 3. Was daran anders ist als an seinem Vorgänger, sieht der Laie vermutlich nicht, denn aussehen tut er fast gleich. Aber »neun von zehn Teilen sind neu«, heißt es. Und das zeigt: Die inneren Werte machen den Unterschied. —

developing and designing, an intention which he voices several times, but refuses to elaborate on. I hope we will be able to develop Bugaboo into a consumer brand, and that we will turn out to be as successful in this endeavor as we are now with our strollers. And, somewhat coyly, he adds: "Two years from now we'll know more." To bridge the gap, Bugaboo's latest masterstroke, the "Cameleon 3," has just been released. Though to the untrained eye it's hard to see what makes this stroller stand out significantly from its predecessor – it doesn't really look all that different – we are informed that "nine out of ten parts are new." A further example of the Bugaboo corporate creed: it's the inner values that count. —

bugaboo

03

Caffè Ferrari
Renato Ferrari

Text **Olivia El Sayed** Photos **Gian Marco Castelberg**

Grossmutters Käfeli
über dem Kohlefeuer geröstet
säurearm
reiner Arabica
Caffè Ferrari
8953 Dietikon, Telefon 044 740 80 11
www.mondialprodukte.ch
Grossmutters Käfeli
über dem Kohlefeuer geröstet
säurearm
reiner Arabica

Ein guter Kaffee braucht mindestens drei Dinge, um sich überhaupt gut nennen zu dürfen: ausgewählte Bohnen, deren richtige Mischung und eine sorgfältige Röstung. Drei zugegebenermaßen relative Faktoren. Renato Ferrari, für den die Qualität seines Kaffees seit jeher mehr als nur ein Beruf ist, verwendet für seinen Kaffee Arabica-Bohnen aus Zentralamerika, sorgt seit Jahrzehnten selbst für die richtige, streng vertrauliche Mischung und überwacht die zeitintensive Röstung, in der vermutlich das Geheimnis der Einzigartigkeit dieses Kaffees schlummert.

A good coffee requires three essential things before it can even hope to qualify as good: choice beans, a perfect blend and meticulous roasting. Three factors that are not easy to measure. To achieve the perfect coffee blend, Renato Ferrari, for whom the quality of his coffee has always been more mission than profession, uses Arabica beans from Central America. He mixes them himself according to a top-secret recipe and supervises the protracted roasting process which might well be the key to his coffee's success.

Es ist Montag früh, sieben Uhr dreißig, und im Halbdunkel ist auf der Türe des alten Bauernhauses »Verbotener Eingang« zu lesen. An der anderen Tür, zum Laden hin, hängt ein Schild mit einem Scherz über Öffnungszeiten, der impliziert, dass eigentlich nie jemand da sei. Von drinnen dringen aber Stimmen und ein Rattern in den noch zwielichtigen Morgen hinaus. Durch das mit Eis beschlagene Fenster ist ein Mann zu sehen, der mit einem Zeitungsstapel beladen zum verbotenen Eingang schreitet – und winkend Einlass in die Rösterei gewährt. Es handelt sich dabei um Mike Schärer, den Neffen von Renato Ferrari, der die Rösterei eines Tages übernehmen wird. Groß, mit freundlichem Gesicht und einem gerollten R ganz weit hinten im Hals, verliert er ein paar Worte zur Begrüßung und schreitet dann voran. An Tischen nahe dem Eingang sind ein paar bunt beschürzte Frauen gerade dabei, Kaffee abzupacken, während der Röster das Kohlefeuer überprüft. Die Maschinen tanzen stampfend im Takt und es duftet nach Kaffee und brennendem Holz.

Early Monday morning, seven thirty, and in the semidarkness a forbidding "No Entry" sign can be made out on the door. On the other door, the shop door, hangs a jokey sign about opening hours, implying that they do not exist at all. But from inside, voices and a clattering sound are audible in the half-light. I screw up my eyes and peer through the windowpane to see whether I can make anything out, and I discover Mike Schärer. Carrying a stack of newspapers, he approaches the forbidden entry door – and beckons me to enter. Mike Schärer is Renato Ferrari's nephew: tall, with a friendly face and a rolling "r" that seems to originate far back in his throat. He leads me into the roasting house where a couple of women package the coffee while the master roaster checks the coal fire. The machines dance and stomp in unison and the smell of coffee and burning wood fills the air.

Wir produzieren nicht den besten Kaffee. Das ist Geschmackssache. Aber wir bieten mit Sicherheit die beste Qualität.

Der alte Herr im dunkelroten Pullover steht immer dabei, wenn zweimal pro Woche die grünen Bohnen aus ihren Jutesäcken im Lager geholt und über dem Kohlefeuer dunkelbraun und ölig glänzend geröstet werden. Seine Pensionierung liegt bald zwanzig Jahre zurück, aber bis auf die Tatsache, dass sein ehemaliger Beruf zu seinem Hobby wurde, hat sich nichts verändert. Der Röstprozess des Ferrari-Kaffees dauerte schon immer überdurchschnittlich lang und tut dies nach wie vor, denn die hundertjährige Röstmaschine erreicht nur eine Höchsttemperatur von zweihundert Grad Celsius. »Dadurch wird den Kaffeebohnen ein erheblicher Teil der Gerbsäure entzogen und die Aromen entwickeln sich langsamer, dafür aber intensiver«, erklärt Renato Ferrari. Das Sicherstellen der Qualität und die Liebe zu diesem Produkt treiben ihn seit jeher an: »Man muss sich schon noch etwas

The old gentleman can always be found here when, twice-weekly, the green beans are brought over from the warehouse in jute sacks and roasted over the coal fire until they take on a dark brown, oily sheen. Though now officially retired for nearly twenty years, besides turning his former profession into his hobby, nothing has really changed for Renato Ferrari. His coffee takes a long time to roast because the centenarian roaster does not reach temperatures over two hundred degree Celsius. This leads to a higher percentage of tannin being extracted and the aromas developing at a slower pace, resulting in a more intensive flavor. The urge to safeguard the quality and his love for the product are the driving factors for him. "They'll just have to be patient until I'm ready to leave," Ferrari laughs. To this day he remains fascinated by his product and is delighted by the renaissance he and his co-workers believe they are witnessing: a new clientele of young customers that find

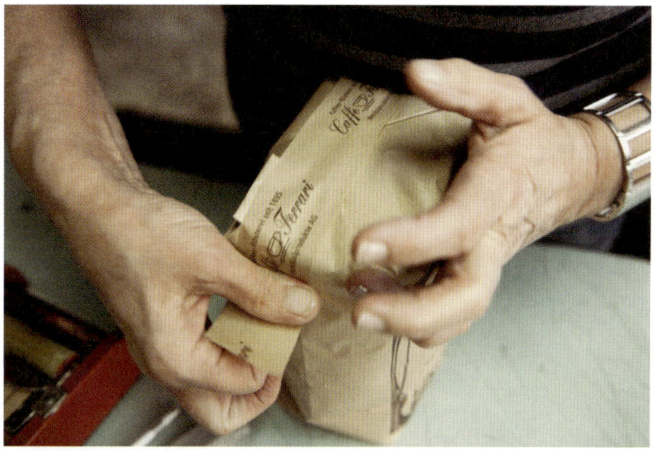

TOLEDO

gedulden, bis ich hier das Feld räume«, lacht er. Heute wie damals fasziniert ihn Kaffee und er freut sich über die Tendenz, die sowohl er als auch seine Mitarbeitenden zu erkennen glauben: Die jungen Leute genießen wieder vermehrt das Erlebnis in der Rösterei Ferrari. Sie treffen hier auf eine Welt, die sie so nicht mehr kennen: die Maschinen, das Handgemachte und der kleine Kaufmannsladen, geführt von Ferraris Frau Bethli. »Es ist die Faszination für diese eigentümliche Welt, die die Jungen wieder zum Kaffeetrinken verleitet«, ist Ferrari überzeugt, »nicht der Kaffee selbst.«

In seinem Büro zündet er sich eine Pfeife an und setzt sich hin. Unter seinem roten Paul & Shark Yachting Pullover trägt er ein weißes Hemd, aus dessen Ausschnitt der goldene Halter eines Montblanc-Stiftes hervorblitzt. Er tippt mit dem Zeigefinger darauf und murmelt, dass alle edlen Produkte etwas gemein hätten. »Etwas Edles kann nur herstellen, wer selbst Stil hat.« Eine italienische Version dieser Aussage wiederholte sein Vater tagtäglich: »Un prodotto buono deve essere fatto con stile.« Sein Vater war ihm, nebst Helmut Schmidt, den er vor allem fürs konsequente Rauchen und seine Sturheit bewundert, immer das größte Vorbild. Ferrari Senior kam ohne die entsprechenden Sprachkenntnisse in die Deutschschweiz. Doch es war die Zeit der italienischen Immigranten. Egal wie groß oder klein ein Lokal im Zürcher Kreis 4 damals war: Gehörte es einem Italiener, so fand sich darin auch eine Espressomaschine, und die wiederum verlangte ausschließlich nach den dunklen Ferrari-Bohnen.

the actual buying experience at the roasting house Ferrari worthwhile in itself. They enjoy entering into this different world with its machines, hands-on manufacturing, and the miniscule shop which is run by Ferrari's wife, Bethli. "It's simply their fascination with our special little world that is luring the young ones back to drinking coffee," states Ferrari with conviction. "And not actually the coffee itself. We don't produce the best coffee. That will always be a question of taste. But we most certainly produce the best quality."

He sits down in his office. Clipped onto his white shirt, the gold cap of a Mont Blanc pen peeks out from beneath the red Paul & Shark Yachting pullover Ferrari is sporting. Unprompted he goes on to declare that, in order to produce a high-class product, you have to have class yourself. Or as his father would say in Italian on a daily basis: "Un prodotto buono deve essere fatto con stile." His father, the man he admires most next to Helmut Schmidt, whom he admires chiefly for his resolute smoking habit and his stubbornness, was his role model. When Ferrari senior arrived in the German-speaking part of Switzerland he could hardly speak a word of the language. But this was in the era of Italian immigration and, no matter how large or small an establishment in Zurich's "Kreis 4" was, if it belonged to an Italian, it was sure to have an espresso machine in it somewhere. And this in turn needed to be kept filled with those dark Ferrari beans.

BE STUBBORN AND SMOKE A LOT.
THEN YOU WILL GROW OLD AND SUCCESSFUL.

Viele der damaligen Kunden sind es heute noch. Auch dank Ferraris Kompromisslosigkeit. »Seien Sie stur und rauchen Sie viel. Dann werden Sie alt und erfolgreich«, flüstert er hinter vorgehaltener Hand. So will er von Mengenrabatt beispielsweise gar nichts wissen. »Stellen Sie sich den Gewinn vor, den jemand machen würde, nur weil er eine größere Menge kauft!« Seine Augen leuchten und in Windeseile fegt der Montblanc über das Papier, begleitet von den feurigen Ausführungen des rechnenden alten Herrn, der resümiert: »Ich komme also lieber jemandem im Preis entgegen, der schon seit vielen Jahren bei uns bestellt.«

Ferraris Freiheit in der Berufswahl war durch seinen Status als einziger Sohn eingeschränkt. Es war immer klar, dass er die Rösterei eines Tages übernehmen würde. Weil er mit Kaffee groß geworden war, schien ihm das aber nie ein Nachteil zu sein. Von seinem Vater hat Ferrari außerdem gelernt, wie wichtig es in einem kleinen Betrieb ist, jede Funktion auch selbst ausführen zu können, um unabhängig zu bleiben. Mit einem Handelsdiplom und kurzen Auslandaufenthalt im Gepäck kam er 1948 als stolzer junger Mann zurück ins beschauliche Dietikon, bereit, in den väterlichen Betrieb einzusteigen. In Gedanken schon ganz Geschäftsmann, betrat er die Rösterei und wollte sich alsbald an den Schreibtisch setzen

Many of those clients have been carried over from that time. In part, this is due to Ferrari's unwillingness to compromise. He does not offer a quantity rebate. "Imagine the profit a person would make just because they buy a larger quantity!" His eyes light up, and with lightening speed he reels off a calculation that leaves me in awe. "If anything, I'd offer a rebate to an old and valued customer."

As an only son, Ferrari's freedom of choice when it came to a career was extremely limited. It was always understood that one day he would take over the roasting house. Growing up in the trade, however, he never considered this to be a disadvantage. He admired his father and the master roaster for their passion. They loved their profession and managed the entire business without any outside help. His father also taught him the importance of being able to execute every step in the process so as to maintain independence as a small establishment. In 1948, after finishing his commercial training and spending a short time abroad, Renato Ferrari came back to the then tranquil town of Dietikon as a proud man, ready to start working in his father's company. Convinced that he had already learned all that needed to be learned about running a business, he entered the roasting house and prepared to make himself comfortable behind a desk. But his father, a work apron draped over his arm, blocked his way and said: "Where do

Zuger Chriesiblueete

und loslegen. Doch sein Vater, eine Schürze über dem Arm, versperrte ihm den Weg und rief: »Du gasch gar nienets ane. Leg dä Schurz a und gang go Chole schufle!« Enttäuscht gehorchte der junge Mann, stellte sich zusammen mit seinem Stolz neben den Kohlehaufen und erlernte das Handwerk des Kaffeeröstens von Grund auf.

Und noch heute ist es mit dem Lernen nicht vorbei. »Plötzlich hieß es, du musst jetzt ins Internet, das ist gut für das Geschäft. Dabei mag ich gar keine Computer«, lamentiert er. Und sein ungutes Gefühl bestätigte sich schnell: Kaum war die Website der Rösterei online, verlangte ein gewisser Herr Cordero di Montezemolo nach ihm und drohte mit einem ordentlichen Prozess. Aus dem ursprünglichen Markennamen »ferrari caffè« sollte »Caffè Ferrari« werden und ein Kaffeetässchen als Bildzeichen sollte überdies verdeutlichen, dass es sich bei diesem Ferrari um nichts anderes als Kaffee handelte. Beim Erzählen tippt sich Ferrari an die Stirn. »Das ist mir doch egal, ob nun Caffè Ferrari oder ferrari caffè – mein Kaffee ist, was er ist, egal was auf der Tüte steht.«

Teuer war es aber trotzdem. Und das, obwohl Ferrari eigentlich auf sein Nutzungsrecht hätte bestehen können. Den Kaffee gibt es nämlich weitaus länger als die pferdestarken Karossen. Aber Renato Ferrari wollte nicht streiten. Offensichtlich hat seine hochgelobte Sturheit auch Grenzen. Dann doch lieber noch eine Pfeife anzünden und dem behaglichen Rattern der Maschinen lauschen. —

you think you're going? Put on this work apron and go shovel coal!"

Disappointed, the young man obeyed and planted himself – along with his pride – next to the pile of coal to learn the ropes of roasting coffee from the bottom up. And he has not stopped learning since. "All of a sudden, everyone was saying that you had to go on the Internet. And I have never liked computers," he complains. His uneasiness soon proved to be justified. The website had hardly been uploaded when a certain Mr. Cordero di Montezemolo called and threatened to take him to court. Capitalizing the "F," placing the word Caffè in front of it, and inserting a coffee cup icon between the words were some of the conditions he had to agree to – to ensure that he would never try to adorn the word Ferrari with a little horse. Ferrari taps his forehead in a typical Italian gesture to express how ridiculous he thinks the whole matter is. "I really do not care about that kind of stuff. Whether Caffè Ferrari or ferrari caffè – my coffee remains what it is, regardless of the name on the package."

It was an expensive lesson, even though Ferrari could probably have stood his ground and claimed his right to the use of the name. After all, his coffee brand existed long before the high-powered sports cars did. But Renato Ferrari decided not to put up a fight. Apparently even his legendary obstinacy has its limits. He would prefer to smoke another pipe. —

04

Campomaggi
Marco Campomaggi

Text **Olivia El Sayed** Photos **Gian Marco Castelberg**

Nur knapp fünfzig Kilometer vom Meer und von Rimini entfernt liegt das kleine Städtchen San Carlo di Cesena, wo die Taschenmarke Campomaggi 1980 von ihrem Namensgeber Marco Campomaggi gegründet wurde. Als Sohn eines Bildhauers war der Designer seit jeher an allem interessiert, was sich mit den eigenen Händen kreieren ließ.

In Italy, just fifty kilometers inland from the Adriatic coast and Rimini, lies the little town of San Carlo di Cesena where, in 1980, a young Marco Campomaggi founded the brand Campomaggi for his beautiful leather bags. As the son of a sculptor, the designer has always been fascinated by things that can be handcrafted, and was blessed with the talent to make this passion work for him.

Glücklich, wer mit Talent gesegnet: Seine ersten Ledertaschen nähte Marco Campomaggi schon als Kind. Er verwendete dafür altes Sattelleder, verzierte die Taschen mit Metallnieten und verkaufte sie auf dem Pausenhof oder nach der Schule auf den Gehsteigen seiner Stadt. Zu seiner eigenen Verwunderung stimmten Nachfrage und Angebot schon damals überein. »Sogar mein Architekturstudium ließ sich auf diese Weise finanzieren«, verrät Marco. Wenn er über seine Arbeit erzählt, entführt er mit seinen Worten in eine Märchenwelt: Er schwärmt vom Geruch von frischem Leder, vom Streunen auf Flohmärkten, vom Suchen und Finden kleiner Schätze an Orten, wo man sie nicht erwartet hätte. Gedankenversunken zupft er am Kuhfell, das den Sessel ziert, auf dem er sitzt, den Blick durch die Fensterfront nach draußen in die Ferne gerichtet.

Campomaggi sewed his first bags from old saddle leather while he was still at school. He decorated them with metal studs and sold them to co-students or hawked them on the sidewalks after school. To his surprise, his creations sold well from the outset, and he was even able to finance his architectural studies with his earnings. When Marco Campomaggi tells you about his work, his words conjure up a fairytale world. He enthuses about the smell of fresh leather, describes how he roams flea markets or tracks down small treasures in the most unexpected locations. Occasionally lapsing into silence as he pursues a line of thought, he absentmindedly tugs at the cowskin that covers the seat of his dark brown armchair and gazes out the window at the distant horizon.

ICH HABE MICH FÜR DAS RICHTIGE PRODUKT ENTSCHIEDEN, WENN ICH BEIM TRAGEN DAS GEFÜHL HABE, ETWAS GUTES AUS EINER MASSE AN UNZÄHLIGEN MÖGLICHKEITEN HERAUSGEFISCHT ZU HABEN.

Bei all den philosophischen Gedanken, die der Italiener anscheinend so unüberlegt von sich gibt, vermutet man fast einen Teleprompter irgendwo am blauen Himmel. Er hat eine ruhige, tiefe Stimme, von der man sich wünscht, sie möge jeden Morgen aus dem Off erklingen und dem Neonlicht des Badezimmerspiegels seine Weisheiten über das Wesen der Zeit entgegenhalten. »Neben den schönen Falten, die ein Gesicht erst definieren, offenbaren auch andere Dinge ihre Schönheit erst mit der Zeit. Je älter man wird, umso reicher ist unser Schatz an Geschichten und Erinnerungen, an Anekdoten, Ideen und Gedanken. Sie machen uns erst wirklich schön – schön im eigentlichen Sinne des Wortes.« Die Produkte von Campomaggi verkörpern genau diese Idee: Die Zeit nimmt ihnen nichts weg, sondern bedeutet immer einen Mehrwert. Deshalb lautet der aktuelle Slogan der Marke auch »Il tempo non toglie, ma dà«. Produkte zu schaffen, die zeitlos sind, ist das, was Campomaggi mit seiner Arbeit verfolgt, und er sagt: »Mich inspiriert das Gebrauchte; Objekte, denen man ansieht, dass sie etwas zu erzählen haben.« Oft kauft er in Trödelläden oder auf Flohmärkten alte Arbeitertaschen und studiert diese. Was sind die funktionalen Aspekte einer solchen Tasche? Was daran ist

Considering the quantity of philosophical cogitations this Italian exudes straight off the cuff, we half expect to espy a Teleprompter somewhere in the vast blue skies. Marco Campomaggi has a calm, deep voice, and you find yourself wishing to hear his wise words about the essence of time piped in voice-over to counterbalance the message of harsh reality encountered each morning upon looking into the bathroom mirror. "Next to the beautiful lines that, with time, decorate a face, there are other things that only unfold their charm as time goes by. The older we get, the more abundant our wealth of stories and memories, anecdotes, ideas and thoughts become. They are what make us truly beautiful – beautiful in the most real sense of the word," he says. Campomaggi's products embody the selfsame principle. Time does not diminish them; to the contrary, it actually adds to their value. This is underscored by the brand's current slogan: "Il tempo non toglie, ma dà." Marco is dedicated to creating products that are truly timeless. "I find used objects inspiring. Things that clearly show they have a story to tell," he says. Frequently, Campomaggi buys old leather work bags at flea markets or thrift shops and inspects them carefully to determine exactly which aspects are functional, and which mere frills. "Nowadays so many things are made that are completely

Schnickschnack? »Heute werden so viele Dinge gemacht, die keinen tieferen Sinn haben«, bemerkt er. Entsprechend gering ist deshalb auch sein Interesse an der Konkurrenz und an aktuellen Modetrends. Beim Frühstückskaffee beobachtet er zu Recherchezwecken Leute mit gutem Stil und überlegt sich, mit welcher Tasche jemand noch besser aussehen könnte. Solch kleine Augenblicke reichen ihm als Inspiration. »Ich mache ja nichts Weltbewegendes. Ich mache einfach nur Taschen«, schmunzelt er. Dass viele berühmte Designer sich so verhalten, als würden sie mit ihren Kreationen Leben retten, versteht er nicht. Er sieht die Sache eher pragmatisch: »Taschen sind dazu da, Objekte von einem Ort zum anderen zu transportieren. Wenn ich zur Optik dieses Mittels etwas Positives beitragen kann und jemandem damit Freude bereite, umso besser.«

Campomaggi selbst achtet nicht auf Marken. Er hält für sich selbst vor allem Ausschau nach anonymen Sachen wie Militär- oder Arbeiterkleidung. Seine eigenen Produkte sollen auch nicht gekauft werden, weil es die Mode so vorschreibt. Viel eher sollen sie die Fähigkeit des Individuums unterstreichen, selbst bestimmen zu können. Die Modewelt birgt für Marco die Gefahr, dass sie den Leuten die Fähigkeit aberkennt, zu entscheiden, was gut für jeden Einzelnen ist. «Sie wählen nicht das, was ihnen am besten gefällt, sondern denken schon beim Kauf daran, womit andere sie wohl am meisten schätzen würden. Das erzeugt ein enormes Ungleichgewicht im eigenen Geschmackssinn. Das finde ich eine beunruhigende

meaningless," he deplores. Consequently, he is neither overly interested in what the competition does nor what the current fashion trends are. His research consists mainly in keeping his eyes open and attuned to everyday life. While he drinks his morning coffee in one of the little neighborhood cafés, he observes people whose style he likes and imagines what kind of bag would make them look even better. He then draws on these musings for inspiration. "It's not as if I'm doing anything extraordinary. I just create bags," he grins. Although not a few celebrated designers behave as if their creations were of vital importance, this attitude baffles Campomaggi. Ever a pragmatist, he says: "Bags are made to transport things from one place to another. If I can improve their look and make somebody happy in the process, so much the better."

Campomaggi himself is not interested in brand articles – as a rule he buys anonymous items such as army surplus or worker's clothing for himself – nor does he think his products should be bought just because they have become fashionable. He would prefer his bag to be seen as a sign of individuality, the ability to decide for oneself. The world of fashion, according to Marco Campomaggi, poses the danger that it can stop people from making their own choices and lead them to blindly follow what the latest trend is. "Rather than choosing based on what they like best, people buy what they think others will rate highest." This is detrimental to an individual sense of taste, a trend he finds alarming. "When what I put on makes me feel as if I've managed to extract some-

Tendenz.« Bei Campomaggi nimmt man sich deshalb die Freiheit, sich nicht jedem Modetrend zu beugen. Dafür muss die Qualität immer stimmen. »Unsere Kunden erwarten Substanz und Natürlichkeit«, weiß Marco. Der kleine Betrieb benutzt für die Produktion seiner Taschen noch immer dasselbe Leder wie früher, als er anfing. Zusammen mit seiner Frau entwickelte er im Lauf der Zeit eine Waschung des Leders, die zu einer speziellen Färbung führt. Für die Verarbeitung werden anschließend nur pflanzliche Fette und Öle verwendet. Die Taschenmodelle aus den verschiedenen Jahren unterscheiden sich tatsächlich nur wenig. Sie sind schlicht, natürlich, meist braun, olivgrün oder schwarz und in Form und Größe recht ähnlich. Als Designer achtet Marco Campomaggi am meisten auf die Verarbeitung und das Material bei einem Produkt.

thing good out of a mountain of infinite possibilities, then I know I have chosen the right article." At Campomaggi's, the liberty of not slavishly following every fashion trend is a given. Something they never take liberties with, however, is quality. "Our customers expect a certain character and a natural look," says Campomaggi. The small company still uses the same leather to manufacture bags that it did when Campomaggi first started. As a team, he and his wife have developed a procedure using only vegetable oils to treat the leather that creates their distinctive coloring. In truth, the models only display minimal changes from year to year. With almost no frills, they have a no-nonsense, authentic look about them. And, besides being very similar in shape and size, they are usually brown, olive-green or black. As a designer, Marco Campomaggi pays utmost attention to the materials and the craftsmanship that go into making a new model.

QUALITY FOR ME DEFINES ITSELF IN FOUR ASPECTS: MATERIAL, IDEA, EXECUTION, PURPOSE.

Er ist jedoch überzeugt, dass das Qualitätsverständnis eines Menschen immer davon abhängig ist, wie man sein Leben bisher gelebt hat. »Qualität definiert sich für mich über vier Dinge: Material, Idee, Umsetzung, Zweck. Je nach persönlichen Umständen erwartet man mehr von dem einen oder eben von dem anderen Teilaspekt.« Während seine Studienkollegen sich noch überlegten, was sie mit ihrem Leben anfangen wollten, beschäftigte er sich mit seinen Taschen, ohne zu bemerken, dass er damit die Frage für sich schon beantwortet hatte. »Die Art und Weise, wie ich anfing, Taschen herzustellen, hat etwas von einem Hippie. Ich war unbeschwert und enthusiastisch«, erinnert er sich. Sein persönlicher Weg hat auch den seiner Marke geprägt: Die Leidenschaft für das Alte, das Natürliche und das Streben nach Zeitlosigkeit spiegeln den Charakter des Markenmachers in seinen Produkten. —

Even so, he is convinced that quality is not a tangible matter. In his opinion, a customer's expectations will always base in how they have lived their life. The expectations we have are formed by our personal history. When Campomaggi was younger and his fellow students were busy trying to find out what they were going to do with their lives, he was busy making his bags. "I guess the way I started producing bags was kind of hippie. I was light-hearted and enthusiastic," he recalls. The question of his future settled itself without him even noticing. And so a brand was established with products created out of a passion for things from the past, a quest for timelessness, and a naturalness that all reflect the creator's character and philosophy. —

05

Carine Gilson
Carine Gilson

Text **Olivia El Sayed** Photos **Gian Marco Castelberg**

CARINE
GILSON
LINGERIE COUTURE

Die in Belgien geborene Designerin Carine Gilson entführt mit kostbarer Lyoner Seide und französischer Spitze aus Chantilly in eine Traumwelt: Ihre hauchdünnen, handbestickten Kreationen umwehen den weiblichen Körper in pfirsichfarbenen Tönen oder verzücken die Sinne mit himmlischem Türkis und betörendem Fuchsia. Fast scheint sich die verspielte Lingerie zu mokieren über die unausweichlich auftretende Unentschlossenheit eines jeden Betrachters. »Schauen Sie noch oder wollen Sie schon?«, flüstert sie. Entscheiden aber geht nicht mehr.

Made using sumptuous Lyon silk and Chantilly lace, the lingerie of Belgian-born designer Carine Gilson transports to an enchanted world. Her gossamer, hand-embroidered creations envelope female curves in peach-colored hues and delight the senses with heavenly turquoise and tantalizing fuchsia touches. And the playful lingerie almost seems to poke fun at the beholder's inevitable indecision. "Are you still at the looking stage or are you ready for more?" it whispers. But, by now, reaching any kind of decision is completely out of the question.

Würde man Carine Gilson zufällig treffen und aus Verlegenheit, die zufällige Begegnungen manchmal mit sich bringen, Beruferaten spielen, lägen die Chancen relativ hoch, dass man sich vertippt. Umweltaktivistin, Jazzmusikerin, Landschaftsgärtnerin, dies sind die vorgefertigten Fettnäpfchen. Carine Gilson erscheint mit zerzaustem Haar, ungeschminkt, in Jeans und einem weißen Shirt, dem man ohne Etikettenspick nicht ansehen würde, ob es nun ein teures ist, das so sein muss, oder ein normales, das so nicht mehr sein müsste. Sie hat viel zu tun und weiß eigentlich auch gar nicht genau, worum es geht, freut sich aber sichtlich über den Spontanbesuch in ihrem Brüsseler Atelier und auf die damit verbundenen Fragen. Beim Beantworten klopft sie mit den beturnschuhten Füßen unentwegt einen munteren Takt gegen das Schreibtischbein.

Es ist die Faszination für diese feine, durchbrochene Erscheinungsform der Spitze, die Carine Gilson schon früh ihren Weg offenbaren sollte. Von Kindsbeinen an war sie mit Stoffen, Borten und Bändern vertraut, denn ihre Mutter verdiente ihr Geld als Damenschneiderin. Auf dem heimischen Wohnzimmertisch fanden sich immer Nadel und Faden, Nähmuster, Knöpfe und Stoffe aller Art, die es nach der Schule ausführlich zu bestaunen galt. Carine beobachtete

If you were to encounter Carine Gilson by chance and, on a whim, start hazarding a guess at what she does for a living, odds are you would not even come close. An environmental activist, a jazz musician or a landscape designer are only a few of the more obvious mistaken conclusions you might reach. She opens her atelier door to us with tousled hair, no makeup, jeans and a white shirt that leaves you wondering whether it's an expensive one meant to look that way, or a normal one that should not. A question that is resolved by a quick glimpse of the label. Although Carine is very busy and not entirely sure what exactly we are after, she is nevertheless visibly delighted by our unannounced visit to her workshop in Brussels and the questions we pose. While answering them, she taps a sneaker-clad foot in a lively tact against the desk leg.

Her fascination, already at a young age, with the fine, openwork structures of lace proved to be a prime indicator of the path Carine Gilson was eventually to follow. From her earliest childhood she was accustomed to being surrounded by the fabrics, trimmings and ribbons her mother used in her work as a seamstress. There were always needle and thread, sewing patterns, buttons and fabrics of all kinds spread on the dining room table to be inspected in detail at the end of a school day, and Carine would often look on while her mother sewed, daily feeding her own desire to work with the same material. She says: "I have a passion for

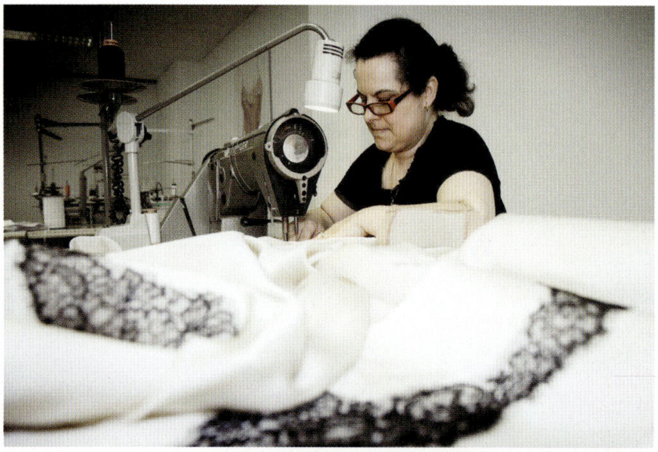

CARINE
GILSON

ihre Mutter oft bei der Arbeit und ihr eigener Wunsch, einmal mit demselben Material zu arbeiten, wuchs mit jedem Tag. »Ich hege eine Leidenschaft für alles, was perfekt ist. Deshalb auch meine Liebe zu französischer Spitze.« Schneiderin zu sein war zur damaligen Zeit aber kein Beruf, den man sich für seine Tochter wünschte, denn es war keine angesehene Tätigkeit, sondern eine für Arbeiterinnen – dies zumindest war die Meinung der Mutter. Doch Carine Gilson sah in nichts anderem eine Alternative und folgte ihrem Willen, studierte an der Kunstakademie in Antwerpen und arbeitete anschließend als Freelancerin für verschiedene Prêt-à-porter-Labels. Lange glücklich war sie damit jedoch nicht.

all that is perfect. Which is why French lace will always remain my first love." Her mother, however, objected strongly to Carine's wish to become a dressmaker. She did not consider it a suitable profession for her daughter. In her opinion, this sort of work was more suited to the working class. Yet, Gilson herself could not imagine choosing another profession; and so, following her heart, she studied at the Art Academy in Antwerp and then went on to work for various prêt-à-porter labels as a freelancer. She soon came to realize, however, that this type of work was not right for her. "I have an extremely independent character, so setting up for myself was a logical choice," she explains herself.

Mein Wesen könnte nicht unabhängiger sein, es war für mich nur natürlich, etwas Eigenes zu machen.

Mit 23 Jahren kaufte sie sich ihr eigenes Atelier und begann, damals noch unter dem Namen »Vanité«, Lingerie zu produzieren. »Dieser Name gefiel mir, die Eitelkeit der Frau empfand ich stets als etwas sehr Starkes.« Doch viele Leute rieten ihr dazu, die Marke unter ihrem eigenen Namen zu vermarkten. »Unterwäsche mit meinem Namen? Das schien mir am Anfang ein merkwürdiger Gedanke. Aber im Grunde ist es meine Inspiration, meine Essenz, mein Stil, da hatten die Leute schon Recht, die mir das nahelegten.« So benannte sie ihr Unternehmen schließlich doch nach sich selbst: Carine Gilson.

»Eine Marke beabsichtigte ich nie zu schaffen, sondern ein Universum, das zum Träumen anregt», sagt Carine Gilson heute. Inspiration für ihre Markenwelt fand sie ursprünglich in der Mode der Dreißigerjahre, im Art-déco-Stil sowie im russischen Ballett. All das ließ sie subtil in ihre Kreationen mit einfließen. »Heute suche ich nicht mehr nach Inspiration, die Spitze an sich inspiriert mich schon genug.« Was nicht heißt, dass es nicht auch Menschen gibt, deren Lebenswerk Carine Gilson als Quelle der Inspiration sieht. So bewundert sie zum Beispiel Madame Grès, eine der größten Couturières der Modegeschichte, die für ihre römisch anmutenden, fließenden Gewänder berühmt war, in die sich Frauen wie Marlene Dietrich, Greta Garbo und Jacqueline Kennedy hüllten. Und auch der Einfluss der eigenen Mutter ist ihr bewusst: »Wir haben nicht viele Gemeinsamkeiten, aber die Liebe für gut gemachte Arbeit verbindet uns. Es ist meine Mutter, die mich dazu inspiriert, in meiner Arbeit stets nach Perfektion zu streben.« So märchenhaft und verspielt die Lingerie von Carine Gilson daherkommen mag, hinter dem Teil der Marke, der für die Außenwelt ersichtlich ist, stecken auch viele Ungereimtheiten, die mit der Abgerundetheit von Märchen nur wenig zu tun haben. Carine Gilson gesteht sich selbst ein, »eigentlich das Gegenteil von dem zu sein, was meine Marke suggeriert. Das ist das Paradoxe am Künstlerdasein. Wir müssen hart arbeiten, damit die anderen träumen können.«

At the age of 23 she bought her own atelier and started to produce lingerie. Initially, she named her label "Vanité.""I liked the name. I've always considered female vanity a very strong force." However, not a few friends and colleagues advised her to market the brand under her own name. "Underwear with my name on it? That seemed a very strange idea at first. But, basically, it is my inspiration, my essence, my style that flows into the brand. So, in that sense, those people were giving me the right advice." And, in the end, she decided to give the enterprise her name after all: Carine Gilson.

"I never intended to establish a brand, more a universe that evokes dreams," Carine says. Originally, she drew the inspiration for her brand environment from the fashion of the 1930s, the Art Deco style and Russian ballet. She then delicately imbued her creations with the spirit of these images. "Today, I don't have to look for inspiration anymore. The lace itself acts as a catalyst for fresh ideas." Which is not to say that Carine Gilson does not see certain people's lifework as a source of creativity as well. One of them is Madame Grès, one of the greatest couturières in the fashion business, whose Roman-style flowing robes adorned sophisticated women such as Marlene Dietrich, Greta Garbo and Jacqueline Kennedy. And Carine is equally aware of her mother's influence. "We do not have a lot in common, but our love for fine craftsmanship connects us. It's my mother who inspires me to continually strive for perfection in my work," Gilson confirms. Though her lingerie may appear to be the light-hearted stuff of dreams, behind the visible face of the brand there exist a number of incongruities that belie the apparent fairytale-like simplicity of the label. Carine Gilson concedes that she is "actually the opposite of what her brand transports."

Right from the start, Gilson realized that selling dreams entails a lot of work and personal commitment; as a result, pursuing her private dreams is currently not an issue, but rather something she has put aside for later. Which is not to say that she is a stranger

CARINE
GILSON
72% Polyamide-28% Spandex
Wash 30°
Made in Belgium
S

That's the typical paradox of an artist's existence. We have to work hard to provide others with dreams.

Dass das Verkaufen von Träumen viel Arbeit und persönliches Engagement erfordert, war ihr von Anfang an bewusst, deshalb ist für sie das Ausleben der eigenen Träume aktuell kein Thema, sondern etwas, was sie sich für später aufhebt. Nicht dass ihr die verträumten Märchenwelten voller Verführung und Neugierde fremd wären, es ist das, wovon auch eine Carine Gilson selbst träumt, und das jeden Tag sehr gern, wie sie mit amüsiertem Blick erzählt. Vor allem, wenn sie nicht arbeite, obwohl das so oft auch nicht vorkomme, denn »wenn ich nicht arbeite, analysiere ich meine Arbeit, ich plane und studiere daran herum. Aber vor allem hinterfrage ich mich, so oft es nur geht.« Das ist ein schwieriger Prozess, wenn man ihn ernst nimmt: »Wenn ich mich und meine Arbeit immer und immer wieder in Frage stelle, garantiert mir das nicht den Erfolg, aber es bestätigt mich in meinem Glauben an den Erfolg meiner Ideen.«

to the enchanted world of seduction and curiosity. These are equally the stuff of Carine Gilson's own dreams, and she enjoys indulging in them – as she reveals with a smile. Especially when she is not working, although, of course, this does not happen very often – because, as she says, "When I'm not working, I'm analyzing my work, making plans and rethinking them. But, most of all, I question what I do as often as I can." A demanding process if you go about it seriously. "Questioning myself and my work over and over again does not guarantee success, but it confirms my belief in my ideas to myself. And believing in your ideas is the key prerequisite for success."

Es ist die Grundvoraussetzung für Erfolg, dass man an seine Ideen glaubt.

Und das tut offensichtlich nicht nur sie, denn mit ihrer Lingerie ist Carine Gilson regelmäßig in der »Vogue« vertreten und verkauft ihre Kreationen – deren Kilopreis nur unwesentlich tiefer liegen dürfte als derjenige von Gold – in Brüssel, Paris und ab September auch in London. Überrascht ob der fortgeschrittenen Zeit lacht sie plötzlich auf, kramt nach einer Visitenkarte, streicht den Namen darauf durch, schreibt ihren eigenen darüber und streckt in einer Emsigkeit die Karte von sich, dass ihre Haare wie elektrisiert um den Kopf fliegen. In der anderen Hand klingelt das Handy und Carine Gilson verabschiedet sich mit einer Herzlichkeit, wie sie spontane Begegnungen nur ganz selten mit sich bringen. —

Clearly she is not the only one to believe in her success. Carine Gilson's lingerie regularly features in "Vogue", and her creations are available – at a kilo price probably only slightly lower than that of gold – in Brussels, Pari, and, from September onwards, in London as well. Suddenly, surprised at how quickly time has passed, Carine Gilson laughs, rummages for a business card and crosses out the name on it, replacing it with her own. She hands over her card with such vigor that her tousled hair actually flies around her head. While her cell rings in her other hand, Carine Gilson says her good-byes with a genuine warmth seldom experienced in a spontaneous encounter. —

06

Casa Fagliano

Héctor, Germán, Rodolfo & Eduardo Fagliano

Text **Karen Naundorf** Photos **Marco Vernaschi**

Detailgenau wie immer, beinahe liebevoll hatten die Faglianos die ungewöhnlichen Füße ausgemessen. Und die Form des Stiefels angepasst, so wie sie es seit über hundert Jahren machen, immer neu, für jeden Fuß. Doch der Mann mit den sechszehigen Füßen starb, bevor er seine Stiefel abholen konnte. »Sie hätten ihn sicher sehr glücklich gemacht«, sagt Héctor Fagliano, in seinem Gesicht spiegelt sich ehrliches Bedauern. Er trägt eine dunkelgrüne Schürze und wiegt die Stiefel, die es nicht aus seiner Werkstatt schafften, behutsam in der Hand. Dann stellt er sie zurück auf das Naturholzregal und greift zu einem schweren Hammer, mit dem er wenig später Bronzenägel in die Sohlen eines maßgefertigten Polostiefels versenkt.

The Faglianos had measured the unusual feet with a customary precision that borders on devotion. The shape of the boot had been adjusted – a new fit for every foot – in keeping with over one hundred years of tradition. But the man with the six-toed feet died before he could pick up his boots. "I'm sure they would have made him very happy," says Héctor Fagliano, sincere regret mirrored in his face. Wearing a dark-green apron, he gently cradles the boots that did not make it out of his workshop. He then carefully returns them to the rustic wooden shelf and reaches for a heavy hammer. Soon, he is driving brass nails into the sole of a bespoke polo boot.

Es riecht nach Leder, Holzspänen, Schuhcreme und Kleber. Durch die Fenster und die weit geöffnete Flügeltür zum Garten dringt milde das Sonnenlicht in den Raum. Und in der Luft liegt Tradition. Perfektion. Und eine bescheidene Noblesse. Die Faglianos kamen als Handwerker nach Argentinien. Sie sind es noch heute. »Es ging uns nie ums Geld, es ging immer nur um die Stiefel«, sagt Eduardo Fagliano, Héctors älterer Bruder. »Sie sind Teil der Familie, ich erkenne sie aus Tausenden heraus.« Der 52-Jährige ist heute das Gesicht des Traditionsunternehmens. Er fährt auf Poloturniere, begrüßt dort Kunden, empfängt sie in der Werkstatt und wählt mit ihnen gemeinsam das beste, in Quebracho-Extrakt gegerbte Leder aus. Sein Vater schneidet es zu. Sohn Germán fügt die Lederteile zusammen. Bruder Héctor fertigt die Sohlen. Und wenn der Kunde es wünscht, stickt Eduardo ganz am Ende von Hand, mit einer einst von europäischen Einwanderern auf dem Schiff nach Argentinien gebrachten Vorkriegsnähmaschine der Marke Dürkopp, die Initialen oder das Logo auf den Schaft. Vier bis sechs Monate Geduld müssen Kunden mitbringen. Und seit der Polostil nicht nur in Argentinien in Mode ist, manchmal noch mehr.

The smell of leather, wood shavings, shoe polish and glue permeates the workshop. Shimmering in through the windows and wide-open French doors leading to the garden, the sun casts a gentle glow into the premises. The scent of tradition is in the air. Excellence. And an unassuming sense of refinement. The Faglianos came to Argentina as craftsmen, and that is what they have remained. "It was never about money for us; it has always been about the boots," says Eduardo Fagliano, Héctor's older brother. "They are like members of the family, I can pick them out among thousands of others." The 52-year-old is the face of the traditional establishment. He attends polo tournaments, greets clients and receives them at the workshop where, together, they select the sought-after material from only the best leather, tanned exclusively with quebracho extract. His father cuts the leather, son Germán joins the pieces, brother Héctor produces the soles, and at the very end of the process, if the client wishes, Eduardo stitches initials or a logo on the boot shaft using the ancient Dürkopp sewing machine brought to Argentina by European immigrants. Clients, for their part, need to contribute four to six months of patience. And, now that polo boots have become fashionable outside Argentina, sometimes even more. "Each boot must be perfect. That is the best advertisement," says Eduardo.

JEDER STIEFEL MUSS PERFEKT SEIN. DAS IST DIE BESTE WERBUNG.

Die Faglianos machen vieles anders als die Konkurrenz. Sie schalten keine Werbeanzeigen, vertrauen auf Mundpropaganda. Und Eduardo weiß: »An einer Marke arbeitet man jeden Tag neu.« Die Faglianos sind langsam, für ein paar Stiefel brauchen sie mehr als vierzig Arbeitsstunden. Sie verwenden Nähmaschinen und Werkzeuge der Großeltern, weil sie nicht glauben, dass neue Technik ihr Produkt verbessern würde. Und sie sind weit weg vom Kunden. In Hurlingham, einem Vorort von Buenos Aires, gegründet

The Faglianos do many things differently to their competitors. They do not run advertisements, preferring to trust in word of mouth. They work slowly, spending over forty hours on one pair of boots. They use the sewing machines and tools their grandparents used because they doubt that new techniques could improve their product. And, situated in Hurlingham, a suburb of Buenos Aires, founded by British engineers in the middle of the 19th century, they are far away from their clients. In 1892, the first Faglianos arrived from Italy where they had worked as

16
30

A BRAND MUST BE IMPROVED EVERY SINGLE DAY.

von britischen Ingenieuren Mitte des 19. Jahrhunderts. 1892 kamen die ersten Faglianos aus Italien nach Hurlingham, schon in der Heimat hatten sie als Schuster gearbeitet. Um 1920 herum bat sie ein englischer Polospieler, seine Stiefel zu reparieren. Und später fragte er, ob sie nicht welche für ihn anfertigen könnten.

Die Faglianos hatten keine Pferde. Polo, das war Sache der Gutsherren, der Bessergestellten. Bis heute halten sie sich vom Spielfeld fern. »Wir machen das, was wir am besten können. Das sind die Stiefel«, sagt Eduardo. »Wir sind nicht einmal Fans eines einzelnen Teams, unsere Kunden sind überall.« Er greift zu einem schmalen, langen Notizbuch. Mehr als zwanzig dieser gebundenen Hefte stehen im Regal, in ihnen die Daten aller Kunden und eine Zeichnung ihrer Fußform. Mit seinem Kugelschreiber umrandete Eduardo schon die Füße von Prinz Harry von Wales, von Schauspieler Tommy Lee Jones, von Adolfo Cambiaso, einem der besten Polospieler der Welt. Der König von Spanien trägt Stiefel und Mokassins der Faglianos. Prinz Charles hat welche in seiner Sammlung. Der Sultan von Brunei bestellte vor ein paar Jahren 120 Paar Stiefel, alle auf einmal. Der gute Ruf der Faglianos erreichte vor ein paar Jahren auch die Schweiz: Die Privatbank Julius Bär bot den Argentiniern eine Partnerschaft an. »Sie sagten uns, dass sie wie wir nach Exzellenz streben, das überzeugte uns«, sagt Eduardo. Gerade haben die Faglianos weiße Stiefel für einen chinesischen Geschäftsmann fertiggestellt. »Er bat uns um ein Stickemblem auf dem Schaft, das Ferrari-Logo«, sagt Eduardo, der den Wunsch des Kunden erfüllte. Mit der alten Dürkopp, die ihn noch nie im Stich ließ.

Seinen ersten Schuh entwarf Eduardo Fagliano, als er elf Jahre alt war. Wie das ging, hatte ihm sein Vater erklärt. Der wusste es von seinem Vater. Und der wiederum von seinem. Der etwas unbeholfen vernähte Mokassin aus beigem Rindsleder steht in einem Regal in der Werkstatt. Dem kleinen Eduardo gefiel das Schusterhandwerk. Schnell war ihm klar, dass er im Familienunternehmen bleiben würde, trotzdem studierte er als junger Mann Maschinenbau. »Für alle Fälle, um noch eine andere Ausbildung zu haben«, sagt Eduardo, der an Sonntagen im Kirchenchor singt. »Aber mein Herz sagte mir immer, dass mein Platz hier ist, in unserer Werkstatt.« Seine schwarzen Lederschuhe sind perfekt geputzt, natürlich Marke Fagliano. —

cobblers. Around 1920, a British polo player stopped by the family business to have his boots repaired. And later he returned, asking whether the Faglianos could make him a new pair.

The Faglianos did not own any horses. Polo was a sport for the wellborn and the wealthy. To this day, the family stays away from the playing fields. "We stick with what we do best. Which is making boots," says Eduardo. "We're not even fans of a specific team. Our clients are everywhere." He reaches for a long, narrow notebook. More than twenty of these bound notebooks line a shelf and contain client details along with an outline of their feet. Using a simple ballpoint pen, Eduardo has outlined the feet of Prince Harry of Wales, actor Tommy Lee Jones and Adolfo Cambiaso, one of the world's best polo players. The King of Spain wears boots and moccasins made by the Faglianos. Prince Charles has a pair in his collection. Several years ago, the Sultan of Brunei ordered 120 pairs of boots in one go. The Faglianos' good reputation reached Switzerland a few years ago. Private bank Julius Bär offered the Argentines a partnership. "They told us they strive for excellence, just as we do. We were convinced," says Eduardo. Right now, the Faglianos have just finished making a white pair of boots for a Chinese businessman. "He has asked us to stitch an emblem on the shaft, the Ferrari logo," says Eduardo as he fulfills the customer's wish – naturally with the old Dürkopp which has never let him down.

Eduardo Fagliano designed his first shoe when he was eleven years old after learning the craft from his father. Who had been taught by his father. Who, in his turn, had been taught by his father. The somewhat clumsily sewn moccasin made of beige leather decorates a shelf in the workshop. Young Eduardo liked shoemaking, and it soon became clear that he, too, would join the family business. Nevertheless, he decided to study engineering first. "Just in case, to have another trade to fall back on," says Eduardo, the thoughtful artisan who sings in the church choir on Sundays. "But my heart always tells me that this is where I belong: in our workshop." His black leather shoes are polished to perfection, and, naturally, made by Fagliano. —

07

Conditorei Schober-Péclard
Michel Péclard

Text **Olivia El Sayed** Photos **Gian Marco Castelberg**

Die Boutique in der kopfsteingepflasterten Napfgasse aus der vorletzten Jahrhundertwende hat eine lange Geschichte. 1874 kam sie in den Besitz ihres Namensgebers Theodor Schober. Zwei Generationen prägten den Familienbetrieb, bis schließlich die Erbengemeinschaft Schober die Konditorei an die Confiserie Teuscher verpachtete. Der Name »Schober« blieb stets Bestandteil der Marke, die heute vom aktuellen Pächter Michel Péclard neu definiert wird.

The "boutique café" that can be discovered in the quaint cobblestoned Napfgasse looks back on a long history. In 1874, it became the property of the eponymous Theodor Schober who installed his family business that ran for the next two generations. Schober's descendants then leased the property to the Confiserie Teuscher, but the name Schober remained – and still remains – an inextricable component of the brand, although now redefined by Michel Péclard.

Wo würde Proust hier wohl mit Beschreiben beginnen, wenn er schon für ein simples Madeleine mehrere Seiten benötigte? Die Konditorei Schober fesselt mit ihren Details: Die stuckbesetzte Decke mit dem imposanten Leuchter, der dunkle Holzboden und all die assortierten Köstlichkeiten auf silbernen Etageren lassen einen innehalten. Kindern gleich will man alles stehen und liegen lassen, die schönen Schachteln im uralten Provence-Schrank bestaunen, ausprobieren, ob diese alte Silberkasse tatsächlich in Betrieb ist, und dann eins, zwei, fünf dieser schillernden Patisseriestückchen kosten!

Vermutlich ginge es uns mit der Unfähigkeit zur verbalen Zurückhaltung wie Proust, hätten wir uns denn schon einmal etwas Vergleichbares auf der Zunge zergehen lassen. Und genau das Unvergleichbare ist es, was Michel Péclard in seinem Café den Spagat zwischen Mehrheitsfähigkeit und Einzigartigkeit vollziehen lässt. Nirgendwo sonst soll es in der Stadt ähnlich gute Patisserie geben. Doch bevor sich Michel Péclard den Feinheiten und Qualitätsansprüchen seines Cafés widmen konnte, gab es einige grobe Hürden zu überspringen. Allein schon der Druck, der ein derart traditionsreiches Unternehmen mit sich bringt, schien ihm schlicht zu groß: »In Zürich gibt es drei Große: die Kronenhalle, das Odeon und den Schober«, erklärt er. »Da überlegt man sich schon zweimal, ob man derjenige sein möchte, der so etwas unter Umständen in den Sand setzt.«

Erst als ein guter Freund ihm mitteilte, dass der Schober, wenn er selbst ihn nicht übernehme, fortan ein Dasein als Filiale einer Billigkleiderkette fristen sollte, übermannte ihn seine tief verankerte Verbundenheit für Zürich und er nahm die Herausforderung an. Selbige war mindestens so facettenreich wie Monsieur selbst: Erbschaftsstreitigkeiten, Probleme mit dem Namen »Schober«, den Teuscher für sich als Marke hatte schützen lassen, Geschmacksrichtungen, die bipolare Ziele anstrebten, und Vorschläge, die den impulsiven Unternehmer schlichtweg die Wände hochgehen ließen. Seine Stimme überschlägt sich: »Manche wollten den Schober mit Corbusier-Stühlen füllen und die Wände mit Neonfarben streichen. Das hatten wir doch alles schon tausendmal. Was für ein Graus!« Nicht selten ließ Péclard während der Renovation den einen oder anderen mit offenem Mund stehen. Für die Gestaltung wollte er nämlich partout keine Designer engagieren, sondern Bühnenbildner, die Kulissen bauen. Auf diese Weise sollten

How would Proust even begin describing this splendor, if to describe one small Madeleine he all but used up several pages? Upon entering Café Schober, a multitude of impressions vie for your attention: the impressive white stuccoed ceiling hung with an enormous chandelier, the wonderful dark wooden flooring, and the vast selection of scrumptious pastries and sweets appetizingly displayed on sterling silver cake stands. Instantly transported back to childhood, you develop a spontaneous urge to peek in those tantalizing boxes sitting on the shelves in the antique cupboards, or to see if the old silver till still works and then, quickly now, try one, two, five pieces of the toothsome array of pastry.

Just as Proust could not check his tribute, you, too, will be challenged to not start singing the confectioner's praises once you have tasted these one-of-a-kind delicacies. Which precisely reflects the one-of-a-kind mark Michel Péclard has succeeded on setting in his café – sparking old tradition with fresh individuality. Nowhere, they say, can you find pastries and sweets that even come close. Yet, before Michel Péclard was actually able to dedicate himself to the myriad details and strict dictates of quality such an enterprise involves, he had to overcome several large obstacles. Just the sheer pressure to succeed when taking on an establishment so steeped in tradition appeared to him as challenging as if he were getting ready to climb the Matterhorn. "In Zurich, the three big names are: Kronenhalle. Odeon. And Schober. So you think twice before volunteering to take on a challenge that may well leave you with the reputation as the guy who made Schober go under," he explains.

But after hearing from a close friend that plans were afoot to turn the time-honored premises of Schober into a new venue for a popular clothes brand outlet, the need to save this Zurich landmark overcame his fear of the obstacle and Péclard met the challenge head-on. A challenge that in its diversity proved to be a worthy undertaking for a man of his caliber: disputes amongst the Schober descendants, complications with the brand name "Schober" which Teuscher had protected for its own use, questions of taste that could be taxed as bipolar, and interior design concepts that literally drove the spontaneous entrepreneur up the wall: "Some people suggested refurbishing Schober with Corbusier chairs and putting in neon-colored walls. As if that hasn't been done a thousand times before. What a nightmare!" During the renovation, Péclard caused jaws to drop on several occasions. Instead of hiring an interior designer, he insisted on employing a set designer to construct a fantasy world like a fairytale, a place to dream with

péclard

sie mit ihm eine Erlebniswelt wie im Märchen erschaffen, wo ungehemmt geträumt werden darf: vom Baden in Schokolade, vom Fliegen und vom Königsein. Eine Welt so verführerisch wie Prousts verlockendes Madeleine, bei dessen Verzehr Erinnerungen und Wünsche plötzlich zum Greifen nah scheinen.

open eyes: of bathing in chocolate, of soaring high above the world, or of being a king – in short, a world as seductive as the one Proust's delicate little Madeleine conjured up, evoking memories and desires and making them appear within reach.

Nennen Sie mir einen Menschen, der als Kind nicht davon geträumt hat, König oder Königin zu sein. Diesen Traum möchte ich für einen Moment für jeden wahr werden lassen.

Und im Salon Rouge geschieht eben dies. An der niedrigen Decke wechseln sich massive Querverstrebungen aus Holz mit samtüberzogenen Kissen ab, angebracht, um die Akustik des Raumes zu optimieren (was nicht wirklich funktioniert, denn man hört die Musik – die im Übrigen in einem Fahrstuhl ohnehin besser aufgehoben wäre – nur bei genauem Hinhören). Stehlämpchen mit cremefarben befransten Stoffschirmchen stehen auf Beistelltischchen und Bilder hängen in dicken Goldrahmen, manch eines davon ziemlich schief, an den zinnoberroten Wänden. Man fühlt sich tatsächlich königlich riesig in diesem Raum. Und wie man so wohlig in den Tiefen der Polstersitze versinkt, ertappt man sich dabei, wie man in die Backstube dieses Cafés ein altes, tatteriges Ehepaar projiziert, wie sie da stünden und mit der naturgegebenen Langsamkeit ihres Alters Törtchen um Törtchen verzierten.

Zurück in die Realität bringt uns erst die Backstube. Sie ist hell beleuchtet, Hunderte von Blechformen und riesige Schwingbesen hängen an den Wänden. Kolossale Öfen und Kühltruhen bilden eine silberne Front, die heizt und piept und kühlt. Das Radio läuft, es ist gefühlte 36 Grad Celsius heiß und zwei Jugendliche stehen sich wortlos gegenüber und arbeiten. Sie hantieren mit Bunsenbrennern und besprühen ausgewählte Patisserie mit modernster Airbrush-Technik. Sie schweigen kein Wort, und alles läuft, obwohl sie allein sind. Der Chefpatissier Marc Döhring, der älteste in dieser Backstube, ist abwesend. Er feiert seinen zweiundzwanzigsten Geburtstag.

Und hierhin, in diese sehr reale, industrielle und schnelllebige Welt passt Michel Péclard, den man abgesehen vom Nachnamen nicht unbedingt in die verschnörkelte Pariser Welt der Patisserie einordnen würde. Er hat wache, leuchtend blaue Augen und ein Lachen, das die Tassen im Schrank erzittern lässt. Er verästelt seine Geschichten bis ins Unendliche und reiht Anekdote an Anekdote, ohne dass man auch nur einmal eine Frage stellt. Sein Tatendrang und seine Leidenschaft für seine Arbeit springen einen förmlich an und finden sich in all den Details des Cafés wieder. »Ich liebe Süssigkeiten. Ich liebe das Reisen. Ich liebe Inspiration. Dieses Café. Meine

"Show me a person who never dreamt of being a prince or a princess as a child! I want to make that dream come true for everyone, even if only for a moment!" And that is exactly what happens in the "Salon Rouge." The low ceiling is made of massive crossed wooden beams that alternate with velvet padding, placed there in an attempt to improve the acoustics. (It doesn't really succeed. The music, more suitable for an elevator anyway, can only be heard if you strain your ears.) Table lamps with ecru-colored tasseled lampshades decorate the coffee tables, and paintings with thick golden frames hang, some decidedly crooked, on vermilion walls. A wondrously regal sensation permeates your senses, and, while you relax luxuriously in the deep cushioned armchairs, you can almost see an elderly couple, conjured up by your surroundings, standing in the kitchens busily decorating piece after piece of pastry.

Once in the kitchens, however, you are brought down to earth with a thump. Bright overhead lighting, hundreds of baking trays and enormous whisks hanging from the walls, and humongous ovens and freezers form a no-nonsense metallic front. A radio is playing, it is extremely hot – at least 36 degrees Celsius – and two young people are silently working at a counter opposite each other. Using Bunsen burners and airbrush techniques they decorate pastries. Not a word is spoken as they work, despite being on their own today. Pastry chef Marc Döhrig, the oldest employee in the kitchens, is away, celebrating his 22nd birthday.

And here, in this very real, fast-paced world, is where Michel Péclard fits in, a man who aside from his surname doesn't have anything in common with the ornate Parisian world of pâtissiers. With alert, bright blue eyes and a belly laugh that makes the kitchenware tremble in the cupboards, he tells story after story, one tale leading to another, and strings along one anecdote to the next without any prompting. His energy and passion for his work spark off him and can be found in every detail of his café. "I have at least another hundred ideas that I'd like to try out," Péclard reveals. One of those ideas is to offer space to makers of sweet delights to display their wares – for example those unique jars of exclusive "Gelée de Champagne" produced in the South of France, far away from the city's bustle, by the culinary couple

I LOVE GOODIES. I LOVE TRAVELING. I LOVE INSPIRATION. THIS CAFÉ. MY WORK. I LOVE EVERYTHING I DO AND I HAVE AT LEAST ANOTHER HUNDRED IDEAS THAT I'D LIKE TO TRY OUT AND SEE IF THEY WORK.

Arbeit. Ich liebe alles, was ich tue, und ich habe noch mindestens hundert Ideen, die ich umsetzen möchte!« Eine dieser Ideen war, verschiedenen Produzenten einen Rahmen für eigene Produkte zu bieten. So stammen die ausgefallenen Marmeladengläser aus Südfrankreich; das Pärchen Catherine und Delphine fertigt dort fernab von jedem Trubel den exklusiven Gelée de Champagne. Und der Starpatissier Patrick Mésiano aus Monte Carlo zeigt sich federführend für die Patisserie und empfängt dann und wann eines von Péclards Backstubenküken, auf dass sie vom Besten lernen und im Idealfall die Kreationen mit eigenen Ideen verfeinern. Es scheint dies der Königsweg, einer traditionsreichen Marke innovativen Wind einzuhauchen.

—

Catherine and Delphine. And Master Pastry Chef, Patrick Mésiano, responsible for the choice selection of pastry, occasionally receives one of Péclard's fledgling pastry chefs at his kitchens in Monte Carlo where they can learn from the very best – and maybe one day improve the maestro's creations with their own ideas. It seems to be the enchanted path to sweeten this traditional brand Schober with the flavor of innovation.

—

08

Cook in Boots
Ravinder Bhogal

Text **Olivia El Sayed** Photos **Reto Caduff**

Bevor die ehemalige Mode- und Beauty-Journalistin Ravinder Bhogal einen vom britischen Channel 4 übertragenen Kochwettbewerb gewann, nutzte sie ihre Küche vor allem nachts, wenn sie nicht schrieb, und verzückte mit ihren nächtlichen Kreationen Familie und Freunde. Als eines von fünf Kindern eines orthodoxen indischen Ehepaares in Kenia aufgewachsen, war sie jedoch schon von Kindesbeinen an vertraut mit Lebensmitteln aus aller Welt. Heute lebt und kocht sie vor allem in London. Die berühmte Sendung »F Word« mit Gordon Ramsay, bei der Ravinder 2008 als Siegerin hervorging, veränderte ihr Leben auf einen Schlag. Sie veröffentlichte ihr preisgekröntes Rezeptbuch »Cook in Boots«, kocht sich seither durch Fernsehsendungen und Hotelküchen und träumt vom ersten eigenen Restaurant.

Before Ravinder Bhogal won a British Channel 4 cooking competition, she could be found in her kitchen mainly at night, whenever she was able to steal time away from her work as a beauty and fashion editor. Friends and family were always delighted to receive the fruits of her nocturnal labors. Growing up in Kenya as one of five children of an orthodox Punjabi couple, she was introduced to foods and ingredients from all over the world at a very early age. Today, she lives and cooks mainly in London. The notorious program "F Word" with Gordon Ramsay, which Ravinder won in 2008, changed her life from one day to the next: she has since published her award-winning recipe book "Cook in Boots" and cooks her way through TV shows and hotel kitchens while dreaming of opening her first restaurant.

So unvorhergesehen wie die plötzliche mediale Aufmerksamkeit ihrem Leben eine neue Wende gab, so unkompliziert geht die heute 34-Jährige damit um. »Vielleicht war es auch einfach Schicksal«, lacht Ravinder offen. Und wem bis dahin ihr Mund noch nicht aufgefallen ist, der wird sich spätestens ab jetzt in den Reigen derjenigen einreihen, die ihren Blick nicht mehr davon abwenden möchten. »Ich habe eine Freundin, die mich damals anrief und sagte, hör zu, es gibt da diese Sendung ›Find Me a Fanny‹, dort sucht Gordon Ramsay eine weibliche Küchenchefin. Meld dich da an, ich habe so eine Vorahnung, dass du gewinnen wirst.« Der zweideutige Titel des Programms bezieht sich auf Fanny Cradock, eine britische Köchin und Restaurantkritikerin, die 1994 verstarb. Mit ihrer erfrischend frechen Art und nie darum verlegen, einen Geschmack oder ein Gericht als »unglaublich sexy« zu bezeichnen, lenkt Ravinder den Fokus der Zuschauer immer wieder auf den sinnlichen Aspekt des Essens, was ihr schon damals viel Sympathie einbrachte. Und so war es am Ende Ravinder, der aus Tausenden von Teilnehmerinnen das begehrte Küchenzepter überreicht wurde. »Hätte mir vor fünf Jahren jemand gesagt, dass ich heute hauptsächlich in Restaurants am Herd stehe, ich hätte gesagt: ›Du spinnst!‹. Aber nun ist es genau so und ich bin sehr glücklich darüber.«

Zu kochen begann Ravinder schon im zarten Alter von fünf Jahren, damals aber nicht aus Leidenschaft, sondern einfach, um ihrem Appetit gerecht zu werden. »Wenn du hungrig bist, dann koch dir was«, lehrte die Mutter ihr unersättliches Töchterlein, einen zusätzlichen Hintergedanken hegend. »Wer einen Ehemann finden will, muss kochen können, sonst wird das nichts«, zitiert Ravinder ihre Mutter mit erhobenem, rot lackiertem Zeigefinger und schräg geneigtem Kopf. Und so, wie Ravinder kocht, hätte sie sich eigentlich gemäß der Gleichung ihrer Mutter einen kompletten männlichen Harem verdient: Ihre Gerichte sind stark geprägt von der indischen Küche, haben einen mediterranen Einfluss und bedienen sich oft der Gewürze des Nahen Ostens, was nicht nur geschmacklich einen feuerwerksgleichen Einfluss auf die Speisen hat; farbenfroh, einladend und sinnlich sieht alles aus, was Ravinders

Despite the sudden media attention which turned her life completely upside-down, the 34-year-old has remained refreshingly unaffected by it all. "I think it was fate really," Ravinder says laughingly. (If you hadn't noticed Ravinder's generous mouth before, this is the moment when you join the ranks of those who find it almost impossible to avert their gaze from it.) "I have this really good friend, who phoned me up and said, 'you know Gordon Ramsey is planning this competition called 'Find me a Fanny' where he's looking for a female cook. You have to enter, I just have this real feeling that if you do you are going to win.'" The intentionally suggestive title of the program allegedly refers to Fanny Cradock, a British writer, restaurant critic and TV cook who died in 1994, and sets the tone for this uniquely British production with plenty of innuendo. With her fresh butter-won't-melt-in-my-mouth looks that make her saucy comments all the more piquant, Ravinder was an unqualified success. Never shy to call a flavor or a dish sexy, she constantly draws attention to the more sensual aspects of great cooking and delectable foods. And so it was Ravinder who was selected from thousands of competitors and awarded the coveted kitchen scepter. "Had somebody told me five years ago that I'd be cooking in restaurant kitchens everywhere today, I would have said they were crazy. But now here I am and I'm very happy about it."

Ravinder started cooking at the tender age of five, not out of inner passion, but simply to satisfy her appetite. "If you're hungry, then cook something for yourself," her mother would say and taught her insatiable daughter to cook – albeit with an ulterior motive. "To get a husband you must be able to cook, otherwise you won't find anybody," Ravinder quotes her mother brandishing an index finger topped with bright red nail polish and imitates an admonishing look. If her mother's predictions had been correct, Ravinder's cooking mastery would have won her an entire male harem by now. Her dishes are strongly influenced by Indian cuisine with a Mediterranean slant, and often include spices from the Middle East. The results are not only a firework of flavor, but also extremely colorful and enticing. Everything that emerges from Ravinder's steaming pots and pans is mouthwateringly appetizing. She stirs, spices, tastes

WE ARE
LICENSED
TO PLAY
RECORDED
MUSIC.
EN
-FRI
PM

I
BRIXTON
NO SMOKING.
It is against the law to smoke in these premises
SCORES ON THE DOORS
CLOSED
Hours of Business
closed

dampfende Töpfe und Pfannen verlässt. Sie rührt, würzt und probiert und schüttelt heftig die riesige Bratpfanne, die für ihre feinen Handgelenke eigentlich viel zu schwer scheint – es passiert aber nichts. Erst als sie sich über den Tisch lehnt, um an die Schokolade zu gelangen, fällt ein Stück Butter zu Boden. Sie stößt einen kleinen Schrei aus. »Ich wirke wohl wie die ungeschickteste Köchin, nicht?«, ruft sie durch den Raum und schiebt hinterher: »Das liegt aber nur an meiner Ungeduld!« Die Leidenschaft, mit der Ravinder kocht, schmeckt man in jedem einzelnen Bissen. »Es ist einfach das tollste Gefühl der Welt, wenn man jemanden bekochen darf«, schwärmt sie und nascht flink eine geröstete und zuvor mit Ahornsirup beträufelte Mandel. »Man bekommt so viel Liebe und Dankbarkeit«, und sie beginnt erneut zu lachen. »Ich bin richtig süchtig danach. Und ja, wenn ich es mir recht überlege, mache ich es eigentlich nur der Komplimente wegen.«

and energetically shakes the enormous frying pans that look much too heavy for her delicate wrists – all without the slightest mishap. Then, as she reaches over the table for a piece of chocolate, a chunk of butter falls to the ground. Uttering a little cry, she says: "I must seem like the clumsiest chef, mustn't I? I actually am, I have no patience at all!" The passion Ravinder puts in her cooking can be tasted in every single bite. "It's the most satisfying feeling in the world when you cook for people," she enthuses and chomps on a roasted almond coated in maple syrup. "I love the difference you can make to someone's day if you give them a beautiful bowl of cooked pasta, a curry or a lovingly prepared stew. They feel so grateful to you and they give you so much love," she says as she starts laughing again. "I'm addicted to receiving that. So when I think about it, I just do it for the compliments!"

ICH LIEBE ES, WIE SEHR MAN JEMANDEM DEN TAG VERSÜSSEN KANN, WENN MAN IHM EINE SCHALE FRISCHER PASTA, EIN CURRY ODER EINEN LIEBEVOLL ZUBEREITETEN EINTOPF VOR DIE NASE STELLT. MAN BEKOMMT SO VIEL LIEBE UND DANKBARKEIT.

Egal, worüber Ravinder spricht, ihre positive Ausstrahlung fegt alle anders gepolten Energien im Umkreis von mindestens hundert Kilometern vom Feld und jedes Thema wird zum Vergnügen. Beim Mittagessen in einem nahe gelegenen Diner plaudert sie über die Kausalität ihrer beiden Laster, hohe Absätze und Taxis, ihre letzte Zusammenarbeit mit Guy&Max Diamonds, als sie mit einem essbaren Goldspray ihre berühmten selbstgerösteten Nüsse in goldene Diamanten verwandelte (»Am liebsten würde ich seither alles mit diesem Goldspray besprühen, bevor ich es esse!«), oder die lange Liste ihrer kochenden Inspirationsfiguren. Sie spricht und erzählt mit einer Leichtigkeit, dass man sich nicht wundern würde, wenn sie sich bei der Altersangabe um zehn Jahre älter geschummelt hätte. Und selbst dem glibberigen Sandwich, das man ihr in dem heruntergekommenen Lokal vorsetzt, kann sie etwas Gutes abgewinnen und isst es bis auf den letzten Krümel auf, bedankt sich mit einer umwerfenden Herzlichkeit beim geplätteten Inhaber und tingelt auf ihren hohen Schuhen aus dem Laden. Nur den Tee lässt sie zwinkernd stehen. »Der war nun doch etwas zu speziell für mich«, witzelt sie.

Am liebsten hört man Ravinder aber zu, wenn sie über Menschen spricht, die sie mag, dann leuchten ihre dunklen Augen unter den pechschwarzen Haaren hervor. Da ist beispielsweise ihr Bruder, »kein so guter Koch«, und ihre drei Schwestern, »allesamt brillante Köchinnen«, von denen eine in Indien lebt. »Das ist wunderbar«, findet Ravinder, die generell viel und mindestens einmal pro Jahr nach Indien reist. »Jetzt habe ich da immer ein Zuhause.« Wem

No matter what subject Ravinder talks about, her optimism sweeps away any negative vibes within a radius of at least one hundred kilometers. During our lunch in a nearby diner she chats about the connection between her two vices, high heels and taxis, her recent cooperation with Guy&Max in which she transformed her famed roasted nuts into golden diamonds using edible gold spray ("Ever since, I'd really like to spray it on everything I eat!") and a long list of cooks that inspire her. Appearing to be in her mid-twenties at most with her youthful and refreshingly lighthearted persona, she even finds something positive to say about the rubbery sandwich they dish up at the seedy café while polishing off the last crumb. Then, thanking the slightly stunned proprietor effusively, Ravinder skips out on her high heels, leaving only the tea untouched. There she makes a joking comment with a wink: "That was a bit too much."

Ravinder is particularly enchanting when she talks about the people she loves, and her eyes begin to glow from behind her ebony-black bangs. For example, about her brother, who's "not really a good cook," and her three sisters, "all brilliant cooks," one of whom lives in India. "It's fantastic," says Ravinder, who travels frequently in general, and at least once a year to India. "Now I have a home there, too." No one, however, comes close to Ravinder's mother in the kitchen. A mother who never went to school, yet ironically taught Ravinder nearly everything she needs to know to earn her livelihood. "My mother is a magical cook. Anything that passes through her hands tastes incredibly good. Even if she peels a piece of fruit for you, it tastes better because it has been in her hands. She is completely magical." Ravinder's father, whose photo can be found in her first cookbook,

I would really love to stand for ethical luxury. Pleasure and responsibility do not have to be mutually exclusive.

aber niemand das Wasser zu reichen vermag, ist Ravinders Mutter, die selbst nie zur Schule ging, Ravinder aber all das beibrachte, womit diese nun ihren Lebensunterhalt verdient. »Meine Mutter ist eine zauberhafte Köchin. Alles, was sie mit ihren Händen berührt, schmeckt gut. Selbst wenn sie dir eine Frucht schält, schmeckt diese Frucht besser als alles andere, allein deshalb, weil sie in ihren Händen war. Sie ist einfach nur magisch.« Ravinders Vater, dessen Foto in ihrem ersten Kochbuch auf einer der ersten Seiten zu sehen ist, verstarb kürzlich. »Er hatte einen Traum für mich«, erzählt sie. »Als ich noch als Mode- und Beauty-Journalistin arbeitete, konnte er sich darunter nie richtig etwas vorstellen. Mein Berufsleben spielte sich in einer Welt ab, die ihm völlig fremd war. Aber als ich dann mit Essen zu arbeiten begann, machte ihn das richtig stolz und er freute sich sehr«, erinnert sie sich. »Ich möchte diesen Traum auch ein Stück weit für ihn weiterleben.«

Und dieser Traum ist nicht einfach nur ein eigenes Restaurant. »Klar, das wäre wundervoll und ich verdiene mir derweil in diversen von Männern dominierten Küchen meine Sporen ab«, erzählt sie. Die mediale Aufmerksamkeit, die der schönen Köchin zuteil wird, will sie aber auch in einem größeren Kontext für ihre Marke nutzen. »Ich möchte für ethischen Luxus stehen. Genuss und Verantwortung sollen sich nicht ausschließen«, ist Ravinder überzeugt. »Ich möchte für die Leute einstehen, die für ihre Produkte keinen fairen Preis bezahlt bekommen. Und ohne dass ich in das Leben von irgendwem eingreifen oder den Mahnfinger erheben möchte, will ich zeigen, wie viel Unterschied manchmal nur schon zehn Cents machen können, denn jeder Kaufakt ist eine Entscheidung, mit der man etwas bewirken kann.« Dass sie ihre Füße zum Weltverbessern nicht in Ökosandalen stecken muss, freut sie dabei sicherlich. —

died recently. "He had this dream for me," she says. "When I was a beauty journalist he didn't really understand what I did and complained about that. My work took place in a world that was completely foreign to him. Then, when I started to do food, he was so proud and excited. He was very happy," she recalls. "I want to live this dream for him a bit as well."

A dream that is not just about owning a restaurant. "Of course, that would be wonderful and right now I'm really earning my stripes at the moment, going into these male-dominated kitchens and working very hard." However, this gorgeous and talented cook also wants to channel the enormous media attention she's receiving so that her brand will also benefit the greater good. "I want to stand up for people who are not being paid a fair wage for the food they produce. And, without interfering with other people's lives or being judgmental, I want to show what a difference even only 10 pence more can make. Every decision to buy is also a decision that can make a difference." Luckily for her, scaling back to eco-friendly footwear is not essential in her mission to improve the world. —

09

Dean & DeLuca
Giorgio DeLuca

Text **René Allemann** Photos **Marc Gerritsen**

DEAN & DELUCA
DEAN & DELUCA
DEAN & DELUCA

Im September 1977 eröffneten Joel Dean und Giorgio Deluca ihren Feinkostladen im New Yorker Stadtteil Soho und lösten damit im kulinarischen Wilden Westen der Siebzigerjahre eine kleine Revolution aus. Heute gilt Dean & Deluca als die beste Adresse für Feinschmecker, und das weit über New York hinaus.

In September of 1977, Joel Dean and Giorgio Deluca opened a small, high-end grocery store in New York's SoHo neighborhood and instigated a minor revolution in the culinary abyss of the seventies. Today, Dean & Deluca is the address for gourmets and famed far beyond the city limits of New York.

Wir schreiben das Jahr 1977. New Yorks Stadtteil Soho erlebt seine erste Blütezeit. Eine Generation junger, aufstrebender Künstler und Intellektueller erschafft sich einen neuen Mikrokosmos. Es ist die Zeit der Kreativen, des Weins und der Käsepartys. In ganz Soho feiern sich die Stars und Starlets der neuen Bohème mit französischer Feinkost.

Giorgio Deluca, Sohn einer Familie italienisch-amerikanischer Abstammung, hing seinen Beruf als Geschichtslehrer nach knapp einem Jahr an den Nagel, denn er wollte mit dem schäbigen Bildungssystem nichts mehr zu tun haben. Giorgio war mit einem außergewöhnlichen kulinarischen Repertoire aufgewachsen: Sein Vater, ein Banker, hatte sich 1945 zusätzlich auf den Import italienischer Lebensmittel spezialisiert. Darin erkannte auch der junge Deluca seine Chance und eröffnete mitten im aufstrebenden Soho einen eigenen kleinen Käseladen. So wurde er binnen weniger Monate für die Künstler zu »Mister Cheese«. Vier Jahre später, im September 1977, erweiterte er sein Sortiment, eröffnete einen neuen Laden und holte seinen Freund Joel an Bord – die Geburtsstunde von Dean & Deluca.

Einer strengen Linie folgend, boten sie eine Auswahl hochwertiger Lebensmittel und Küchenwaren an. Dean & Deluca richtete sich seit den ersten Tagen an ein anspruchsvolles Publikum. Und dies in einer Zeit, in der das Essen in Amerika vorwiegend aus der Tiefkühltruhe kam und in den Läden alles aus Plastik war. Erschwinglichkeit, Geschwindigkeit und Bequemlichkeit waren die Schlagworte der damaligen Esskultur. »Die meisten hatten ja keine Ahnung, was es da draußen in der Welt alles Fantastisches gab – so fixiert waren sie auf den eigenen Tiefkühler, dass sie vergaßen, dass frisch zubereitetem Gemüse ein ganz anderer Genuss innewohnt. Unsere Mission war es, die Qualität im Lebensmittelbereich wieder einzuführen. Ein Verständnis dafür zu schaffen, was gut und was sehr gut ist. Wir wollten den Menschen zeigen, dass sie mehr Möglichkeiten haben, als sie selber ahnten», so Deluca über seine Vision von damals.

Dean & Deluca sollte nicht bloß ein Name auf der Verpackung von exotischen Gewürzen sein, sondern für ein Lebensgefühl stehen. Dabei achtete Deluca bewusst darauf, nicht schick, ausgefallen oder trendy zu sein. Er wollte mit allen Mitteln verhindern, dass man sie als Snobs abstempelte. Denn ihm war klar, wie kurzlebig das gewesen wäre. »Wir wollten Produkte präsentieren, von denen wir überzeugt waren, dass es die besten sind. Und das in einem Umfeld, das den Produkten und ihrer Herkunft gerecht wurde.« Die beiden überließen

The scene is set in New York, 1977, where the SoHo district is becoming increasingly popular as it fills up with a new generation of young, ambitious artists and intellectuals intent on creating their own microcosm. It is the era of creativity, of wine and cheese parties, and the burgeoning downtown bohemian scene celebrates itself with French gourmet food.

Giorgio Deluca, the son of a first generation Italian-American family, quits his job as a history teacher after a year and decides to wash his hands of the sordid educational system. Having grown up in an extraordinarily rich culinary environment, courtesy of his father, a banker, who joined a food brokerage business specializing in Italian food imports in 1945, young Deluca decides that this business may have potential and opens a small cheese shop in SoHo. Within a couple of months, Giorgio has become "Mr. Cheese" to the neighborhood artists. Four years later, in September of 1977, he broadens his range of products and reopens at a new location close by, taking his friend Joel on board: Dean & Deluca are born.

Through a vigorous editing process they offered a selection of worthy foodstuffs and kitchen wares – from good to very best. From day one, Dean & Deluca targeted a discerning clientele with a keen taste both for gourmet food and aesthetics. And this in an era when food in America came predominantly out of the freezer and stores were almost exclusively decorated with plastic trimmings. Quick, affordable and convenient were the marketing slogans of the day. "Most people did not have a clue about all the superb food out there – they were so fixed on their own freezer they completely forgot that freshly prepared food has a different flavor altogether. Nobody seemed to know what quality was anymore. So we made it our mission to reintroduce excellence into the food sector. And to create an understanding of what is good and what is very good. We wanted to show people that they had more options than they realized," is how Deluca describes the vision he had.

Dean & Deluca did not just want to become a name on a can of exotic spices. The brand was supposed to stand for a way of life, for quality and aesthetics. At the same time, Deluca was careful not to become too chic, too offbeat, too trendy. "Your name is your most valuable capital. Your reputation should always come first, before the money," he says. At all costs Dean and Deluca wanted to avoid being labeled snobs, knowing that would have short-lived potential at best. "We wanted to offer products we were convinced were the very best. And display them in surroundings that did them and their provenance justice." They left absolutely nothing up to chance. At a time when nobody had heard of integrated

nichts dem Zufall. Zu einer Zeit, als man weder von integrierter Kommunikation noch von der Wichtigkeit eines einheitlichen Markenerlebnisses sprach, verstanden sie, wie man alle fünf Sinne der Konsumenten ansprach. So waren Dean und Deluca bald nicht nur für die herausragende Qualität ihrer Produkte bekannt, sondern auch für ihre ästhetischen Verpackungen, die Musikauswahl und den Einsatz echter Materialien im Laden sowie für das beste Personal. Dies alles ließ über die Jahre eine einzigartige Erlebniswelt entstehen, die selbst im heutigen Amerika, zumindest in der Nahrungsmittelindustrie, noch darauf wartet, übertroffen zu werden.

communication or of holistic brand experiences, Dean and Deluca were catering to their customers' five senses. Soon the partners were known not only for the excellent quality of their products, but also for their aesthetic packaging, their choice of music, the use of authentic decorations in their shop, and their qualified staff. Over the years, they created a unique food experience for their customers that remains unequaled even in latter-day America – at least in the food business.

IT WAS MY TASK TO OFFER A CHOICE. TO DISPLAY A SELECTION OF THE BEST PRODUCTS, SO CUSTOMERS WOULD DARE TO TRY SOMETHING NEW, ALLOW THEMSELVES TO BE TEMPTED INTO EXPERIENCING SOMETHING EXTRAORDINARY AND ONE-OF-A-KIND.

Doch damit allein lässt sich der Erfolg nicht erklären. Es waren mehr als nur die Waren und der Ort, an dem diese verkauft wurden. Alles war echt und authentisch an Dean & Deluca, die Produkte und die Macher. Die beiden Geschäftspartner standen mit ihrem Namen für die Integrität des Angebots. Das hatte schon damals eine starke Wirkung. Und sie verstanden noch etwas anderes: Die Menschen sind dankbar für angebotene Hilfe bei der Auswahl. Gut, dass Deluca ein Vordenker mit wachem Verstand ist, ein kritischer Beobachter, der es sich zur Aufgabe gemacht hat, Trends frühzeitig zu erkennen. »Meine Aufgabe war es, den Menschen eine Selektion zu bieten, für sie die besten Dinge auszuwählen, damit sie sich trauten, Neues auszuprobieren, sich einzulassen auf das Spezielle, das Gute und Einmalige.«

Es scheint, als sei sich Deluca in all den Jahren treu geblieben. Vielleicht auch deshalb, weil er sich seine Position im Leben hart erarbeiten musste und sie ihm nicht in den Schoß gefallen ist. Seine Selbständigkeit hat ihn aus der vertrackten Depression seiner Kindheit, wie er selbst sagt, herauskatapultiert. Aufzuwachsen mit dem Vater und der Stiefmutter, nachdem seine leibliche Mutter gestorben war, als er erst zwei Jahre alt war, das hat ihn blockiert. Da habe sein Entscheid, einen eigenen Laden aufzumachen, seine Persönlichkeit wie eine Rakete gezündet.

Deluca ist noch heute überrascht vom schnellen Erfolg. Seine Leidenschaft für sein Lebenswerk, aber auch für Qualität und Ästhetik generell sind auch heute noch spürbar. Auch wenn er sich aus dem operativen Geschäft bei Dean & Deluca bereits vor einigen Jahren zurückgezogen hat, lebt er seinen Traum vom perfekten kulinarischen Erlebnis weiter: in seinem neuen Restaurant »Giorgione«. Und es würde nicht verwundern,

But that alone does not explain their success. It was more than just the right products in the right venue. Everything felt honest and authentic at Dean & Deluca: the products and the men who sold them. Both business partners vouched for the quality of their goods and lived by their convictions. This sent a powerful message. Another thing they understood was that most people are grateful for advice when it comes to trying something new. Luckily, Deluca is the archetypal forward thinker, a critical observer who prides himself in catching trends early.

It would appear that Deluca has remained true to type over the years. Maybe this is the result of all the hard work he put into his personal and professional life: success was not handed to him on a platter. His professional achievements catapulted him out of the confounded depression of his childhood – as he puts it – caused by growing up with his father and stepmother after his mother died when he was only two. His decision to start his own store acted as a catalyst on his personal development.

Even today, Deluca is surprised by their meteoric success that went far beyond his wildest dreams. And yet, despite this success, his passion not only for his life's work, but also for quality and aesthetics in general has not flagged. Although he withdrew from the operating business of Dean & Deluca a few years ago, he continues to live his dream of the perfect culinary experience in his new restaurant "Giorgione." Still brimming with ideas, it would come as no surprise if he were to open another shop with an entirely new concept. Slowly but surely he is becoming a brand himself.

In terms of all-embracing aesthetics, Dean & Deluca remains matchless. To be sure, the brand has lost a little of its sheen during the last few years: expanding to new locations and markets has

Betrachte deinen Namen als dein wichtigstes Kapital. Vor dem Geld kommt immer dein Ruf.

wenn er da und dort wieder einen neuen Laden mit einem neuen Konzept eröffnen würde. Ideen hätte er jedenfalls genug. Und so macht er sich selbst langsam, aber sicher zur Marke. Die Gesamtästhetik von Dean & Deluca hat bis heute kaum jemand übertroffen, auch wenn die Marke in den letzten Jahren etwas von ihrem Glanz eingebüßt hat. Die Qualität hat unter der Expansion an neue Standorte und in neue Märkte gelitten. Doch die Marke bietet noch heute ein stimmiges Erlebnis und sie lebt vom guten Ruf der Gründungszeit. Das ist nicht ungefährlich, zumal die damaligen Gründer nicht mehr aktiv sind. Bleibt zu hoffen, dass die heutigen Manager die Geschichte und das Selbstverständnis der Marke wirklich erfasst haben und nicht dem kurzfristigen und mutlosen Gewinnstreben erliegen. —

affected quality to a small extent. Nevertheless, the brand's concept remains intact and is sustained by the good name it has carried over from its founding years. This is not entirely unproblematic, given that both of the founders have retired from the operating business. It remains to be seen whether the new managers have really grasped the brand's history and identity in all its details. Hopefully, they, too, will not succumb to the temptation of making nearsighted and uninspired decisions in the interest of short-term profits – and so carry on the founders' tradition of intuition, originality and quality. —

10

Edsor Kronen
Jan-Henrik M. Scheper-Stuke

Text **Olivia El Sayed** Photos **Gian Marco Castelberg**

Bereits über hundert Jahre alt ist die Tradition dieser Marke. 1909 wurde sie unter dem Namen »Kronenmarke« aus der Faszination für Aristokratie heraus gegründet. Ab 1911 war das Unternehmen gar Haus- und Hoflieferant von Kaiser Wilhelm II. Die beiden Weltkriege erschwerten ihren Werdegang, denn kaum erwachte in den Zwanzigerjahren das Bedürfnis, Kleiderkultur zu leben, wurde es vom darauffolgenden Krieg wieder verdrängt. Überflüssig, die Folgen im Detail zu nennen: Danach Marken mit deutschem Namen etablieren zu wollen war mehr als schwer. Edward Windsor diente daher als Inspiration – nicht nur für die die Marke nährende Ideologie, sondern auch für ihren Namen. Aus den ersten zwei und den letzen drei Buchstaben des Gentlemans der Fünfziger- und Sechzigerjahre entstand der fiktive Markenname »Edsor«.

The brand Edsor Kronen draws on more than one hundred years of tradition. Originally established in 1909 under the label "Kronenmarke," literally meaning the Crown's brand, the name was chosen to reflect a fascination for the aristocracy. In 1911, the company was even appointed as purveyor to the court of Kaiser Wilhelm II. Then came the two World Wars, each making a significant impact on the company's development. As the demand for elegant clothing rekindled in the 1920s, it was almost immediately extinguished again by the following war. After World War II, brands with a German name found it especially hard to find their footing again. While seeking a solution, the company was inspired by Edward Windsor. In a tribute to this mid-20th century nobleman, the tie manufacturers decided to create the fictive brand name "Edsor" by using the first and the last syllable of the royal name.

Im Innenhof der traditionsreichen Hackeschen Höfe tippeln elegant bestrumpfte Promibeine neben nobel beschuhten Herrenfüßen über das blau beleuchtete Kopfsteinpflaster. Ein paar lokale Glanzlichter umschwirren die runden Tischchen, die vor dem neu eröffneten Edsor Flagship Store stehen, Kameras klicken und es klirrt das Eis in den gereichten Cocktailgläsern, während sich Jan-Henrik M. Scheper-Stuke nach unzähligen geschüttelten Händen seinen Weg vom roten Teppich durch die Menge ins Licht bahnt. Nicht nur er, Inhaber und Testimonial der Marke, spricht zu diesem Anlass ein paar Worte, sondern auch Dr. Philipp Rösler, Bundesminister für Wirtschaft und Technologie, gibt sich die Ehre und betont in seiner Rede die Wichtigkeit von Familienbetrieben in der heutigen Zeit. Ein Toast, Musik, und der Abend nimmt seinen Lauf. Ein weiterer Schritt in der langen Markengeschichte von Edsor.

Die Manufaktur selbst befindet sich in einem fast schon provozierend unauffälligen Hinterhof in Kreuzberg. Ein paar Treppenstufen über Boden, im Wartezimmer und Showroom, spürt man die Erlebniswelt der Marke dann jedoch deutlich. Sie haftet förmlich an den WMF-Vasen und flüstert aus den alten Schränken und Kommoden, die den Raum definieren. Zwei Pferdeköpfe in Silber zieren die Wände, in ihren Mäulern hauseigene Krawatten. Daneben ein Sofa, auf dessen dunkelrotem Bezug sich ein paar müde Sonnenstrahlen, die sich früher an diesem Tag ihren Weg durch die hohen Fenster gebahnt haben, ausruhen. Noch ist es unbesetzt. Nach einer halben Stunde eilt uns ein junger Mann entgegen. Blass wie ein Spannbettlaken und offensichtlich etwas angeschlagen begrüßt er uns, dies aber wider Erwarten sprudelnd eloquent. Er benötigt nur ein paar Sekunden, um uns eine vollumfängliche Erklärung, einem Syntaxfeuerwerk gleich, zu liefern, die mehr als verständlich macht, warum er es nicht früher schaffte. Vor lauter Überraschung, dass aus dem müden Gesicht so viele Worte kommen, kann man sich den Inhalt der Erklärung ohne Nachfragen dann aber doch nicht so recht merken. Schleife zu eng gebunden, keine Luft mehr, zu viel

In an inner courtyard of the Hackeschen Höfe, a complex of traditional buildings and courtyards in the center of Berlin, elegant legs trip lightly over the blue-lit cobblestones, keeping time with dapper male feet shod in bespoke shoes. A few local celebrities can be observed mingling at the bistro tables in front of the brand-new Edsor Flagship Store. Cameras click and ice cubes tinkle in cocktail glasses as Jan-Henrik M. Scheper-Stuke walks down the red carpet toward the lights. Passing through the crowd he shakes countless hands and then goes on to address the audience in his capacity as the brand's figurehead. He is followed by Federal Minister of Economics and Technology, Dr. Philipp Rösler, whose speech is an endorsement of family establishments in this day and age. A toast, some music, and the evening is well underway. Yet another step forward in Edsor's time-honored brand history.

The manufactory is located in an anonymous courtyard in Berlin's Kreuzberg district, a setting so humble as to be almost provocative. However, a few steps up, in the waiting room and the showroom, the brand experience makes itself clearly felt – indeed it is almost clinging to the WMF vases and whispering among the antique cupboards and cabinets that give the venue its character. Two silver horse-head figures are mounted on the wall, each with an exclusive cravat dangling from its mouth. Next to them a sofa with dark red upholstery on which a few tired sunbeams rest after having found their way through the high windows earlier during the day. As yet, it is unoccupied. Half an hour later, a young man comes rushing into the waiting room, white as a sheet and obviously somewhat under the weather. His greeting words, however, are surprisingly energetic. Within seconds he has delivered a complete explanation for his lateness with an overwhelming display of syntactical fireworks. In our surprise that such an exhausted-looking person could immediately start firing off a long and convoluted monologue, we find it difficult to follow his account from start to finish: bow too tight, no air, too much work, two years without a break, it had to happen, a stay at the hospital, but now it's time to continue, opening tomorrow – some water? No chance to get in a word edgewise, let alone ask questions, before Jan-Henrik M. Scheper-

LODEN-FREY
FÜR

gearbeitet, seit zwei Jahren ununterbrochen, so musste es ja kommen, bis eben im Krankenhaus, nun aber weiter, morgen die Eröffnung – ein Wasser? Nachhaken geht nicht, denn Jan-Henrik M. Scheper-Stuke ist schon wieder drei Schritte weiter. Für die Verspätung entschuldigt er sich dann so vornehm, dass man sich schon fast schämt, die offensichtlich immer etwas zu knapp bemessene Zeit des jungen Herrn in Anspruch zu nehmen. Nach einem kurzen, aber freundlichen Hallo in den Nebenraum, wo sich noch einige Mitarbeitende aufhalten, erzählt er über das, was sein Leben bestimmt – die Marke Edsor und deren Entwicklung.

Stuke has already latched on to the next topic. His apologies for the delay are so profuse that we are almost ashamed to demand more time from the obviously packed schedule of this extremely busy young man. After calling out a brief, yet friendly greeting to several employees who are busy in the next room, he starts telling us what it is that has taken over his life so completely these past two years: Edsor and its development.

ICH HATTE NIEMALS DIESEN DRANG ZU REBELLIEREN. ICH HÄTTE GAR NICHT GEWUSST, WAS ICH SONST HÄTTE MACHEN SOLLEN. DROGEN FAND ICH ANSTRENGEND UND NICHT ANSPRECHEND. NICHT DER BESTE SEIN ZU WOLLEN LAG BEI UNS NICHT DRIN UND MITTELMASS FAND ICH IMMER DOOF.

»Mein Vater hatte einen eigenen landwirtschaftlichen Betrieb, den jetzt einer meiner Brüder übernommen hat. Er lebt für die Jagd, für die Schweine- und Rinderzucht«, erzählt er. »Das ist schön, aber nicht meine Welt. Wie der liebe Gott will, gab es auch diesen anderen Teil der Familie, der sich der Ästhetik verschrieben hatte. Das hat dann auch komplett mein Interesse geweckt.« Schon während seiner Zeit im Internat war Jan-Henrik anders – statt des Binders, den damals alle tragen mussten, band er sich aus demselben Stoff eine Schleife. Und aufgrund der langjährigen Tradition und dem Hintergrund seiner Familie war und blieb er auch der einzige, dem dies gestattet wurde. Seither sieht man ihn selten ohne Schleife. »Dementsprechend lebe ich seit diesem Zeitpunkt eigentlich schon unsere Marke.« Knapp war seine Zeit schon immer, »gereicht hat es aber dennoch für alles.« Schülerpräsident und Fachschaftsratsvorsitzender, von Haus aus gelernter Bankbetriebswirt – immer vorne, immer rechtzeitig und noch keine dreißig. »Ich habe keine Angst vor dem Alter. Wer nicht älter werden will, will auch die Entwicklung nicht sehen.« Definitiv zum Luxusgut (»Hätte ich Zeit, würde ich wieder mehr Golf spielen. Und das nicht schlecht.«) wurde seine Zeit dann, als er sich dazu entschloss, mit der Marke einen neuen Kurs einzuschlagen: das Gute gut zu lassen, das Verstaubte zu entstauben und selbst zum Markenbotschafter zu werden, und das mit Haut und Haar. So ist es er selbst, der von den Plakatwänden und Broschüren blickt (»Die feinen Gesichtszüge habe ich von meiner Mutter geerbt.«), sich der kompletten Kommunikation annimmt und die Marke zum international gefragten Nischenprodukt führen will. »Wenn die Marke einmal verbrannt ist, braucht man mindestens fünf Jahre, um sie wiederherzustellen.«

"My father ran his own agricultural holding which one of my brothers has taken over in the meantime. Hunting as well as breeding pigs and cattle are his passion. Which is fine, but not at all my world. Mercifully there is another side to the family that is dedicated to aesthetics. This is where my passions lie." Already during his time at boarding school Jan-Henrik stood out from the rest. "I never had the urge to rebel. There was nothing I really wanted to change. Doing drugs never appealed to me, and not wanting to excel was not an option. I find mediocrity dull," he says. So instead of wearing the tie that was part of the dress code at boarding school, he preferred to knot himself a bow tie from the same material. Thanks to his family's background and their long-standing tradition, Jan-Henrik was and remains the only student ever to receive permission for this. Since that day he has hardly ever been seen without a bow tie. "In fact, one can say that from that point in time onwards I started living our brand." He's never had a lot of spare time, but "always time enough to do everything." Class representative, student body president – always at the top, always on time, and not yet thirty. Time definitely has become a luxury ("If I had time, I'd play more golf again. And not badly either.") since he decided to lead the brand in a new direction. His aim is to leave what works, but to infuse new zest into those divisions that need a boost. His strategy of choice has been to become the brand ambassador himself. Something he does with enormous conviction. And which explains why it is his face we see looking at us from billboards and in brochures. ("I inherited the good bone structure of my mother.") Taking charge of communications entirely, he plans to recreate the brand as an internationally sought-after niche product. "When a brand has fallen into decline, it takes at least five years for it to recover."

Text Wirtschaft

Edsor
Edsor
für Feuerwehr

Günther H. Stelly, sein Patenonkel und ehemaliger Geschäftsführer des Betriebs, führte den ambitionierten Jüngling in das Manufakturleben ein. 2010 bereits übernahm er dann die Position des Geschäftsführers, während Günther H. Stelly seinen Posten als Chefdesigner nach wie vor innehält und sich für die über dreitausend jährlich kreierten Stoffmuster verantwortlich zeigt. Es ist inzwischen kurz vor drei Uhr: Die Verspätung hat zur Folge, dass viele der Mitarbeitenden nicht mehr anwesend sind. Viel wird in der Manufaktur noch von Heimarbeiterinnen erledigt, die um die Mittagszeit ihre Sachen abholen oder zugestellt bekommen, so dass es nun in der Mitte dieses Nachmittags schon sehr still ist. Jan-Henrik M. Scheper-Stuke greift zum Telefon, das auf dem Art-déco-Tischchen steht. Dass sich hier alle siezen, fällt zunächst gar nicht auf. »Es gibt ein viel verbindlicheres Sie als ein gewolltes Du. Es erzeugt einen respektvolleren Umgang miteinander.«

Günther H. Stelly, his godfather and the former managing director of the company, introduced the ambitious young man to manufacturing. In 2010, he assumed the role of managing director while Günther H. Stelly continued as the leading designer, responsible for the three thousand fabric patterns they design annually. Meanwhile, due to our initial delay, it is almost three o'clock. A large number of the employees have already left. Many of the wares are produced by homeworkers who deliver and pick up their assignments around noon. By the middle of the afternoon, the premises have become very quiet indeed. Jan-Henrik M. Scheper-Stuke reaches for the phone that stands on an Art Deco side table. And suddenly, we become aware that the mode of conduct in this establishment is extremely formal. "We prefer to employ a formal mode of address. In our opinion, it leads to a more respectful business relationship than the over-familiar tones that are generally adopted nowadays."

GETTING OLDER DOES NOT WORRY ME. PEOPLE WHO DON'T WANT TO GROW OLDER DON'T WANT TO EXPERIENCE DEVELOPMENT.

Adrett gekämmt, die Kleidung selbstverständlich knitter- und einwandfrei, von Kopf bis Fuß auf Aristokratie eingestellt, würde ein Du auch fast zu jovial wirken. Was dann aber doch ins Auge sticht – oder einfach nur von einer konsistenten Erlebniswelt zeugt, ist die Beschriftung des Telefons. Selbst die Tasten sind alle nach dem Schema Frau / Herr plus Nachname beschriftet. Er wählt die Taste »Frau Hartmann«. »Frau Hartmann, hallo, ich bin's. Sie wollten gerade gehen? – Mhm. Meinen Sie, Sie könnten den Herrschaften noch etwas zeigen?« Wir winken ab. Er winkt zurück. Mit seiner feinen Hand verdeckt er die Hörmuschel und raunt uns zu: »Sie macht alles für mich, keine Sorge.« Ein wenig wirkt er, als hätte er sich selbst erfunden.

Oben im Atelier schneidert Frau Hartmann in feinster Handarbeit geduldig eine Krawatte vor. Sie wirkt, als könnte sie es auch mit geschlossenen Augen. Pro Jahr fertigt die Kronen-Manufaktur zwischen achtzig- und hunderttausend Teile, für welche seit jeher ausschließlich feinste italienische Seide verarbeitet wird. Als Scheper-Stuke telefonierend hinter ein paar bunten Stoffballen verschwindet, lächelt sie und sagt: »Es ist schon alles ein bisschen hektischer geworden, seit er hier ist.« Und dann schneidert sie ruhig weiter. —

In truth, it's a bit hard to imagine lighthearted banter on first-name terms between this carefully groomed and faultlessly attired epitome of aristocratic style and his employees. What does catch our eye – although this may be just an example of a consistent brand experience – is the listing of names next to the pushbuttons on the telephone: all names are prefixed with "Herr" or "Frau." Jan-Henrik M. Scheper-Stuke presses the pushbutton labeled Frau Hartmann. "Mrs. Hartmann, hello, it's me. You were just on your way out? – Ah, I see. Would you mind giving our guests a short demonstration?" We give a wave to indicate it is not that important. But he waves back at us. Lowering the phone and covering the mouthpiece with a slender hand, he whispers: "She'll do anything for me, don't worry," playing the role he has created for himself to perfection.

Up in the atelier, Mrs. Hartmann patiently stitches a cravat for us with precise, exquisite craftsmanship. Her movements reveal years of practice, and she could probably tailor a tie with her eyes shut. Annually, the manufacturer Edsor Kronen prepares two exclusive collections made of the finest Italian silks, their fabric of choice from the very beginning. As Scheper-Stuke disappears behind a few brightly colored fabric bales to conduct a phone call, Mrs. Hartmann smiles and says: "It has become a tad more hectic since he joined us," and then continues to stitch in calm, precise movements. —

11

MAISON FABRE
JEAN-MARC & OLIVIER FABRE

Text **Barbara Markert** Photos **Kai Jünemann**

Den Handschuhmacher Fabre gibt es seit fast einem Jahrhundert, doch erst seit kurzer Zeit findet man seine erlesenen Produkte auf den Seiten von Modezeitschriften wieder. Nach einer wechselhaften Firmengeschichte, die vom Auf und Ab des Handschuhs in der Mode zeugt, kämpfen heute in der vierten Generation zwei entschlossene Brüder mit einer klaren Luxus- und Modestrategie erfolgreich gegen warme Winter und handschuhlose Sommer an.

Though glove maker Fabre has existed for almost a century, their exquisite products have only recently started appearing in fashion magazines. Now, after a checkered company history that reflects the ups and downs of glove fashion, two determined brothers are fighting back with a clearly defined strategy to make a name for themselves in the luxury and fashion segment.

Solange Pinaud fixiert durch ihre Brille hindurch das knallrote Leder in ihren Händen. Ohne den Blick abzuwenden, greift sie nach rechts und dreht sanft das Rad ihrer antiken Nähmaschine. Sofort saust die Nadel für drei klitzekleine Stiche herab und durchbohrt das samtig weiche Material, dann hält Solange inne und schiebt das Leder ein paar Millimeter nach vorne. Die Sisyphusarbeit nennt sich Piqué-anglais-Naht und Solange gehört zu den wenigen, die sie in Perfektion beherrschen. Mit 68 Jahren sollte die weißhaarige Dame längst in Rente sein. Sie ist es auch, sie helfe nur immer wieder mal aus – in dem Betrieb, in dem sie ihr ganzes Berufsleben verbrachte. Seit 45 Jahren sitzt Madame an exakt diesem Platz, an exakt dieser Nähmaschine. Missratene Handschuhe kennt sie nicht. »Ausschuss? Haben wir kaum.«

Peering through her glasses, Solange Pinaud fixes her eyes on the piece of bright red leather in her hands. Without looking, she reaches up and gently turns the wheel of her ancient sewing machine. Instantly, the needle darts down and thrusts through the soft, supple leather to make three minute stitches. Solange pauses, and then pushes the leather forward a couple of millimeters. This excruciatingly slow work is called piqué-anglais (English stitch), and Solange is one of the few who have mastered it. At the age of 68, however, she should have retired some time ago. Which she did – but she enjoys helping out every now and then in the company where she spent her entire working life. Madame Pinaud has been sitting in exactly this spot, behind this same machine for 45 years. Faulty work is not in her vocabulary. "Rejects? Practically never."

Bei uns werden alle Handschuhe wie vor hundert Jahren noch von Hand gefertigt. Alles, was wir produzieren, geht in den Verkauf, unser Lagerbestand ist null.

Solange arbeitet beim Handschuhmacher Fabre in Millau. Das kleine, verschlafene Städtchen mit zwanzigtausend Einwohnern im Südwesten Frankreichs galt einst als Hauptstadt der Handschuhe. Damals, als Damen ohne das modische Accessoire nicht ordnungsgemäß gekleidet waren, ratterten hier in über sechzig Werkstätten ganze Hundertschaften von Nähmaschinen. Heute sind davon fünf Unternehmen übrig. Fabre ist der zweitälteste Handwerksbetrieb und der einzige, der noch in der Hand seiner Gründer ist. Die vierte Generation, bestehend aus den Brüdern Jean-Marc und Olivier, versucht mit einer Handvoll Mitarbeiter in einer Zeit zu bestehen, in der Handschuhe schon lange kein modisches Muss mehr sind. Nur zehn weitere Angestellte arbeiten neben Solange in Fabres Atelier. Die meisten sind Frauen, die mit museumsreifen Gerätschaften hantieren oder per Hand Stickereien anfertigen. Im Eingangsbereich stapeln sich Pappkartons und Holzkisten, auf denen Post-its kleben mit handschriftlichen Bemerkungen wie »Phyton bordeaux« oder »Schlange haselnussbraun«. Gleich neben der fertigen Ware tropft es von der Decke. An der Rückwand des Ateliers füllen alte Garnspulen ein Schrank-

Solange works for the glove makers – or glovers – Fabre in Millau. A small, sleepy town in the southwest of France with a population of about twenthy thousand that was once the country's glove-making capital. In those days – when ladies were considered improperly dressed if they left the house without gloves – over sixty workshops had hundreds of sewing machines rattling away. Today, a total of five glove makers remain. Fabre is the second-oldest atelier and the only one still in the hands of its founders. The fourth generation, consisting of brothers Jean-Marc and Olivier and a handful of employees, are trying to survive in a time when gloves have long ceased to be a fashion dictate. Besides Solange there are only ten further employees working in the Fabre atelier. Most of the glovers are women who either work at dated machines or embroider by hand. In the entrance hall cardboard boxes and wooden cases are piled on top of each other, each bearing Post-its with hand-written labels such as "Phyton bordeaux" or "Snake hazelnut brown." Water leaks down from the roof, just next to the finished wares. At the back of the workshop, a cupboard is overbrimming with yarn bobbins. Judging by the dust on them, some have been sitting there for some time. Jean-Marc Fabre, who is in charge of

brother

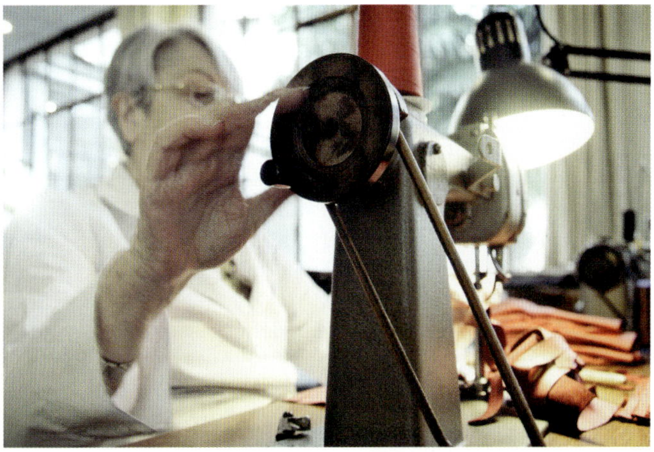

regal. Manche haben bereits Staub angesetzt. Jean-Marc Fabre, im Betrieb zuständig für die Produktion, meint: »Wir brauchen nur kleine Mengen, wie sie heute kaum noch einer verkauft, also heben wir alles auf.« Durch die hohen Fenster scheint die milde Herbstsonne, ein zarter Ledergeruch strömt durch den Raum. Außer dem monotonen, anheimelnden Tackern zweier Nähmaschinen ist es ganz still. Die Herstellung von Handschuhen erfordert höchste Konzentration, auch wenn die Mitarbeiter ihre Handgriffe blind beherrschen. Bis auf eine Auszubildende sind alle seit Jahrzehnten im Betrieb. Die meisten nähern sich der Rente oder machen wie Solange auch danach noch weiter. Freiwillig, weil sie ihren Arbeitgeber schätzen und irgendwie zur Familie gehören.

Die Geschichte der Familie beginnt mit Etienne, der sich 1924 auf Handschuhe aus dem weißen Leder der Zicklein, die rund um Millau herum auf den Hochweiden grasen, spezialisiert. Etiennes Business beginnt zu laufen, als der Zweite Weltkrieg ausbricht, in dem einer seiner beiden Söhne, Louis, ums Leben kommt. Dessen Zwillingsbruder Denis heiratet Rose, die ab 1947 erst nur mithilft und dann die Leitung übernimmt. Ihre Enkel kommen ins Schwärmen, wenn sie von ihrer energiegeladenen Oma sprechen: »Sie ist wie auf Red Bull. Großmutter war damals die einzige Firmenchefin am Ort. Sie hatte zwar kein Wahlrecht, dirigierte aber 350 Mitarbeiter.« Unter der Autodidaktin blüht die Firma auf. Von Reisen bringt Rose neue Modellideen mit, sie kooperiert mit Hermès, Dior oder Yves Saint Laurent und verkauft die eigene Linie bei Harrod's in London und Saks in New York. Zweitausend Modelle hat das Haus in diesen glorreichen Tagen im Angebot, pro Woche werden über tausend Tierhäute verarbeitet. »Damals verschickten wir unsere Handschuhe nach ganz Europa«, schwelgt die heute 93-Jährige in Erinnerungen. »Madame Pompidou fuhr zusammen mit Madame Funès im Rolls-Royce vor und lud den Kofferraum voll«, erinnert sie sich.

Rose Fabre sitzt dezent geschminkt und frisch frisiert auf einem kleinen Schemel neben Solange und hält mit ihrer langjährigen Mitarbeiterin ein Schwätzchen. Den Gehstock hat sie lässig an die Stanzeisen-Maschine gelehnt. Die alte Dame schaut gern im Atelier vorbei und ihr Wort zählt noch immer. Sie gibt ihren Segen, als ihr Sohn Louis in den Siebziger- und Achtzigerjahren Teile des einstigen Ateliers in Mietwohnungen umwandelt und die Produktion auf Sicherheitshandschuhe umstellt. Mit einem zusätzlichen Auftrag für die Armee navigiert Louis Fabre den Betrieb durch die Handschuh-Krise, die für die meisten Mitbewerber das Ende bedeutet. Doch Louis' Kampf ums Überleben der Firma reibt ihn auf. Als sein Sohn Olivier sich 1997 entschließt, seinen Berufstraum Politjournalist an den Nagel zu hängen, gibt der Vater ohne Zögern die Führung ab. Jean-Marc und Olivier übernehmen die Firma in schweren Zeiten. Der Armee-Auftrag bricht weg, neue Geschäftsideen sind gefragt. Durch einen Zufall lernt Olivier einen Designer von Yves Saint Laurent kennen. »Von ihm habe ich alles über Farbe gelernt. Er hat uns auf einen neuen Weg gebracht, den der Mode und des Luxus.« Die Neuorientierung in Richtung Prêt-à-porter ist gewagt. »Wir mussten vieles umstellen, jahrelang nur investieren und uns mühsam ein Image aufbauen.« Mit Exklusivmodellen für Lady

production, explains, "Often we only need small quantities, and almost nobody delivers like that nowadays. So we save everything." A mild autumn sun streams through the high window, and the faint smell of leather fills the air. Except for the monotonous clacking of two sewing machines, it is completely quiet. Crafting gloves requires a high level of concentration despite the fact that the employees are well-versed professionals who – aside from one trainee – have worked for the company for decades. Most of them are approaching retirement age, and some, like Solange, have carried on beyond that. Voluntarily, because of their deep-rooted affection for their employer and out of loyalty to the trade.

The family fortunes started with Etienne, who was specialized in making gloves from white kid leather of which there was a steady supply from the goats that grazed on the high plateaus surrounding Millau. Etienne's business was well on its way when World War II broke out and one of his sons, Louis, was killed during the war. After the war, Louis's twin brother Denis married Rose, who started helping along in the business in 1947 and then went on to take charge of the entire company. Her grandsons start rhapsodizing when the topic of their energy-laden grandmother comes up, saying she acts like she's flying on Red Bull. "Grandma was the only businesswoman running a company in the region. She didn't have the right to vote, but she did have 350 employees working for her." Under the wings of this determined woman who, with no formal training, took on the business, the company flourished. Rose brought back ideas for new models from her travels, started working with Hermès, Dior and Yves Saint Laurent, and placed the Fabre's own line with Harrods in London and Saks in New York. In its glory days, the company offered a selection of two thousand different glove models, and more than one thousand animal hides were processed every week. "Our gloves were delivered throughout Europe back then," the 93-year-old remembers with pleasure. "Madame Pompidou, the president's wife, would arrive with her friend Madame Funès in a Rolls Royce and fill the trunk with gloves," she recalls.

Freshly coiffed and with a touch of makeup, Rose sits on a little stool next to Solange and chats with their longtime employee. Her walking stick is nonchalantly leaned on a punching machine. The old lady enjoys looking in on the workshop, and her word still carries weight. She gave her blessing when her son Louis decided to convert parts of the former workshop into rented property and switch to manufacturing safety gloves. Along with an additional military contract, this was how Louis Fabre was able to navigate the company through the glove crisis during which most of the competition was forced to close down. But Louis' fight for the company's survival took its toll. When his son Olivier decided to quit his dream of becoming a political journalist in 1997, Louis was glad to hand over the reins immediately. Jean-Marc and Olivier took over the company in an extremely difficult economic phase. The military contract fell by the wayside and new entrepreneurial vision was required. By coincidence, Oliver became acquainted with a designer at Yves Saint Laurent. "I learned everything about colors from him. He led us in a new direction – to the fashion and luxury segment." However, gearing themselves towards prêt-à-porter came at a price. "We had to change a lot of things, and we have been investing money for years to slowly

OUR CLIENTS MUST NEVER HAVE THE SLIGHTEST REASON TO COMPLAIN.

Gaga und Beth Ditto, Messebesuchen, Kooperationen mit Nachwuchsdesignern sowie sehr viel persönlichem Einsatz aller gelingt die Kehrtwende. Fabre macht 2010 bei zwei Millionen Euro Umsatz erstmals wieder Gewinn. Zwei eigene Läden in Paris dienen als Schaufenster für neueste Kreationen. Namhafte Modedesigner wie Ann Demeulemeester, Walter van Beirendonck, Carven und der Haute-Couture-Stylist Stéphane Rolland greifen inzwischen auf das Knowhow des kleinen Betriebs aus Millau zurück. »Unsere Kunden dürfen niemals Anlass zu Klagen haben«, betont Olivier.

Nach der Eroberung des heimischen Marktes will Fabre wieder international werden. Überall, wo es kalt ist, sollen Boutiquen entstehen. »Für die nächsten Jahre planen wir Neueröffnungen in Moskau, Peking und New York«, erklärt Olivier Fabre aufgeregt und begeistert. Der 39-Jährige hat von der Großmutter den Elan geerbt und übernimmt als PR-, Verkaufs- und Marketingchef die Rolle des Troublemakers, der ständig mit neuen Ideen kommt. Seinen Bruder Jean-Marc, 45, nennt er nur »Mister No, der Bremser«. Doch aktuell hat Jean-Marc in seiner

create a new image." In the end, visiting trade fairs, managing joint projects with young up-and-coming designers, and designing exclusive gloves for Lady Gaga and Beth Ditto all combined with a huge amount of personal commitment finally led to the turnaround. In 2010, Fabre saw its first profit in decades with a turnover of two million euros. Two company stores in Paris act as a showcase for their newest creations. Renowned fashion designers such as Ann Demeulemeester, Walter van Beirendonck, Carven and the celebrated haute couture styliste Stéphane Rolland have meanwhile started to rely on the know-how of the small company from Millau. Yet despite their success, the Fabres have only achieved the first stage of their road map. Ahead of them lies a lot of work and ambitious plans. "We have to further the brand with new materials and introduce new processing methods."

After conquering the national market Fabre would like to become international again. They plan to open boutiques in all the cold regions of the world. "In the coming years we are planning to open stores in locations such as Moscow, Beijing and New York," Oliver Fabre informs us enthusiastically. The 39-year-old obviously

Funktion als Rohstoffeinkäufer und Buchhalter den schwierigeren Job zu meistern. Durch die europäische Wirtschaftskrise wird in Ländern wie Spanien und Portugal weniger Fleisch verzehrt, die Preise für Leder, insbesondere Lammleder, sind um das Dreifache gestiegen. Weil Handschuhmacher nur eine Saison haben, wird außerdem jeder milde Winter zum Cashflow-Problem. »Wenn dann Firmen wie Chanel oder Louis Vuitton klingeln und mit einem Scheck winken, werden viele schwach. Sie verkaufen ihre Firma und geben das Savoir-faire an die Luxuskonzerne«, grummelt Jean-Marc. Auch bei den Fabres klopfte einst Louis Vuitton an – mit einem Großauftrag. Die Fabres sagten nein und sind stolz darauf. »Wir wären nicht bereit gewesen und sind es auch heute nicht.« Fast dreißigtausend Handschuhe verlassen jährlich das kleine Atelier. Verkaufen könnte Fabre rund ein Drittel mehr. Und warum nicht einfach die Produktionsmenge erweitern? »Weil man keine Handschuhmacher mehr findet. Es gibt keine Ausbildungsstätten.« Sechs Monate dauert die Anlernung an für einen Produktionsschritt. Und hinzu kommt: Nach Millau will kaum jemand ziehen. Die Fabres haben nach langer Suche endlich einen Ersatz für ihren lang gedienten Zuschneider gefunden. Olivier Fabre: »Die nächsten Jahre müssen wir mit selbst ausgebildeten Heimwerkerkräften überbrücken. Aber mein Traum wäre, eine Schule für Handschuhmacher ins Leben zu rufen.« Dort könnte dann Solange dem Nachwuchs die englische Naht beibringen: drei Stiche, innehalten, das Leder wenige Millimeter nach vorne schieben, drei Stiche ... und immer so fort. —

inherited his grandmother's zest, and in his role as the PR, sales and marketing manager he acts as a catalyst by continually coming up with new suggestions. He refers to Jean-Marc – the elder by six years – as "Mister No, the wet blanket." But Jean-Marc, in charge of resource purchases and accounting, has an extremely challenging job. Due to the European economic crisis, less meat is being eaten in countries such as Spain and Portugal. As a result the price of leather, especially lamb's leather, has risen threefold. Furthermore, gloves only have one season, which means every mild winter results in a cash flow problem. "Many people find it impossible to resist when a company like Chanel or Louis Vuitton knocks on your door and waves a check. They sell their business and all the know-how flows into the luxury company," Jean-Marc grumbles. Louis Vuitton came knocking on the Fabre's door, too – with a large order. The Fabres are proud that they refused it. "We were not ready yet, and are not ready now either." Nearly thirty thousand pairs of gloves leave the workshop annually. And Fabre could easily sell yet another third again. "All our gloves are made by hand just as they were one hundred years ago. Everything we produce is sold directly, we do not have stock," says Olivier. So why not simply increase the production? "Because there are no glovers anymore. There are no training facilities. Just learning one production step takes up to six months. And besides that, hardly anybody wants to move to Millau." It was only after a long search that the Fabres were able to find a replacement for their trusted cutter. Olivier Fabre continues, "We will have to bridge the next years with workers we train ourselves. But my dream is to establish a glover's school." There Solange could pass along the secrets of the English stitch: three minute stitches, pause, push the leather forward a few millimeters, three minute stitches, pause ... and so on, and so on. —

12

Figlmüller
Hans & Thomas Figlmüller

Text **Olivia El Sayed** Photos **Gian Marco Castelberg**

Es gibt eigentlich nicht viel, was man an der Zubereitung eines Schnitzels verändern kann: klopfen, panieren, braten – es bleibt sich gleich. Schnitzel neu zu erfinden ist also keine Möglichkeit, wenn ein Schnitzel ein Schnitzel bleiben soll. Und das muss es, schließlich ist es das Nationalgericht Österreichs. Bleibt die Option, das beste Schnitzel anzubieten. Und genau das ist es, was sich die Brüder Hans und Thomas Figlmüller zum Ziel gesetzt haben. Qualität und Tradition sind hierbei die beiden wichtigsten Faktoren, die bereits ihrem Vater Hans Figlmüller dabei halfen, das Figlmüller-Schnitzel zum Wiener Kulturgut zu machen.

There's not much room for creativity when it comes to making a schnitzel. Pound a slice of meat, bread it and fry it – nothing new there. Reinventing the schnitzel is simply not an option if the schnitzel is to remain a schnitzel. And, as the schnitzel is Austria's national dish, that's non-negotiable. Which leaves only one option: offering the hands-down best schnitzel in the world. This is the goal Hans and Thomas Figlmüller have set themselves, just as their father, Hans Figlmüller, did before them. He ceaselessly focused on quality and tradition, the two key factors that have made the Figlmüller Schnitzel into a Viennese cultural heirloom.

In der engen Seitenstraße im ersten Bezirk Wiens ist kein Durchkommen. Zahlreiche Menschen stehen vor dem Eingang des »Figlmüller« und warten auf einen der begehrten Plätze und auf das bekannteste Schnitzel der Stadt. Dünner und knuspriger als die Konkurrenz soll es sein und größer als der Teller, auf dem es serviert wird. »Der Horizont beginnt, wo unser Schnitzel endet«, steht deshalb wohl auch in der Speisekarte zu lesen. Und wir lernen (und schmecken): Schnitzel ist eben doch nicht gleich Schnitzel. Für das große Stück Genuss wird in der Figlmüllerschen Variante vor allem Schweinefleisch verwendet, davon im Speziellen die Karreerose, die weniger sehnig ist als herkömmliches Schnitzelfleisch und sich bei der Zubereitung nicht wellt. Geklopft wird das Fleisch so lange, bis es einen Durchmesser von mindestens dreißig Zentimetern hat, danach wird es paniert – und zwar ausschließlich mit »Bröseln von der Kaisersemmel« – und anschließend in Pflanzenöl gebraten. Pro Backvorgang dürfen immer nur wenige Schnitzel in die Pfanne. Und nach jeder Runde wird das Öl ausgetauscht. Die mehreren tausend Liter Öl, die so monatlich in der kleinen Küche verwertet werden, werden später zu Biokraftstoff weiterverarbeitet.

Die Gaststätte ist bis auf den letzten Platz besetzt. Dass die meisten Gäste Touristen sind, merkt man daran, wie interessiert sich alle umsehen. Die Einrichtung des Hauses ist so klassisch wie erwartet: jägergrüne Wände, Holzbänke, auf den Tischen jeweils ein Körbchen mit frischem Brot, umhüllt von einer weißen Serviette und die Lettern des Hauses altmodisch geschwungen wie die gusseisernen Gitter, die den Innen- vom Außenraum trennen. Außer der Wand mit den Pressebeiträgen aus aller Welt fordert eigentlich nichts besonders dazu auf hinzugucken. Und ähnlich verhält es sich auch mit den Brüdern Thomas und Hans Figlmüller. Bescheiden ist ihr Auftreten, unauffällig ihre Erscheinung. Und dass ihnen der Wert der Familie wichtiger ist als szenige Gastrotrends, zeigt sich gleich zu Anfang. Weil seine Tochter derzeit die erste Kindergartenwoche erlebt, erscheint Hans Figlmüller etwas verspätet und aus der Puste zum Interview. Die beiden Brüder sind die nunmehr vierte Generation, die das über hundertjährige Unternehmen führen. Durch die starke Fokussierung auf ein Produkt drängt es sich auf, die altbewährte Strategie fortzusetzen: Um sich zu differenzieren,

Passing through the packed narrow side street in Vienna's First District is almost impossible. A large number of people are lined up in front of the restaurant's entrance waiting for a sought-after seat – and the most celebrated schnitzel in town. "Figlmüller's" boast: a schnitzel that is thinner and crisper than anything the competition can offer – and larger than the plate on which it is served. Which is probably why the menu states: "The horizon starts where our schnitzel ends." We take a bite and realize that there's more to schnitzel than just schnitzel. The Figlmüller variation of this culinary delight is generally made of pork tenderloin which is more tender than the ordinary cuts used for schnitzels and does not curl when fried. The meat is pounded with a mallet until it is over a foot wide in diameter. Then it is breaded – exclusively with "kaiser roll crumbs" – and after that fried in light vegetable oil. Only a few schnitzels are fried in one batch. And after every round, the oil is replaced with fresh oil. The several thousand gallons of oil that the kitchen goes through every month are later processed into biofuel.

The schnitzel house is packed. From the way many of the guests scrutinize their surroundings we deduce the majority must be tourists. After all, the interior is as predictable as it is traditional: forest-green walls, wooden benches and tables, each with a basket of delicious bread wrapped in a fresh white linen napkin, and old-fashioned lettering in line with the wrought-iron room partitions. Aside from one wall displaying press releases from all over the world, there is really nothing to catch your interest – a fact that is entirely in keeping with the outward aspect of Thomas and Hans Figlmüller. Both make a relaxed impression and they do not go out of their way to draw attention to themselves. And the fact that they rate family values higher than fashionable gastro trends is clear from the beginning of our interview when Hans Figlmüller arrives slightly late and out of breath because his daughter has just started her first week at kindergarten.

They are the fourth generation to run the Viennese family business that looks back on over one hundred years of tradition. The strong emphasis on a single product has been a major argument for them to continue using the same strategy: to stand out, they have to be the best. And stand out they do. In part, this is due to the attention they devote to their product, but also a result of stringently upholding the values that have defined the establish-

Es gab bei uns keinen Unterschied zwischen Arbeit und Zuhause, unser Vater war stets derselbe, ob nun der Geschäftsmann und Unternehmer oder eben der Papa.

müssen sie die Besten sein. Und das gelingt vor allem durch die Liebe zum Produkt und dank der Erhaltung eben der Werte, die das Familienunternehmen schon seit 1905 prägen.

2002 übernahmen die beiden Brüder die Leitung des Betriebs, weil ihr Vater aus gesundheitlichen Gründen nicht mehr dazu imstande war. Wirklich geplant war das nie: »Lustigerweise war es für all unsere Freunde nicht überraschend, als wir beschlossen, den Betrieb zu übernehmen. Wir selbst waren die Einzigen, die doch irgendwie staunten, als es dann wirklich so weit war«, sagt Hans. Und Thomas ergänzt: »Die Übernahme des Betriebs war immer ein unausgesprochenes Thema. Und doch stand die Entscheidung zum Verkauf nie wirklich im Raum. Irgendwie führte so eins zum anderen.« Doch der Wechsel an der Spitze ging nicht ganz reibungslos über die

ment since 1905. "In our family there was no difference between work and home. Our father was always the same, whether he was an entrepreneur or simply papa," recalls Thomas.

In the year 2002, the brothers took over the management of the company together when their father was not able to continue running the establishment due to health issues. This was not a step they had planned. "Interestingly enough, none of our friends were surprised when we announced we were taking over the family business. We were the only ones who seemed to be a bit taken aback when it finally happened," grins Hans. And Thomas adds: "Taking over the business was a topic that was never discussed properly. And yet the decision to sell was never seriously considered either. Somehow one thing led to another." But to say the handover went smoothly would be an exaggeration.

ESSEN & TRINKEN
SCHATZ ECKE

Bühne. Auch wenn weder Hans noch Thomas Figlmüller die typischen Merkmale von rebellischen Söhnen zeigen, so trennt sie mindestens die Entwicklung einer ganzen Generation von derjenigen ihres Vaters. »Früher war das Figlmüller keine Marke, sondern ein Gasthof. Über das Thema Marke und Struktur im Betrieb wurde nie konkret nachgedacht«, meint Thomas. »Unser Vater ist einfach noch vom alten Schlag. Er gehörte zur Kriegsgeneration, das war irgendwie diese Cowboymentalität. Damals hatte man noch keine Strategie für den Betrieb, es wurde einfach gearbeitet. Und was mein Vater sagte, wurde einfach gemacht, weil er es sagte.« Hans nickt und fügt hinzu: »Heute werden Entscheidungen anders gefällt und umgesetzt. Sicher nicht immer besser, aber vielleicht schneller als damals.«

Though neither Hans nor Thomas Figlmüller give the impression of being a rebel, they are separated from their father by at least one generation's worth of modern development. In the past, the brand and the business structure had never been thought through, Thomas explains. "Our father is definitely 'old school.' He belongs to the war generation, and they had this 'do it or die' approach. The business didn't have a proper strategy; people just did their job. And if our father gave orders to have something done, it was done because he said so." He nods and adds: "Today we make and implement our decisions differently. Not always better, but maybe more quickly than back then."

QUALITY MEANS CONSISTENCY. BETTER IS ALWAYS GOOD, BUT GOOD MUST BE THE YARDSTICK.

Trotz der angestrebten Änderungen im Unternehmen legen beide Brüder viel Wert darauf, dass die Kernwerte der Marke, die sie schon als kleine Kinder erfuhren, erhalten bleiben, wie Hans erklärt: »In unserer Familie wurden uns Werte wie Aufrichtigkeit gegenüber Menschen, Fairness und ein Sinn für Moral vorgelebt. Das hat uns geprägt.« Und das wiederum prägt die Mitarbeiterkultur: Das Ziel ist, Leute bis zur Pension zu beschäftigen. »In der Gastronomie ist Arbeit normalerweise kurzlebig, aber da versuchen wir gegenzusteuern«, sagt Hans. Und Thomas ergänzt: »Wir lassen Mitarbeitenden viel Freiraum und machen in der Praxis einiges anders, als wir es im Betriebswirtschaftsstudium gelernt haben, als es in der Theorie vor allem darum ging, überall und immer den besseren Preis auszuhandeln. Wir setzen lieber auf lange Partnerschaften mit Lieferanten und ein gutes Verhältnis zu Mitarbeitenden. Wir quetschen nicht das letzte Profitprozent aus den Leuten, das ist es uns nicht wert. Besser ist immer gut, aber gut muss immer gewährleistet sein.« Und Thomas schließt mit den Worten: »Qualität bedeutet Beständigkeit. Wir glauben, dass wir die Beständigkeit, die wir gewähren, von den Leuten zurückbekommen. Die Qualität der Arbeit ist einfach besser, wenn sich niemand über den Tisch gezogen fühlt.« —

Despite the changes they aspire to, the brothers insist on retaining the core values of the brand as they experienced them in their childhood, as Hans explains: "We were taught values such as sincerity, fairness and a sense of morality. That formed us." And that forms their business culture as well. For example, it is the brothers' intention to employ people until they are ready to retire. "In the restaurant business, employment is usually short-lived. We are trying to introduce countermeasures," Hans explains. And Thomas adds, "We give our employees a great deal of freedom and do many things differently from what we were taught during our business administration studies. The current theory seems to be that doing good business is first and foremost a question of negotiating the best price. We prefer to build up long-term partnerships with our suppliers and have a good relationship with our employees. We don't want to squeeze the last ounce of profit out of our people. It's simply not worth it." And Thomas ends the interview with the words: "We believe that the consistency we guarantee is given back to us by the people we work with. The quality of work is simply better when nobody feels they are being stung." —

13

Home
Evan & Oliver Haslegrave

Text **Thomas Escher** Photos **Sari Goodfriend**

HOTEL FRIEDA
& BUNGALOWS
2.2 MILES

Charakterlos rotbraune Backsteinfassaden säumen die menschenleeren Straßen. Befremdliche Stille. Nur ein eisig kalter Wind pfeift sein monotones Lied in der tristen Szenerie. Im Hintergrund sind die Umrisse des Empire State Building zu erkennen. Nahezu hämisch grüßt die Spitze des mondänen Bauwerks herüber nach Greenpoint, einen Ortsteil von Brooklyn. Nur einen Steinwurf vom Epizentrum der Finanz- und Modemetropole entfernt erinnert nichts mehr an das makellos polierte Image Manhattans. Wer hier lebt, tauscht Glamour gegen Authentizität, Designeranzug gegen Blaumann.

Deserted streets lined by plain brownstones. A disconcerting silence interrupted only by an icy wind whistling a monotonous tune through the dismal cityscape. In the distance, the silhouette of the Empire State Building can be made out. The elegant spire of the building seems to throw a disdainful glance down on Greenpoint, a district in Brooklyn. Just a stone's throw away from the city's finance and fashion epicenter, here nothing reminds you of Manhattan's polished image. Living in Greenpoint means trading glamour for authenticity, designer threads for coveralls.

Evan und Oliver Haslegrave sind dieses Tauschgeschäft eingegangen, als sie hier 2009 »hOmE« aus der Taufe hoben. Der Name ist ein Akronym des Haslegraveschen Geschwister-Quartetts, das neben Oliver und Evan aus den Schwestern Hadley und Morgan besteht. Der Markenname ist damit vielmehr eine Hommage an die Familie als eine zielführende Beschreibung ihres unternehmerischen Tuns. Umgangssprachlich würde man hOmE wohl schlicht als Architekturbüro bezeichnen. Doch der unkonventionelle Ansatz der Brüder ist viel mehr als das.

Evan and Oliver Haslegrave made this trade-off in 2009, the year they launched "hOmE." The name is an acronym of the Haslegrave sibling names which, besides Oliver and Evan, include sisters Hadley and Morgan. The brand name is more a homage to the family that an accurate label of their professional activities. In everyday terms, hOmE is an architecture firm. Yet thanks to an unconventional approach, it is so much more than just that. Oliver and Evan Haslegrave do not simply draw up plans and concepts. Here, in the heart of urban Brooklyn, is where craftsmanship melds with interior design.

AM ENDE DES TAGES GEHT ES DARUM, EIN GEFÜHL ZU SCHAFFEN. WIR INSZENIEREN EINEN ORT, DER MENSCHEN AUFGRUND SEINER EINZIGARTIGEN IDENTITÄT ANZIEHT.

Für Oliver und Evan Haslegrave geht es nicht allein um die intellektuelle Aufbereitung einer Idee. Hier, inmitten der Urbanität Brooklyns, trifft Handwerkskunst auf Interior Design.
Eine steile Holztreppe führt hinauf ins Obergeschoß des alten Fabrikspeichers. Die Tür am Ende des Korridors ist offen. An einem langen, braunen Eichentisch sitzen zwei junge

A steep wooden staircase leads to the top floor of the old factory warehouse. The door at the end of the corridor stands wide open. At the end of a long, brown oak table, two young men are seated and eating breakfast. "Hey, I'm Evan," one of them introduces himself, getting up as the last bit of a croissant disappears into his bushy beard. For a brief moment, the entire scene is reminiscent of a movie

Männer und frühstücken. »Hey, ich bin Evan«, stellt sich einer der beiden vor, während der letzte Zipfel seines Buttercroissants hinter seinem hellblonden Vollbart verschwindet. Im ersten Moment erinnert die Szene an ein Treffen der Musketiere, so verblüffend ist die Ähnlichkeit Evans und Olivers mit den Romanfiguren der französischen Leibgarde. Beide tragen sie dichte Vollbärte und offen langes Haar. Nur die Säbel haben sie heute gegen zwei große, schwarze Laptops eingetauscht. Es ist elf Uhr vormittags und die beiden Haslegraves sind gerade erst von einer Geschäftsreise aus Las Vegas zurückgekehrt. Deshalb das späte Frühstück. Worum es bei dem mehrtägigen Treffen in der Hauptstadt des Glücksspiels ging, wollen die beiden nicht verraten. Nur so viel: Ein Restaurantbesitzer verlangt nach einer ganz unkonventionellen Idee für sein Lokal.

Aufträge dieser Güte gehören für Evan und Oliver mittlerweile zum Alltag. Seit der Gründung von hOmE 2009 arbeiten die Brüder ständig an der Umsetzung nonkonformistischer Restaurantkonzepte. Ihr Ansatz könnte dabei generalistischer kaum sein. Wer bei den Haslegraves um ein Interior Design bittet, bekommt mehr als ein läppisches Architekturmodell. Die beiden Mittdreißiger erarbeiten eine komplette Markenidentität, vom Raumdesign bis zur Menükarte. Nicht selten liefern sie einen entsprechenden Vorschlag für den Namen des Lokals gleich mit. Mehr noch als bei haptisch erfahrbaren Produkten geht es bei der Komposition von Gebäuden um die Vermittlung eines Gefühls. Nur wer sich wohlfühlt, kommt zurück, um sein positives Erlebnis zu wiederholen. »Wir erschaffen dieses Gefühl«, bringt Oliver die Idee von hOmE auf den Punkt. »Wir inszenieren einen Ort, der Menschen aufgrund seiner einzigartigen Identität anzieht.«

about the musketeers. Evan and Oliver bear an astonishing resemblance to the 17th-century heroes of the royal French garde du corps. Both have thick beards and long hair, but, thankfully, they seem to have traded their swords for two large black laptops. It is 11 o'clock in the morning and the two Haslegraves have just returned from a business trip to Las Vegas. Hence the late breakfast. Neither wants to reveal what they were doing in the entertainment capital on a business trip that lasted several days. Only this much: a restaurant owner is looking for an extremely unconventional concept for his venue.

Assignments of this nature have become commonplace for Evan and Oliver. Since founding hOmE in 2009, the brothers have continuously realized nonconformist restaurant concepts. Their approach is unusually holistic. If you turn to the Haslegraves for an interior design concept, you get more than a mere architectural model. The two men in their mid-thirties will create an entire concept in which interior design is just the starting point. A concept that may include the style of menus to set on the tables and even suggest a name for the venue. More so than with design objects, a restaurant concept by hOmE conjures up a special emotion and conveys a unique atmosphere. Only customers who feel at home will be back to repeat the positive experience. "We create that feeling," says Oliver, putting the concept behind their firm in a nutshell. "We stage a setting that attracts people by its unique identity."

THE PURPOSE OF WORKING AS A BARTENDER IN THE HOSPITALITY INDUSTRY WAS NOT TO STUDY COMMON INTERIOR DESIGN CONCEPTS: I JUST NEEDED TO PAY RENT.

Dass ein perfekt inszeniertes Restaurant ein magischer Ort sein kann, entdeckte Oliver bereits in frühester Jugend. Als Aushilfskellner kam er damals in seiner Heimatstadt Connecticut zum ersten Mal mit der Gastronomie in Berührung. Doch vom Nebenjob als Kellner bis zum Innenarchitekten für Restaurants sollte es ein langer Weg werden. Ein Filmstudium führte ihn Ende der Neunzigerjahre nach New York. Die Verbindung zum Gaststättengewerbe blieb. Die exorbitanten Lebenshaltungskosten der Metropole forderten ihren Tribut. »Der Grund, warum ich als Barkeeper in der Gastronomie gearbeitet habe, verfolgte keineswegs das übergeordnete Ziel, die Innenarchitektur in Restaurants zu studieren«, resümiert er heute schmunzelnd. »Ich musste einfach meine Miete bezahlen.« Seinem Bruder Evan erging es ähnlich. Ein kurzes Intermezzo am Pratt Institute, der Vorzeigeuniversität für Architektur und Design in New

Oliver discovered early on that a perfectly staged restaurant can be a magical place. His first encounter with the hospitality sector occurred in their hometown in Connecticut where he worked as a waiter. Yet it has been a long haul from waiting tables to becoming an interior designer for restaurants. Originally, Oliver came to New York toward the end of the 1990s to study film. He continued work in the restaurant trade on the side – a necessity dictated by the outrageous cost of living in the metropolis. His brother Evan has a similar background. A short intermezzo at the Pratt Institute, the renowned School of Art and Design in New York, to study architecture was also financed by odd jobs in local bars. After dropping out of school, Evan went on to find employment as a laborer on construction sites around New York – which is how he acquired his manual skills. "The fact that we both have the ability to design and build at the same time makes

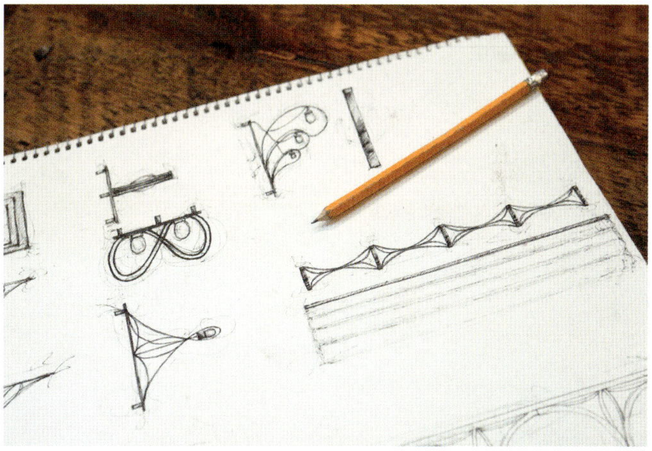

DIE TATSACHE, DASS WIR BEIDE DIE FÄHIGKEIT HABEN, HANDWERK UND DESIGN MITEINANDER ZU KOMBINIEREN, MACHT UNSER KONZEPT BESONDERS UND UNTERSCHEIDET UNS ELEMENTAR VON DEN MEISTEN ANDEREN INNENARCHITEKTEN.

York, finanzierte er sich ebenfalls durch Gelegenheitsjobs in lokalen Bars, bevor er sich später, nach Abbruch des Studiums, mit Hilfsarbeiten auf Baustellen rund um New York seine handwerklichen Fähigkeiten aneignete. Evan: »Die Tatsache, dass wir beide die Fähigkeit haben, Handwerk und Design miteinander zu kombinieren, macht unser Konzept besonders und unterscheidet uns elementar von den meisten anderen Innenarchitekten.« Genau diese Fähigkeiten komplettieren heute den außergewöhnlichen Ansatz von hOmE und verschaffen den beiden Brüdern einen elementaren Wettbewerbsvorteil. Denn wer glaubt, dass mit dem verabschiedeten Architekturkonzept auch Evans und Olivers Arbeit beendet ist, hat die beiden Musketiere unterschätzt, legen diese doch auch bei der handwerklichen Umsetzung im wahrsten Sinne des Wortes Hand an. Obwohl die beiden Allrounder hier

our concept unique and sets us apart from most other interior designers." Precisely these manual skills are what now complete hOmE's unusual approach and give the brothers an edge over their competitors. For whoever thinks that Evan's and Oliver's job ends when their concept has been approved, has drastically underestimated the two musketeers who are involved hands-on with the actual execution of the assignment. Though both generalists also delegate to trusted subcontractors, the pair can frequently be found in their professionally equipped carpenter's workshop. Quite practically, this is integrated directly into the loft they occupy in the old industrial warehouse in Brooklyn. Yet, again, whoever expects to see industrially standardized wooden beams and other conventional sawmill products, will be disappointed once more: the Haslegraves also follow an unusual concept to construct the furniture they design. A concept that begins with

203
309
PROFESSOR
OF
CHEMISTRY

BROOKLYN BRIDGE
1883-1983
MARATHON
MICHAEL LEWIS

nicht selten auf befreundete Subdienstleister zurückgreifen, kommt es ab und an vor, dass man das Gespann nach getaner Computerarbeit in der perfekt eingerichteten Schreinerwerkstatt wiederfindet. Komfortablerweise ist diese direkt in die Loftwohnung des alten Industriespeichers in Brooklyn integriert. Wer hier allerdings nach industriell genormten Holzbalken oder ähnlichen Produktstandards aus der Sägerei sucht, wird einmal mehr enttäuscht. Auch bei der Umsetzung des Möbeldesigns und der damit verbundenen Suche nach geeigneten Rohstoffen verfolgen die Haslegraves einen außergewöhnlichen Ansatz. Die Regel ist einfach: Aus alt mach neu. Jedes neu hergestellte Einrichtungsstück, und sei es noch so klein, wird aus einem Werkstoff geschaffen, der davor schon mal an einem anderen Ort als loser oder eingebauter Gegenstand fungiert hat. Nicht selten verwenden die Brüder dabei Dinge aus ihrem eigenen Interior. »Unsere lange Eichentafel hier könnte durchaus irgendwann als Thekenteil nützlich werden«, erzählt Evan, während er mit der Faust auf die Tischplatte schlägt. Allerdings nur, wenn das Material mit der übergreifenden Idee im Einklang steht. Mit der ständigen Reinterpretation bestehender Dinge halten sich die Brüder geistig flexibel. Und genau das ist es, wonach sie suchen. Nach der ständigen Möglichkeit, etwas Neues zu entdecken. »Am liebsten wäre ich Entdecker geworden«, gibt Evan seinen Kindheitstraum preis. »Dann würde ich heute ständig irgendetwas Unbekanntes erforschen. Aber ich denke, mit der Arbeit als Innenarchitekt ist das ziemlich ähnlich, nicht wahr?« —

their choice of raw materials. The rule is simple, really: new from old. Every single new piece of furniture, however small it may be, is made from something that previously was a part of, or once was, a different object altogether. Occasionally, the brothers even use parts from their own furnishings. "Our long oak table could probably be turned into a useful part of a bar counter," Evan says as he gives it a hard knock. But only if the material is in keeping with the overall design concept. This recurrent reinterpretation of preexisting objects keeps them mentally agile. And something new is what they are perpetually on the lookout for. "I'd rather have been an explorer because you'll constantly discover something new. It's actually kind of the same thing with interior design too, isn't it?" —

14

Horgenglarus
Markus Landolt

Text **Urs Steiner** Photos **Gian Marco Castelberg**

Seit 130 Jahren stellt die Möbelfabrik Horgenglarus seriell Stühle in hoher Qualität her. Spezialität des Hauses ist das Biegen von Holz im Dampf. Es macht die Möbel stabil und schön, spart Material und ist ökologisch nachhaltig. Stühle von Horgenglarus hat man ein Leben lang – danach werden sie vererbt. Sie bleiben jahrzehntelang im Programm, weil sie von namhaften Designern ohne modischen Schnickschnack entworfen wurden. So ist der Katalog von Horgenglarus mit der Zeit zu einer Sammlung von Klassikern geworden.

For over 130 years, the company Horgenglarus has been serially producing high-quality chairs. Their specialty lies in manufacturing wooden furniture using steam bending – a process that creates stable and aesthetic furniture, avoids waste, and is ecologically sustainable. Chairs by Horgenglarus last a lifetime, after which they are handed down to the next generation. No-nonsense design by renowned creators ensures that the models remain on offer for decades and is responsible for turning Horgenglarus' chairs into a collection of classics.

Am Himmel hängt der Glärnisch. Der Hausberg von Glarus, dem Hauptort des Ostschweizer Kantons, türmt sich bedrohlich über der Schreinerei der Firma Horgenglarus auf. Horgen ist weit weg, mit der Gemeinde am linken Zürichseeufer verbindet die kleine Möbelfabrik nur noch der Name. Dort wurde das Unternehmen 1880 in einer ehemaligen Textildruckerei gegründet, im Jahr 1902 kam der Produktionsstandort Glarus dazu, der heutige Geschäftssitz.

The Glärnisch towers in the sky. The prominent mountain near Glarus, the capital of the eponymous canton in eastern Switzerland, looms over the Horgenglarus chairmaking workshop. The first part of the company's name is all that now ties the small furniture manufacturer to distant Horgen, a town on the shore of Lake Zurich. Originally founded there in 1880 in a former textile printer's workshop, the company expanded to include a production site in Glarus, the present place of business, in 1902.

Wir verwenden Laubhölzer, die im rauen Klima des Juras gewachsen sind.

Geblieben ist der einprägsame Name Horgenglarus. Er stammt aus einer Zeit, als Ortschaften noch Pate standen für Unternehmen, auf die man stolz war. Zurich Financial Services ist so geboren, auch die inzwischen verblichene Maschinenfabrik Winterthur oder das Valser Wasser. Heute werden Brands auf komplexere Art kreiert, kein Start-up würde sich mehr »Schlieren« taufen wie einst die Waggon- und Aufzugsfabrik in der Zürcher Agglomerationsgemeinde.

Horgenglarus ist mit seinen vierzig Mitarbeitenden nicht nur der größte, sondern auch der einzige Industriebetrieb im Hauptort des »Zigerschlitz«, so nennt die Restschweiz mehr liebevoll als herablassend das enge voralpine Tal. Entsprechend stolz ist man im Schatten des Glärnisch auf Errungenschaften von Weltruf wie die Stühle von Horgenglarus. Mag sein, dass der Kult um die Produkte, die hier hergestellt werden, nicht von allen verstanden wird. Was macht einen Stuhl aus der Schreinerei beim Bahnhof schon so besonders, dass er von Stararchitekten wie Herzog & de Meuron in exklusiven Gebäuden bis nach Kalifornien eingesetzt wird? Architekten sind halt gelegentlich etwas exzentrisch und lieben das Authentische. Denn nach allem, was man von den hier produzierten Möbeln so zu sehen glaubt, handelt es sich dabei ja um banale Holzstühle, wie sie auch im Restaurant »Kreuz« und im »Hirschen« stehen. Man sieht ihnen nicht einmal an, dass sie von Gestaltern wie Werner Max Moser,

What remains is the quaint name. It dates back to bygone days when the name of a region was considered to add a certain cachet. Zurich Financial Services owes its name to this tradition, as did the now defunct machine factory Winterthur or products such as Valser Wasser, the mineral water brand. Today brands are created in a more sophisticated manner, and no start-up nowadays would christen itself "Schlieren" as did the railway rolling stock and elevator manufacturer from Zurich's suburbs.

With its forty employees, Horgenglarus is not only the largest, but also the only industrial manufacturer in the capital situated in the Zigerschlitz as the rest of Switzerland affectionately calls the narrow alpine valley. The locals here are understandably proud of the worldwide reputation the chairs of Horgenglarus have achieved. It is possible that not everyone understands the cult surrounding the products created here. After all, what is so special about chairs made at a workshop next to the train station in a Swiss village that star architects like Herzog & de Meuron choose them to adorn their exclusive architectural constructions in far-off places like California? Perhaps architects are occasionally somewhat eccentric, but they certainly respect authenticity. To the undiscerning eye, the furniture produced here may seem indistinguishable from the ordinary everyday wooden chairs that can be found in most local taverns. Nothing about them would make you guess that they have been designed by the likes of Werner Max Moser, Max Ernst Haefeli, Max Bill, Hans

Max Ernst Haefeli, Max Bill, Hans Bellmann oder Robert und Trix Haussmann entworfen wurden. Markus Landolt, der den Betrieb vor 13 Jahren gekauft hat und bis im Herbst 2012 führte, öffnet die Tür zur Sägerei, wo ein Schreiner rohe Bretter in handliche Portionen schneidet. Ausgangsmaterial sind alle Laubhölzer von Ahorn bis Kirschbaum, mehrheitlich aber Buche, die Horgenglarus bereits seit neunzig Jahren aus dem jurassischen Vendlincourt bezieht. Die Bäume wachsen in diesem rauen Klima besonders langsam, was ihrem Holz eine schöne Maserung verleiht und es dicht und strapazierfähig macht.

Die zurechtgeschnittenen Holzlatten und Bretter werden dann in Dampftöpfe gelegt, wo sich ihre Feuchtigkeit von zwanzig auf vierzig Prozent erhöht. Jetzt können sie in Schablonen eingespannt und gebogen werden. Nachdem die Rohlinge für Zargen, Beine und Lehnen getrocknet sind und ihre Feuchtigkeit noch acht Prozent beträgt, sind sie formstabil und bereit für eine Weiterverarbeitung. In der Möbelschreinerei werden die Elemente verzapft, verleimt und verschraubt, Lehnen und Sitzflächen werden montiert, Beine auf die passende Höhe gefräst, die Oberflächen geschliffen und danach geölt, geseift oder lackiert.

»Unsere Stärke besteht darin, dass wir alles selber machen«, sagt Markus Landolt. Er legt Wert darauf, dass Leder, Stoffe und Jonc-Geflecht, mit denen seine Stühle ausgerüstet werden, von ebenso hoher Qualität sind wie das tragende Gestell. Max Gimmel aus Arbon kennt sozusagen jede Kuh, deren Leder er nach Glarus liefert. Die Bezugsstoffe stammen vom noblen Textilunternehmen Christian Fischbacher und das Bambusgeflecht für Sitzflächen und Lehnen wird in einer Behindertenwerkstätte von Hand geknüpft. Trotz serieller Produktion ist somit jeder Stuhl ein handgefertigtes Unikat. Dass das Gute immer auch etwas teurer sein darf, versteht sich von selbst. Stühle aus Buchenholz von horgenglarus kosten je nach Modell und Ausführung zwischen fünf- und achthundert Franken das Stück. Damit ist das Unternehmen im Segment der Topqualitätsprodukte durchaus konkurrenzfähig – sofern der Kunde auf Langlebigkeit, Service und Design Wert legt. »Unsere Stärke besteht darin, dass wir alles selbst machen«, sagt Markus Landolt. So ist er nicht abhängig von Lieferanten und deren Qualitätsschwankungen. Am wichtigsten ist ihm jedoch, das Knowhow im Betrieb zu halten. Nur so ist es möglich, Möbel auch nach Jahrzehnten originalgetreu restaurieren zu können. Wie die Sessel im Nationalratssaal des Bundeshauses in Bern, die hundert Jahre nachdem Horgenglarus das Schweizer Parlament ausgerüstet hatte, vom selben Hersteller wieder aufgefrischt wurden.

Neben einer Kundenliste, auf der von der Schweizer Botschaft in Washington, D.C. über die Schweizerische Nationalbank bis zum Fünfsternehotel Suvretta House in St. Moritz lauter klingende Namen aufgeführt sind, ist das Knowhow der Mitarbeitenden das wichtigste Kapital von Horgenglarus. Diesem Erbe trägt Landolt denn auch Sorge, seit er das Unternehmen 1999 übernommen hat. Seine Verbundenheit mit der Firma reicht allerdings wesentlich weiter zurück:

Bellmann, or Robert and Trix Haussmann. Markus Landolt, who runs the enterprise he bought 13 years ago, opens the door to the sawmill where a carpenter is cutting raw planks down to more manageable pieces. The timber used consists exclusively of hardwoods, ranging from maple to cherry. For the past ninty years, however, Horgenglarus has mainly chosen beechwood from the Jurassian region Vendlincourt. The trees grow particularly slowly in the harsh climate there, lending the wood beautiful markings and making it dense and long-lasting.

In a next step, the prepared wooden slats and planks are put into steam vats where their natural degree of moisture is increased from the original twenty percent to forty percent. Now they can be fitted into templates and bent. After the frames, legs and backs have dried and their core humidity has been reduced to eight percent, the pieces are stable and ready for further processing. Later in the workshop, the elements are assembled: backs and seats are joined, legs are tailored to the right height, surfaces are polished, and, finally, the chairs are oiled, soaped or varnished.

"Our strength lies in being in charge of every step of the production process," says Markus Landolt. He considers it essential that the leather, upholstery materials and the wickerwork used in his products are of the same solid Swiss quality as the chair frames. And so he chooses to work with suppliers like Max Gimmel of Arbon, who practically knows the name of each cow that provides the leather he delivers, and high-end textile manufacturer Christian Fischbacher in St. Gallen, who produces the upholstery material. The wickerwork is from the Flechterei Seestern in Männedorf, a workshop for disabled people who weave the bamboo wickerwork by hand. This means that – despite serial production – every chair made by Horgenglarus is basically handmade and thus a unique specimen. Obviously this comes at a price. Beechwood chairs, depending on the model and the features, cost between five and eight hundred Swiss francs each. Despite these prices, the enterprise remains competitive in a high-end market where clients value longevity, service and design. "Our involvement in every step of the process is what makes us successful," states Markus Landolt. This means the business is not at the mercy of suppliers and fluctuations in quality. He is convinced that the key to a flourishing business is keeping know-how in the company. This is the only way to ensure that furniture can be restored faithfully even after decades. One example are the chairs for the National Council in Bern: hundred years after Horgenglarus first delivered furniture to Switzerland's parliament, they were asked to refurbish the original chairs.

Along with a client list that features a large number of prestigious names – including the Swiss embassy in Washington, D.C., the Swiss National Bank, or the five-star hotel Suvretta in St. Moritz – company know-how is the most important asset. And Landolt has been careful to preserve this legacy since taking over the company in 1999. The proprietor and CEO's connections with the company, however, go back to a much earlier date: he initially did his commercial training here. After earning a degree in business administration, it was almost by chance that he had the opportunity to take over the business a couple of decades later. Landolt started hiring young employees who were subsequently trained by the veteran, and, in many cases, soon-to-be retired, craftsmen, thus

Der langjährige Inhaber und CEO hatte seinerzeit seine kaufmännische Lehre bei Horgenglarus absolviert, bevor er Jahrzehnte später als ausgebildeter Betriebsökonom und Treuhänder fast zufällig die Gelegenheit erhielt, den Betrieb zu übernehmen. Landolt zog junges Personal nach, das die Fähigkeiten und das Wissen der altgedienten, in vielen Fällen kurz vor der Pensionierung stehenden Mitarbeitenden erlernen konnte. Dass der Maschinenpark mehrheitlich veraltet war, eröffnete die Möglichkeit von Investitionen in elektronisch gesteuerte CNC-Werkzeugmaschinen, ohne bedeutende Abschreibungen machen zu müssen. Heute beschäftigt Horgenglarus eine junge Belegschaft, die stolz ist auf ihre Produkte. Eine ähnliche Verjüngungskur verordnete Landolt auch seinem Möbelprogramm. So entwickelte der Zürcher Designer Hannes Wettstein (1958 –2008) eine komplett neue Produktelinie für das Unternehmen. »Es geht mir darum, die Kollektion zu schärfen«, sagt Landolt. Der Adelstitel »Horgenglarus« wird nicht so schnell vergeben.

Landolt schreitet durch seinen Showroom und unterzieht die Produkte wie so oft einer kritischen Begutachtung. Die Stühle von Max Bill sind gegenwärtig weniger gefragt als die älteren Modelle aus der Zwischenkriegszeit. Die Moden wechseln auch im Geschäft mit Klassikern, das weiß Landolt, aber er nimmt es gelassen. Bei Horgenglarus dauert eine Saison eine Generation lang. Und selbst wenn ein längst nicht mehr produziertes Modell wieder nachgefragt werden sollte: Die Originalmaquetten davon hängen noch immer an den Wänden. Ein paar Wochen nur – und schon steht jedes noch so ausgefallene Modell in der Spedition. Ein Blick aus dem Bürofenster bestätigt: Der Glärnisch wacht zuverlässig am Himmel über das Wohl der Firma. Und wenn nicht alles täuscht, sitzt über dem ewigen Fels der Liebe Gott auf einem Thron von Horgenglarus. —

ensuring that their knowledge could be passed on. As the machinery was generally outdated, he seized the opportunity to invest in electronic CNC machine tools without suffering great write-off losses. Today, Horgenglarus employs a young workforce that is proud of the products it manufactures. The furniture range underwent a similar rejuvenation. Zurich designer Hannes Wettstein (1958–2008) was asked to produce an entire new line that drew on the Horgenglarus tradition. "I want to give the collection a cutting edge," Landolt explains. "Horgenglarus" is a title that is not lightly bestowed.

Landolt strides through the showroom and subjects his products to a ritual inspection. At present, the Max Bill chairs are less in demand than the models dating from the twenties and thirties of the last century. Yet that does not really worry him. At Horgenglarus, a season can last an entire generation. And it poses no problem whatsoever should a long-discontinued model unexpectedly come back into demand. The original templates still hang on the walls. In a matter of weeks any model, no matter how unusual, can be ready for delivery. A brief glance through the CEO's office window confirms that the Glärnisch remains on watch over the welfare of the company. And, for a moment, it's as if we catch a glimpse of the Almighty himself seated on the eternal rock in a throne made by Horgenglarus. —

15

Hôtel Americano

Carlos Couturier

Text **Simone Ott** Photos **Reto Caduff**

HÔTEL
AMERICAN

Carlos Couturier, der Mitbegründer und kreative Kopf der mexikanischen Boutiquehotelkette Grupo Habita, ist ein gutes Beispiel dafür, wie man aus einer zufällig hingeworfenen Idee eine Gelegenheit wahrnimmt und daraus mit konsequenter Haltung etwas Außergewöhnliches schafft.

Carlos Couturier, co-founder and creative mind behind the Mexican boutique hotel chain Grupo Habita, sets a prime example. Triggered by a casual remark, he followed through rigorously with hard work – and achieved miraculous results.

Um Carlos Couturier wahrzunehmen, braucht man nicht zu sehen, um ihn. Seine Präsenz manifestiert sich über ein Energiefeld, das sich auch außerhalb der Sichtweite erstreckt. Man nimmt es als leichtes Vibrieren wahr. Oder als weit reichende Aura, für feinstofflich Orientierte. Zumindest hört man ihn. Seine Stimme ist tief, kratzig, unverkennbar. Auf einem schwarzen Bertoia-Outdoorstuhl auf der Terrasse des »Hôtel Americano« im New Yorker Galerien- und Künstlerviertel Chelsea sitzt er nicht einfach, sondern regiert. Führt sein kleines, stetig wachsendes Hotelimperium. Gibt hier einen laut kommentierten Handschlag, dort einem Kellner leise Instruktionen. Carlos Couturier ist der neue »King of Boutique Hotels«. Gleich nach dem das Genre definierenden Ian Schrager und Szenehoteliers wie André Balazs. Und das zunächst ohne Plan und ohne Absicht.

You can sense Carlos Couturier before you see him. His presence creates an energy field that is tangible even when he is not in eyeshot. First you sense a low-key buzzing. Or, for the more esoteric among us, a far-reaching aura can be discerned – well, at least you hear him. His voice is deep, raspy, one-of-a-kind. Seated in a black Bertoia patio chair on the terrace of the "Hôtel Americano" in Chelsea, New York's artist and gallery district, Couturier reigns over his select, ever-growing hotel empire. With a jovial handshake here, a sotto voce instruction to a waiter there, Carlos Couturier is the new "King of Boutique Hotels," positioned just behind genre-defining Ian Schrager and luxury boutique hotelier André Balazs. And this initially without plan or intention.

Unsere lateinamerikanische Kultur spürt man überall: Beim Service, beim Essen, bei der Hotelmusik. Egal wo wir sind, wir bleiben unserer Herkunft treu.

Er ist spät dran. Seine Assistentin hat Termine durcheinandergebracht und in knapp drei Stunden hebt sein Flieger nach Mexiko ab. Doch Carlos Couturier, ganz Latin Gentleman, bleibt auch unter Zeitdruck zuvorkommend und die Ruhe selbst. »Natürlich war ich bei diesem Projekt nervös«, sagt er über das Hôtel Americano, sein elftes Hotel und das erste außerhalb Mexikos. »New Yorker sind kritisch und ungeduldig. Wer es nicht auf Anhieb richtig macht, kann gleich wieder einpacken. Eine zweite Chance bekommt man hier nicht.« Die US-Hochglanzmagazine begeisterten sich jedoch nach der Eröffnung über die »design revolution«, attestierten Couturiers Grupo Habita eine »beeindruckend hohe Designsensibilität« und setzten den Newcomer aus Mexiko ganz oben auf ihre Hotlists. »Ich glaube«, meint Couturier, »das Hôtel Americano funktioniert, weil wir uns dabei selbst treu geblieben sind und uns auf keinen Fall anbiedern wollten.« Damit meint er, dass er als passionierter Sammler zeitgenössischer Kunst in Chelsea die richtige Umgebung gefunden, die Inneneinrichtung jedoch bewusst minimalistisch, fast kühl gehalten hat, so wie eine noch unbestückte Galerie – »weil jede Art von Kunst in einem Hotel, das in der Nachbarschaft von international renom-

He is running late. Something to do with conflicting appointments and a plane to Mexico City that leaves in three hours. Yet, ever the caballero, Carlos Couturier remains courteous and relaxed under time pressure. "Naturally, I was nervous about this project," he says about Hôtel Americano, his eleventh hotel and the first one outside of Mexico. "New Yorkers are very critical, they have no patience and they don't give you a second chance. Either you do it right or they dump you." But following the opening, US glossy publications reported enthusiastically about the "design revolution" and attested Couturier's Grupo Habita an "impressively high design sensitivity," placing the Mexican newcomer right at the top of their hot lists. "I think Hôtel Americano works because it's honest, we deliver what we believe in," says Couturier. "We don't want to pretend to be something we're not." By this he's referring to the fact that as a passionate collector of contemporary art, Chelsea is the perfect habitat for him. And yet, the interior design of the hotel is intentionally minimalistic, almost cold, like an empty art gallery. "It is an art-free hotel, because the art surrounds us. Gagosian. Paul Kasmin. Whatever you do would be an imposition on someone's mind." Also, though his taste for sophisticated architecture and

mierten Galeristen wie Paul Kasmin oder Gagosian liegt, nur peinlich wäre.« Er meint damit auch, dass er mit seinen Ansprüchen an hochstehende Architektur und erstklassiges Design zwar gut nach New York passt, dabei aber seine lateinamerikanische Herkunft und Lebensfreude nicht etwa versteckt, sondern ganz selbstverständlich integriert: »Wir sind keine Trendsetter, kopieren aber auch niemanden. Wir gehen konsequent unseren eigenen Weg.«

Couturier ist von Haus aus Zitrusfarmer. Die ersten Lebensjahre verbrachte er in San Rafael, Veracruz, am Golf von Mexiko, umgeben von Orangenplantagen seiner Familie. Die Finca aus dem 19. Jahrhundert seiner aus Frankreich nach Mexiko ausgewanderten Großeltern gehört heute zu Couturiers Hotelkette. Die »Maison Couturier« ist ein Gasthaus wie aus dem Bilderbuch – die materialisierte Städterfantasie eines einfachen und dennoch luxuriösen Landlebens. Später, »ich war etwa sieben«, zog die Familie Couturier nach Puebla, einer pittoresken Stadt aus dem 16. Jahrhundert etwa 130 Kilometer südöstlich von Mexiko-Stadt. Aus einer ehemaligen Wasserreinigungsanlage aus dem 19. Jahrhundert hat Couturier im historischen Kern des Kolonialstädtchens das Hotel »La Purificadora« geschaffen. Modernes Design des inzwischen verstorbenen Architekten und Barragán-Schülers Ricardo Legorreta trifft auf historisches Industriegemäuer. Bei einem Hotel der Grupo Habita spielt nicht nur das Interior Design eine wichtige Rolle: Ästhetik, Architektur, Grafik, Musik,

first-class design fits in well with New York, he doesn't hide his Latin American background and zest for life, integrating these aspects equally as a matter of course: "You feel our Latin American culture in all the details. The service, the cuisine and the music. Wherever we are, we remain true to our roots."

Couturier comes from a family of citrus farmers, and spent the first years of his life in San Rafael, Veracruz, by the Gulf of Mexico on the family orange plantation. His grandparents came to Mexico from France, and their 19th-century finca has meanwhile been incorporated into Couturier's hotel chain. The "Maison Couturier" is a hotel straight out of a picture book – a city dweller's come-to-life fantasy of the simple, yet luxurious country life. Later on ("I was probably seven") the Couturier family moved to Puebla, a picturesque 16th-century town about eighty miles south of Mexico City. Out of an erstwhile 19th century water purification installation there, Couturier created the hotel "La Purificadora" in the old center of the colonial town. It is a fusion of modern design: the meanwhile deceased architect and Barragán scholar Ricardo Legorreta meets historical industrial construction. "We make sure that architecture is part of the hotel. Not only interior design, the whole space. The aesthetics, graphic design and the music. In a way that is unique and special." The soul of the individual Grupo Habita hotels results from Couturier's almost personal relationship with each of his projects. "Hotels are like a family," he says. "Every hotel is like a new baby. You have to take care of all your babies, and there is always a drama."

ohm
rentals

HÔTEL AMERICANO
HÔTEL AMERICANO
HÔTEL AMERICANO
HÔTEL
AMERICANO

We don't copy. We are no trendsetters. We are going our own way.

alles spielt zusammen und ergibt etwas Einzigartiges, die Seele der Grupo Habita. Zu jedem einzelnen Hotel hat Couturier eine persönliche Beziehung. »Es ist wie mit einer Familie«, meint er. »Man zieht die Kinder mit viel Liebe groß, muss jedem ganz viel Aufmerksamkeit schenken, freut sich an ihnen und erlebt auch ganz viel Ärger.«

Die Idee, ein Hotel zu bauen, kam Couturier durch Zufall. »Ich suchte in Mexiko-Stadt Bürolokalitäten für unser Zitrusbusiness«, erzählt er, sonnengebräunt und in blütenweißen Hosen, T-Shirt, Sneakers und indigoblauem Blazer. Sein Studienkollege Moises Micha, ein Investmentbanker, half ihm dabei. »Und plötzlich war ich Besitzer eines wunderschönen alten Hauses im Stadtteil Polanco.« Auf eins folgten mehrere. Micha und Couturier bauten zusammen ein Immobilienportfolio auf. Die renovierten Häuser vermieteten sie an ausländische Businessleute. »Die Wirtschaft in Mexiko blühte zu dieser Zeit auf. Es kamen viele Ausländer, die Geschäfte machen wollten«, erinnert sich Couturier. Und die waren offenbar von den stilvoll renoviertern Häusern begeistert. »Viele fragten uns, ob es denn nicht so etwas Ähnliches geben würde als Hotel, wo sie ihre internationalen Besucher unterbringen könnten. Also bauten Moises und ich eins.«

The idea to build a hotel was based on coincidence more than anything else. "Initially I was looking for office space for our citrus business in Mexico City," Couturier relates, looking very tanned and sleek in immaculate white trousers, a white T-shirt and white sneakers contrasted by an indigo-blue blazer. A friend from college, Moises Micha, then an investment banker, helped him look. "And before I knew it I owned this beautiful old house in the Polanco district." Others soon followed as Micha and Couturier built up a real estate portfolio. The houses were renovated and rented out to foreign business people. "The economy had just opened up in this time and they were flowing into Mexico looking for business opportunities," Couturier recalls. And the tenants appeared to be delighted with the stylishly renovated houses. "Many asked us, don't you have something similar, like a hotel, where our friends and business visitors could stay. So Moises and I built one."

Image ist extrem wichtig. Jedes Detail muss stimmen. Ein unmotivierter Kellner, und sei es nur ein einziger, kann das ganze Erlebnis, das wir vermitteln wollen, zunichte machen.

Das »Hotel Habita« – der Name ist eine Abkürzung von ›habitación‹, spanisch für Zimmer – wurde 2000 in Polanco eröffnet: eine schwebende Glasbox mit 36 Zimmern, entworfen vom renommierten mexikanischen Architekten Enrique Norten. »Rückblickend ein ziemlich romantisches Unterfangen«, lacht Couturier – auch nach langer Plauderzeit noch immer ohne wahrnehmbaren Zeitdruck. »Wir wollten ganz einfach ein Zuhause weg von zuhause schaffen, einen Ort, wo auch wir gern Gäste wären.« Dass keine externe Firma die operative Führung des neuen Boutiquehotels übernehmen wollte, damit hatten die Neulinge nicht gerechnet. »Wir seien zu klein und damit kein gutes Geschäft«, erinnert sich Couturier an die Absagen. »So mussten wir alles selbst machen.« Damals gab es kein einziges Boutiquehotel in Mexiko und ganz Lateinamerika: »Mexiko-Stadt hatte ein schlechtes Image, die Stadt galt als chaotisch, schmutzig und gefährlich. Unser Hotel sollte eine Oase sein, wo man sich wohl und sicher fühlen konnte. Und ein Ort, wo sich Gäste aus dem Ausland auch mit

Hotel Habita – short for "habitación," the word for room in Spanish – was opened in Polanco in the year 2000. A floating glass box with 36 rooms designed by the noted Mexican architect Enrique Norten. "It was quite romantic as an experience," Couturier reminisces – still not restless despite the length of our conversation. "We wanted to build a home away from home. A place we would like as a customer in a Latin American city." What the newcomers hadn't factored in was that they couldn't find an external hotel management service to operate the new boutique hotel. "Nobody wanted to do it because we were so small," Couturier recalls the refusals. "So we did it ourselves." At that time there was not one single boutique hotel in Mexico, in all of Latin America. "Mexico City was perceived by the world as being polluted, chaotic. Our hotel was to be an oasis, a place you could enjoy and feel safe. A place were visitors could interact with locals," he explains. That it would develop into a hub for creative people to hang out was not planned: "We built the first one out of passion. We did it out of instinct. But you have to stay

Einheimischen treffen konnten.« Dass daraus ein Hipster Hangout werden sollte, war nicht geplant: »Es steckte unsere persönliche Leidenschaft dahinter und wir verließen uns auf nichts anderes als unseren Instinkt.«

Wenn eine gute Idee auf richtiges Timing trifft, ergibt das eine starke Zündung. Die Eröffnung des Hotel Habita fiel in die Zeit, als mexikanische Regisseure wie Alfonso Cuarón (Y Tu Mamá También) und Alejandro González Iñárritu (Amores Perros) mit ihren Stars Gabriel García Bernal und Diego Luna international für Aufsehen sorgten. Dazu kam eine innovative Kunstszene rund um den Künstler Gabriel Orozco und Galeristen wie Monica Manzutto. In Mexiko-Stadt blubberte eine Aufbruchstimmung – und das Hotel Habita mittendrin. »Wir hatten so viel Erfolg damit, dass wir gleich ein zweites Stadthotel, das »Condesa df« im Condesa-Viertel und unser erstes Beachresort ›Básico‹ in Playa del Carmen umsetzten«, erzählt Couturier. Heute ist die Gruppe mit 13 Hotels, zwei weitere sind in Planung, ein bunter Mix aus urbanen Hang-outs und relaxten Beachresorts, zigfachen ausgezeichnet mit Designpreisen.

very focused – image is very important. A bad waiter might screw up the whole experience we're trying to create."

A good idea at the right moment can trigger a chain reaction. The opening of the Hotel Habita coincided with the period in which Mexican movie directors such as Alfonso Cuarón (Y Tu Mamá También) and Alejandro González Iñárritu (Amores Perros) and their stars Gabriel García Bernal and Diego Luna were attracting international attention. Add to this an innovative art scene with artists like Gabriel Orozco and gallery owners such as Monica Manzutto. An upbeat mood had taken hold in Mexico City and Hotel Habita was at the center of the action. "We were so successful that we immediately built a second city hotel, the 'Condesa df' in the Condesa district and our first beach resort 'Bàsico' in Playa del Carmen," Couturier tells us. Today the group comprises 13 hotels, two more are in planning stage, a colorful combination of urban hangouts and relaxed beach resorts that have received innumerable design awards. Different though they may be, they all boast the same attention to quality that ranges from the architecture and the interior design on to the guest service.

EACH OF OUR HOTELS IS AN EXTENSION OF ITS NEIGHBORHOOD. WE WANT TO CREATE AUTHENTICITY.

Allen gemeinsam ist die hohe qualitative Substanz, die sich von der Architektur über das Design bis zum Service hin durchzieht. »Jedes unserer Hotels ist ein verlängerter Teil seiner Umgebung. Es geht uns darum, Authentizität zu schaffen.« Nur noch zwei Stunden bis zum Abflug – die Fahrt zum Flughafen dauert eine Stunde, mindestens. Carlos Couturier lässt sich unbeirrt für die Fotos aufs Dach kommandieren, vor den Eingang, in die Lobby. Posiert für die Kamera, tippt ein paar SMS, erzählt von der Neueröffnung des Habita-Luxus-Camping-Resorts »Endémico« in Baja California, »mit dem Auto gut von Los Angeles aus erreichbar«. Und dann ist er plötzlich weg. Hat sich wie von Zauberhand aus einem kräftigen Händedruck in Nichts aufgelöst. Zurück bleiben die energischen Couturier-Vibes, die neben sanften Bossa-Nova-Klängen in der Lobby weiterschwingen. —

Only two hours left until take-off – and the trip to the airport will take at least an hour. Unperturbed, Carlos Couturier lets us direct him to the roof terrace, in front of the entrance and to the lobby to have some pictures taken. He poses for the camera, writes a few text messages, tells us about the opening of the Habita eco-friendly cabin resort "Endémico" in Baja California, that's "easy to reach by car from Los Angeles." And then, all of a sudden, he's gone. A vigorous handshake and, in an instant, he disappears as if by magic. Dynamic Couturier vibes linger behind in the lobby, fusing with the bossa nova rhythms in the background. —

HÔTEL
AMERICANO
CHELSEA NEW YORK

16

KITON
Antonio de Matteis

Text **Olivia El Sayed** Photos **Gian Marco Castelberg**

HAND PRINTED IN ENGLAND FOR Kiton

Antonio de Matteis trinkt seinen Kaffee ohne Zucker. »Der napoletanische Kaffee ist gut, er braucht keine Zusatzstoffe«, sagt er trocken. Zu spät für uns, die bereits entleerten Zuckertütchen unbeobachtet verschwinden zu lassen. De Matteis' Blick ist hinter dem Gentleman-Lächeln etwas gehetzt. Er lehnt im Ledersessel, der sich ihm widerstandslos anpasst, schaut auf die Uhr und hebt die Augenbrauen. Wohl der Startschuss.

Antonio de Matteis drinks his coffee black. "Neapolitan coffee is so good, it doesn't need anything else," he says dryly, making us wish we could hide our already-emptied sugar sachets unobtrusively – but it's too late. Behind his gentlemanly smile, de Matteis seems somewhat harried. He leans back in the leather armchair that ensconces him comfortably, looks at his watch, and lifts his eyebrows – which we take to be the starting signal.

Für das Interview ist de Matteis aus Mailand angereist. Und dahin kehrt er zurück, sobald er hier fertig ist. Lange ist es noch nicht her, dass er zum CEO von Kiton berufen wurde. Patron und Gründer Ciro Paone, sein Onkel, hat sich erst vor ein paar Jahren aus dem operativen Geschäft zurückgezogen, so diktierte es ihm seine Gesundheit. Aus seinen 18 möglichen Nachfolgern, darunter ausschließlich Nichten, Neffen, Schwiegersöhne und eigene Kinder, wählte Paone insgesamt fünf aus, »die fünf besten«, die nun den Konzern Kiton leiten. Dazu gehört auch der Neffe Antonio Paone, der das Unternehmen in New York führt. In Neapel, dem Herzen des Unternehmens, sitzen seine Tochter Maria Giovanna und eben Antonio de Matteis in den Chefsesseln. Er weiß, warum er zu den fünf Auserwählten zählt: »Qualität ist nicht vererbbar. Ein Verständnis für Qualität und Ästhetik hingegen ist lernbar.«

De Matteis has come from Milan especially for the interview, and that is where he will return as soon as he is finished here. He has not been CEO at Kiton for long. Owner and founder Ciro Paone, his uncle, only withdrew from the operative business a few years ago after reluctantly obeying the dictates of health. From a list of 18 potential successors that consisted entirely of nieces, nephews, sons-in-law and children, Paone chose five – "the five best" – who now run the Kiton concern between them. These five include Paone's nephew, Antonio Paone, who runs the branch in New York, his daughter Maria Giovanna, who manages the business headquarters in Naples, and Antonio de Matteis in the director's seat.

Wir nähen nicht einfach unsere Etiketten in ein bestehendes Produkt. Wir kreieren es von Grund auf. Nur so kann es unseren Erwartungen entsprechen.

Von Signor Kiton, wie Ciro Paone noch oft bezeichnet wird, lernte de Matteis vieles; darunter auch den Wert der Familie und die damit verbundenen Vorteile für das Geschäft: Die Firmenhierarchie ist identisch mit derjenigen der traditionell italienischen Familie. Sie ist unantastbar. Der Weg der Entscheidungen ist kurz und klar, und so werden sie schneller umgesetzt als anderswo. Nichtsdestotrotz bringt der Generationenwechsel an der Führungsspitze von Kiton Neuerungen mit sich. Das Sortiment wird erweitert, dann und wann eröffnet ein neues Geschäft in einer weiteren Fashionmetropole, hinzu kommt ein Duft, der Ausbau der Kiton-Frauenlinie, und dennoch geschieht nichts überstürzt. Die Grundidee der Marke, die Tradition der Luxusschneiderei in Neapel, soll als Kern bestehen bleiben. Seit jeher galt diese Produktionsstätte als Garant für weltweit feinste und edelste Anzüge und Herrenhemden. Teuer, italienisch und exklusiv. An diesem Ruf soll sich nichts ändern. »Das Beste vom Besten + 1«, mit diesem Slogan bewarb die Marke 2009 und 2010 ihre Kollektionen. Es war die logische Folge des früheren Slogans »Das Beste ist

De Matteis learned a lot from Signore Kiton, as Ciro Paone is still often referred to, including the value of family and the advantages this provides a company. The company's hierarchy is identical with that of the traditional Italian family. Indeed, it is sacrosanct. This means the decision-making process is short and transparent, and decisions can be realized more quickly than elsewhere. All the same, the new generation at the head of Kiton has brought innovations as well. The product range is expanding, every once in a while a new store is opened in yet another fashion metropolis, a fragrance has been added, the Kiton women's line is being further developed – and yet nothing happens in unseemly haste. The original brand concept of a traditional and upscale sartorial enterprise in Naples remains intact at the core. From the beginning, this manufacturer has stood for quality in suits and men's shirts. Expensive, Italian and exclusive. A reputation that will be upheld. "The best of the best + 1," was the slogan the brand used for advertising their collection in 2009 and 2010. A logical step up from their earlier slogan "The best is simply

BUON NATALE
FELICE ANNO
1996

einfach nicht gut genug«. Wesentlicher Bestandteil dieses einen Extras ist die Exklusivität. Selbst die einzelnen Elemente, die zum Endprodukt führen, sind exklusiv: Die Stoffe werden eigens für Kiton produziert. Eine andere Marke, die denselben Stoff verwendet, ist somit ausgeschlossen. Am Saum eines jeden Stoffballens findet sich das Versprechen sogar eingewoben: »Hand printed for Kiton«. An der New York Fashion Week 2010 gab de Matteis außerdem bekannt, das Unternehmen »Carlo Barbera« aufgekauft zu haben. Das passt: Der namhafte Stoffproduzent setzt bei der Produktion seiner edlen Tuche nur auf Wolle, Mohair und Kaschmir.

not good enough." The major brand component implied by the extra plus in the slogan is exclusivity. "We don't just sew our labels into an existing suit. We create the suit from the bottom up. Only then can it meet our expectations," explains de Matteis. All the basic materials that go into making the final product are select. The material itself is produced only for Kiton. This eliminates the possibility of another brand using the same cloth. Each bale of cloth has the guarantee "Hand printed for Kiton," woven into its border. And at last year's New York Fashion Week, de Matteis revealed that they had taken over the company Carlo Barbera. A sensible move. The prestigious textile producer uses only wool, mohair, and cashmere to create their quality cloth.

QUALITY IS NOT INHERITED. AN UNDERSTANDING FOR QUALITY AND AESTHETICS, HOWEVER, CAN BE ACQUIRED.

Durch die Fabrikhallen von Kiton führt Francesca Capotosti, die Assistentin von de Matteis. In hohen Stiefeln und im kurzen Kiton-Kleid hastet die frischgebackene Mutter gertenschlank und auf beneidenswerten Beinen durch die Räumlichkeiten und erzählt in einem rasanten Tempo, was mit den für Kiton gefertigten Stoffen hier passiert. »25 Stunden braucht es insgesamt, bis ein Anzug fertig genäht ist«, erzählt Capotosti, »und 45 Arbeitsschritte, bis er fertig ist.« Und für jeden Schritt einen eigens darauf spezialisierten Schneider. »So verliert man nie das Auge fürs Detail«, lacht sie. In der größten aller Hallen arbeiten Hunderte von Schneidern und Näherinnen. In Gruppen sitzen sie um Tische herum, die Beine gekreuzt, mit Stoff über den Knien, und nähen. Vor ihnen Fadenspulen, hie und da ein batteriebetriebenes Küchenradio und Trinkflaschen, die sie für die langen Tage im künstlichen Licht mitgebracht haben. An den Tischbeinen: ausgeschnittene Heiligenbildchen und aufgeklebte Fußballhelden. Während die einen damit beschäftigt sind, Knopflöcher zu stanzen, bügeln andere einzelne Stoffteile, die von wieder anderen von Hand zusammengefügt werden. Capotostis dunkelbraun gelocktes Haar wippt im schnellen Takt ihrer Bleistiftabsätze sprungfederngleich auf und ab, während sie im Gehen weitererzählt. Während sie spricht, liest sie E-Mails und reagiert gekonnt auf die erfreuten Rufe aus allen Ecken: »Ciao, Franci, ciao!« – dort ein anerkennender Pfiff, Komplimente, die sie gar nicht mehr hört, weil sie schon wieder eine Station weiter ist. Besonders schnell passiert sie die zwei Tische mit den Nähmaschinen. Sie passen nicht ins wohlbehütete Bild der »Alles von Hand«-Philosophie. Benötigt werden sie einzig dafür, zwei Einzelteile zusammenzufügen, bei denen ein flexibler Saum nicht nötig ist – was an nur gerade einer einzigen Stelle der Fall ist. Manuelles Nähen birgt den ausschlaggebenden Vorteil, dass der Saum der Anzüge flexibler bleibt. Er passt sich so mit der Zeit dem Körper seines Trägers an.

Zurück in de Matteis' Büro. Die Leidenschaft dieses Mannes für seine Marke grenzt an Sturheit. Konkurrenz? Interessiert

Francesca Capotosti, de Matteis' assistant, leads us through the factory halls of Kiton. Wearing high boots and a short Kiton dress, the slim, young mother strides with her enviable legs through the facilities giving explanations. At a rapid pace, she tells us what is being done with the cloth that is specially produced for Kiton each step of the way. "It takes a total of 25 hours to sew a suit, and 45 separate steps to make it. And every single step is executed by a different person," Capotosti explains. "That way you never lose your eye for detail," she laughs. In the largest of the halls, hundreds of tailors and seamstresses are at work. They sit on low stools around tables with their legs crossed, the cloth spread over their knees, and sew. In front of them lay spools of thread, here and there a battery-operated kitchen radio, and beverages that they have brought along with them for a long day's work under artificial lights. Pictures of saints and football heroes are stuck to the table legs. Whilst some are punching out buttonholes, others are ironing small cuts of material in order that these can be sewn together by yet again others. Capotosti's brunette locks bob in rapid tact, her pencil-thin heels clattering briskly as she leads the way, continuing her explanations all the while. As she speaks, she is also checking e-mails and ably fielding the hellos that can be heard from every corner: "Ciao, Franci, ciao!" – along with an occasional appreciative whistle. Compliments that she does not really take in because she has already gone on to the next thing. She whisks by two tables bearing sewing machines particularly quickly. They do not fit in well with the select image conveyed by the "entirely handmade" philosophy. However, the sewing machines are only used to join two single pieces that do not need a flexible seam – and this in just one place. Hand sewing offers the decisive advantage that the seams of a suit remain more flexible. With these, the suit will adjust to the wearer's body over time.

Back in de Matteis' office we get the impression that the man's passion for his brand borders on the stubborn. He is utterly uninterested in what the competition does. Kiton, after all, has its own benchmarks. He couldn't care less about advertising.

ihn nicht. Kiton arbeitet mit eigenen Maßstäben. Werbung? Interessiert ihn ebenso wenig. Das Produkt und sein Wert sind bekannt. Und obwohl er viel reist – andere Städte? Inspirieren ihn nicht. Und er meint: »Ich will da etwas bewegen, wo ich bin. Diese Stadt mag ihre offensichtlichen Probleme haben, aber sie ist meine Heimat.« Scheuklappenverhalten? Nein. »Kiton ist das Beste, warum also nach links und rechts schauen? Das lenkt nur ab.« —

The product and its value are wellknown already. And, though he travels a lot, other cities do not inspire him: "I want to make something happen there, where I am. This city may have its problems, but it's my hometown." He refuses to consider that his approach may be just a little bit blinkered. "Kiton is the best, so why look left or right? That would only be distracting." —

17

Königliche Porzellan-Manufaktur

Jörg Woltmann

Text **Franziska Klün** Photos **Henning Bock**

Die Königliche Porzellan-Manufaktur ist eines von wenigen privat geführten Porzellanhäusern. Hier entwarfen schon Schinkel und Schadow. Die Berufe haben sich seit zweihundert Jahren kaum geändert. Dass dieses Kulturgut weiter existiert, ist Jörg Woltmann zu verdanken – und seinem Bauchgefühl.

The Königliche Porzellan-Manufaktur, or Royal Porcelain Manufactory, is one of the few privately run porcelain manufacturing companies in the world. Great German artists and architects such as Schinkel and Schadow designed porcelain here in the past, and the vital craftsmanship has hardly changed in over two hundred years. The porcelain manufacturer is a national treasure that still exists today thanks to Jörg Woltmann – and his gut feeling.

Wer den Retter der Königlichen Porzellan-Manufaktur treffen will, muss die Verabredung auf den Vormittag legen. Nur dann, von halb neun bis halb eins, ist Jörg Woltmann in dem 140 Jahre alten Backsteingebäude mit den modernen, großen Fenstern und dem großzügigen, gepflasterten Innenhof anzutreffen. Hier, in der kaum befahrenen, fast vergessen wirkenden Wegelystraße direkt zwischen Tiergarten und der berühmten Straße des 17. Juni ist die KPM seit 1873 beheimatet. Jörg Woltmann liebt diesen Ort, er inspiriert ihn, doch kann er nur vormittags hier sein, nachmittags muss er zu seinem anderen Unternehmen – seiner Kreditbank.

Seit dem 27. Februar 2006 macht er das so. An dem Tag übernahm der Unternehmer und Bankier Jörg Woltmann die Königliche Porzellan-Manufaktur Berlin als Alleingesellschafter. Nach 244 Jahren Manufakturgeschichte waren an diesem Februartag zwanzig Minuten entscheidend: Sofort kaufen? Oder insolvent gehen lassen und dann kaufen, wie es ihm seine wirtschaftlichen Berater nahegelegt hatten? Jörg Woltmann machte es wie immer, er entschied nach seinem Bauchgefühl. Und das sagte: Kaufen, jetzt. »Wenn so ein Unternehmen erst einmal insolvent ist, dann ist das ein Bruch in der Historie«, meint Woltmann. Damit endete 2006 eine turbulente Ära der Manufaktur, die einst 1763 von Friedrich dem Großen übernommen wurde und seitdem »Königlich« heißt. In den letzten Jahrzehnten hatten Missmanagement und ständige Geschäftsführerwechsel die in dem Zeitraum größtenteils staatliche KPM gebeutelt, die Insolvenz stand unmittelbar bevor. Auch der Prinz von Preußen, dessen Finanzier Woltmann damals war und der durch den Erwerb der KPM an seine eigene Geschichte anknüpfen wollte, hatte sich nach zwei Jahren der Verhandlungen überfordert abgewandt.

An appointment to meet the champion of the Königliche Porzellan Manufaktur, or KPM, can only be made for the morning hours. Jörg Woltmann is only available from eight to twelve thirty at the offices in the 140-year-old brick building with its large windows and impressive cobblestone courtyard. Since 1873, KPM has been located on this quiet, seemingly forgotten street, Wegelystraße, situated directly between the large Tiergarten park and the famed boulevard Straße des 17. Juni. Woltmann loves this place, saying it's always a fresh source of inspiration to him, although he can only be here in the mornings. In the afternoon he has to tend to his other business – his bank.

He has kept up this rhythm since February 27th, 2006, the day the entrepreneur and banker took over the Königliche Porzellan Manufaktur Berlin as sole shareholder. After 244 years of manufacturing history, Woltmann had twenty vital minutes to make a crucial decision. He could either buy now, or wait for the national institution to file for bankruptcy and then buy it, the way his financial advisors had advocated. Jörg Woltmann did what he always does. He went with his gut feeling, which said: buy, and buy now. And so in 2006, a turbulent era finally came to an end. An era whose beginnings predate 1763, the year Frederick the Great took over the works, thereby allowing the porcelain manufacturing company to add the word "royal" to its name. In the late 20th century however, mismanagement and continual changes in leadership weakened the meanwhile largely state-owned KPM and led it to the brink of bankruptcy. Even the Prince of Prussia, to whom Woltmann was advisor in those days and who wanted to close a gap in his family history by repurchasing KPM, turned his back on the proposition after two years of fruitless negotiation.

IF YOU ALLOW A NATIONAL INSTITUTION LIKE THIS TO GO BANKRUPT, YOU CREATE A RUPTURE IN ITS HISTORY.

Jörg Woltmann, 66 Jahre, ungefähr 1 Meter 70 groß, braune, locker zurückgekämmte Haare, dunkler Anzug, Krawatte, helles Einstecktuch, hatte bis dahin nur mit dem »schnöden,

Jörg Woltmann, a trim gentleman in his mid-sixties, is wearing a dark suit and tie with a light-colored handkerchief tucked neatly in his breast pocket. He explains rather bluntly that, until he bought

seelenlosen Geld« zu tun, wie er sagt. Die ersten großen Summen hatte er in den Siebzigerjahren als Unternehmens- und Finanzberater gemacht, 1980 wurde er Gründer der Allgemeinen Beamten Kasse Kreditbank, die heute über hunderttausend Kunden zählt. Für ihn war es der richtige Zeitpunkt, »sich diesen herrlichen Manufakturprodukten zu widmen«. Für den Urberliner »schon immer der Inbegriff des Schönen«, wurde bereits bei seiner Mutter und Großmutter sonntags aus Kurland-Tellern gegessen – dem KPM-Klassiker aus den 1790er Jahren. Woltmanns Finanzen erlaubten den Kauf, seine Frau sagte: »Wenn's gut für dich und Berlin ist, dann machst du das«, und er fragte sich: »Welcher Unternehmer bekommt schon mal die Chance, ein Kulturgut zu übernehmen?«

Woltmann sagt, die Motivation zu kaufen war rein patriotischer Natur. Er wollte das Unternehmen in der Stadt halten, es fit machen für die nächsten hundert bis hundertfünfzig Jahre. Das Luxushaus, für das von Schadow bis Schinkel zahlreiche renommierte Designer entworfen hatten. Mit ruhiger, langsamer Stimme erzählt er, dass er »all das hier« gebaut habe. Er zeigt auf den schwarzen, modern anmutenden Kubus mit der großen Fensterfront, in dem das KPM Café eröffnet hat, auf das dahinter liegende KPM-Museum und den KPM-Verkaufsraum. Durch die Schaffung öffentlicher Orte wie diesen wollte er die Berliner wieder an die Manufaktur heranführen, sie an ihre Existenz erinnern.

Denn die großen Zeiten der Porzellanmanufakturen liegen lange zurück. Bei Häusern wie KPM lebt man von der Tischkultur, davon, dass die Menschen einander einladen, sich präsentieren – und bereit sind, hundert Euro für einen Teller auszugeben. »Gedeckte Tafeln wurden von Coffee to go ersetzt«, sagt Woltmann. Für Porzellan als Luxusprodukt war ab den Neunzigerjahren niemand mehr bereit, viel Geld auszugeben. »Grundsätzlich«, sagt Woltmann, »gibt es keine bedeutende Manufaktur, die schwarze Zahlen schreibt.« Nur ganz langsam sei ein Wertewandel spürbar. Handwerk und Manufakturen erleben eine Renaissance, die Menschen beginnen wieder in Beständigkeit und Qualität zu investieren. Die »Geiz ist geil«-Mentalität sei vorbei, sagt Woltmann. Und dennoch: Die großen Gewinne werden mit solch einer Manufaktur nie zu erzielen sein. »Man stößt an Kapazitätsgrenzen«, sagt Woltmann. »Wenn die gesamte Welt plötzlich KPM bestellen würde, wäre das für uns nicht zu leisten.«

Was er damit meint, wird bei der Besichtigung der insgesamt 170 Arbeitsplätze sichtbar. Das sei der Moment, sagt Jörg Woltmann, in dem er demütig würde »vor all dem, was hier geleistet wird«. Im Wesentlichen haben sich in den vergangenen zweihundert Jahren die meisten Arbeitsweisen im Hause nicht verändert. Ob die Mitarbeiter in der Glasur, der Malerei, der Sortierung, noch immer arbeiten sie so wie ihre Kollegen vor über zweihundert Jahren. Alles wird von Hand gefertigt, jedes einzelne Stück insgesamt drei Mal kontrolliert, bevor es die Manufaktur verlassen darf. Auf die Reklamationsquote von 0,05 Prozent ist man bei KPM besonders stolz. Das Mantra, das über jedem einzelnen Arbeitsschritt hängt, lautet: Porzellan verzeiht keine Fehler. Denn jeder Fehler, und sei er noch so

KPM, he had been busy making "foul, soulless cash." He experienced his first financial successes as a corporate and financial advisor in the seventies. And in 1980, he established the Allgemeine Beamten Kasse Kreditbank, a credit bank that numbers over a hundred thousand clients today. Then in 2006, it was finally the right moment for him to dedicate himself to these – as he puts it – "magnificent porcelain products." Porcelain has always been the epitome of beauty to this native Berliner. He fondly recalls dining as a child with his mother and grandmother on Sundays, the table set with Kurland porcelain – KPM's classic porcelain line whose design dates back to the 1790s. Woltmann's finances were in good order and his wife said: "If this is right for you and Berlin, then go ahead and do it." And he thought to himself: "How often do you get the opportunity to take over a national treasure?"

According to Woltmann, his decision to buy was entirely patriotic. He wanted to keep the company in the city and to groom it into shape so it can take the next one hundred years or so in its stride – all in the interest of the manufacturer of luxury goods and its tradition of fine design. Woltmann goes on to explain that he has built "all of this" and points to a black, modernistic cube displaying a large window front that contains the KPM café as well as to the museum and salerooms located beyond. By creating these public spaces, Woltmann wanted to remind Berliners of the manufacturing company and to get them interested in coming back.

The heyday of porcelain manufacturing lies in the distant past. The livelihood of porcelain manufacturers like KPM is based on a formal table culture, on people inviting each other over and showing off their homes to their best advantage. And it relies on people who are prepared to pay one hundred euros for a single plate. "Beautifully set tables have been replaced by a coffee-to-go-culture," says Woltmann. After the nineties, nobody was ready to spend a lot of money on porcelain as a luxury product. "In principle," says Woltmann, "There is not one significant manufacturer who makes a profit." Recently, a slow change in values can be discerned. Craftwork and artisanal manufacturing are experiencing a renaissance; people are starting to invest in sustainability and quality again. According to Woltmann, the "cheap is sexy" mentality is on the decline. All the same, large profits can never be achieved with artisanal manufacturing of this kind. We reach capacity limits," he explains. "If the whole world suddenly started ordering KPM, we wouldn't be able to deliver."

His point becomes very clear during a tour of the production site with a total of 170 workplaces. This is the moment, says Jörg Woltmann, when he starts to feel very humble "in the face of everything that is created here." Most of the production methods haven't changed significantly during the last two hundred years. Whether in the glazing, painting or sorting department, employees today work pretty much how their colleagues did in past centuries. Everything is produced by hand, and every single item is checked three times before it is deemed to meet the company's exacting standards. Accordingly, KPM boasts an extremely low rate of complaints – a mere 0.05 percent – something they are very proud of. The mantra practiced over each step in the process is: porcelain tolerates no mistakes. Every mistake, however tiny, is discovered immediately, and the faulty piece is sorted out. Trying to speed up the process will never work under KPM's roof.

winzig, wird entdeckt und das entsprechende Stück aussortiert. Sich beeilen, schneller machen – so etwas funktioniert im Hause KPM nicht. Zeit ist hier relativ. Das liegt zum einen an der konzentrierten Stille, die in jedem Winkel steckt. Porzellan verzeiht keine Fehler, keine nervösen Hände, keine Zerstreutheit. Zum anderen liegt es an den Lebensläufen der Mitarbeiter. Zu KPM kommt man, um zu bleiben. Strategische Wechsel des Arbeitsgebers, die vermeintlich unverzichtbaren Eigenschaften Flexibilität und Mobilität – all das ist bei KPM nicht gefragt. Kürzlich, erzählt Woltmann, haben sie einen Ausstand nach fünfzig Jahren gefeiert. Seitdem konzentriert sich Woltmann auf seine Ziele. Das ist kurzfristig »eine schwarze Null am Ende des Jahres«. Langfristig will er »eine optimale Betriebsgröße erreichen und im positiven Ergebnisbereich liegen«. Sein Anspruch ist es, als beste Porzellanmanufaktur der Welt anerkannt zu werden. Die Konzentration auf den Export soll dabei helfen, auch Kooperationen mit Marken wie dem Luxuswagenhersteller Bugatti oder der italienischen Modefirma Bottega Veneta.

Seit seiner Übernahme konnte Woltmann den Umsatz um etwa zwanzig Prozent auf zehn Millionen Euro im Jahr steigern. Dennoch, sagt er, könnte er stärker sein. Outlets, Sonderverkäufe – all das will er nicht. Als Alleingesellschafter muss Woltmann niemandem Rechenschaft ablegen, das sei sein großer Vorteil: »Für mich gilt: Am Ende ist die Ente fett.« Und bis dahin denkt er nicht daran, sich aus dem Arbeitsleben zurückzuziehen. Es ist die Neugierde, die ihn antreibt, die Freude daran, Dinge zu gestalten. »Ich arbeite eben gern«, sagt er, »was soll ich sonst machen? Auf dem Golfplatz im Kreis laufen?« —

There is a feeling that time moves at a different pace here. This sense is conveyed in part by the quiet concentration in the air. After all, fine porcelain isn't created by nervous fingers or absentminded craftspeople. The atmosphere is, however, also linked to the employees' life stories. People who apply with KPM sign up for the duration. Change of employer for strategic reasons, flexibility and mobility – all those so-called essential qualities in modern businesses – are not sought-after traits at KPM. Recently, Woltmann relates, they celebrated a leaving party for an employee who was retiring after fifty years. Meanwhile, Woltmann has been concentrating on meeting his business targets. In the short term, the goal is a "black zero by the end of the year." In the long run, he wants to achieve "an optimal operational size and a positive balance." His intentions are for KPM to be recognized as the best porcelain manufacturing company in the world. To get there, KPM is focusing more on export and entering into partnerships with brands such as luxury car producer Bugatti and Italian fashion company Bottega Veneta.

Since his takeover, Woltmann has increased turnover by approximately twenty percent to ten million euros annually, but he's convinced he can do better. Nonetheless, he rejects resorting to strategies that might include outlets or sales. As sole shareholder, Woltmann isn't accountable to anyone, something he sees as his biggest advantage. His motto is "good things take time," and before the time is right, he has no plans of retiring. He is driven by curiosity and his enjoyment of shaping events. "I love my work," he says. "What else would I do? Walk around in circles on the golf course?" —

18

Le Labo
Fabrice Penot

Text **Simone Ott** Photos **Reto Caduff**

PIN 12
ANIS 24
d'intérieur
Fresh until: 3/1/2011

Die Idee, Parfums vor den Augen der Kunden frisch zu mischen, kam Fabrice Penot während einer Ausbildung in Grasse, der Welthauptstadt des Parfums. 2006 eröffnete der in den USA lebende Franzose die erste »Le Labo«-Boutique – und legte damit den Grundstein für einen ungewöhnlichen Erfolg.

The idea to compound perfumes before the very eyes – or under the nose – of the customer came to Fabrice Penot while he was attending a course at Grasse, France, the perfume capital of the world. In 2006, the Frenchman, who now lives in the United States, opened the first "Le Labo" boutique – thus completing the first chapter of a very unusual success story.

Im Ledersessel der im Vintage-Look gestalteten Parfum-Boutique Le Labo an der Third Street in West Hollywood sitzt ein bleistiftdünner junger Mann in Jeans und lockerem T-Shirt-Hemd. Sein wuschliges, dunkelblondes Haar wird von einer verwaschenen Baseballkappe nur etwas gezähmt. Man könnte ihn für einen der in der Gegend häufig anzutreffenden Alternativrockmusiker halten, würde er nicht sofort aus dem Sessel springen und sich mit Bisou-Bisou als Fabrice vorstellen. Die Seele des Alternativrock, der erfolgreicheren Variante des Indie Rock, zeigt sich bei Fabrice Penot, dem Mitbegründer des Parfumhauses Le Labo Fragrances, trotzdem schnell. »Eine Pressemappe? Nein, das haben wir nicht«, erwidert er mit einseitig hochgezogener Braue auf die Anfrage nach einem Facts&Figures-Infoblatt. Die Post-Punk-Attitüde »My way or the highway« wirkt bei Penot keineswegs überheblich, sondern durchaus erfrischend. »Eigentlich«, gibt er dann zu, »ist es so, dass wir uns zu Beginn von Le Labo gar keine PR-Profis leisten konnten. Im Rückblick hat sich das allerdings als gute Strategie erwiesen. Wir mussten ganz auf unser Produkt, und dass es für sich selbst spricht, vertrauen.«

A slender young man clad in jeans and a loose shirt sits in a leather armchair in the vintage-style perfume boutique Le Labo on Third Street in West Hollywood. His tousled, dark blond hair is only partially kept in place by a faded baseball cap. He might easily be mistaken for one of the alternative rock musicians who can be found in abundance in the neighborhood – or he could have if he hadn't immediately jumped up and introduced himself as Fabrice while throwing in a couple of authentic French air kisses. Whether rocker or perfume-maker, it soon becomes apparent that Fabrice Penot, co-founder of "Le Labo Fragrances," dances to a different tune when it comes to entrepreneurship. "A press kit? No, we don't have that kind of thing," he replies with a cocked eyebrow to our query for a facts & figures sheet. His post-punk, "my way or the highway" attitude, however, does not come across as arrogant; if anything, it rings refreshingly sincere. "Actually," he goes on to admit, "when we started with Le Labo we couldn't afford a PR specialist. With hindsight that appears to have been a good thing. We had to put all our efforts into our product and trust that it would speak for itself. Philippe Starck told me once that he would have loved to have done our design. He wanted to know who did it. Truth is, nobody did it. We could not afford it."

PHILIPPE STARCK SAGTE MIR EINMAL, ER WÜNSCHTE, ER HÄTTE LE LABO ENTWORFEN. »WER WAR DENN EUER DESIGNER?« »NIEMAND«, ANTWORTETE ICH, »WIR HATTEN GAR KEIN GELD FÜR EINEN DESIGNER.«

»Das Produkt« besteht aus einer Palette von mittlerweile elf außergewöhnlichen, von den weltweit besten Parfumeuren wie zum Beispiel Frank Voelkl oder Françoise Caron, entwickelten Düften. Sie treten als klares Statement gegenüber Massenparfums auf. Die »Le Labo«-Kreationen sind anders, komplexer, schwieriger als Warenhaus-Parfums, aber auch betörender und faszinierender. Oder wie Penot vergleicht: »Genau wie ein perfekter Mann oder eine perfekte Frau spätestens nach drei Wochen todlangweilig werden, haben auch perfekte Parfums so gar nichts Aufregendes.« In dieser Haltung zeigt sich auch Penots Vorliebe für die japanische Kultur, »besonders für die Wabi-Sabi-Ästhetik, die das Unperfekte und Vergängliche zelebriert. Wir wollen und müssen nicht jedem gefallen«, fährt

Meanwhile, the product consists of a range of 11 extraordinary scents developed by the world's best perfume creators including Frank Voelkl and Françoise Caron – the very opposite of your usual run-of-the-mill, commercial perfume franchise. Le Labo creations are different, more complex and intricate than a department store perfume; they are bewitching and beguiling. Or, as Penot puts it, "just as a perfect man or a perfect woman become boring after three weeks at most, a 'perfect' perfume is not at all exciting." These views mirror Penot's fondness for Japanese culture, especially the wabi-sabi philosophy, which celebrates transience and imperfection. "We don't want to, and we don't have to please everyone," he continues while dipping a blotter into a tester containing their newest creation "Santal 33" – a

GRASSE – NEW YORK
LOS ANGELES

ALL PERSONS
MUST TAKE
SHOWER
WITH HOT WATER AND SOAP
BEFORE ENTERING LE LABO

" When I was a kid I used to pray every night for a new perfume from Le Labo.
Then later I realized God doesn't work that way, so I stole one and prayed for forgiveness."
Emo Philips by LL.
ROYAL

LE LABO
GRASSE – NEW YORK
LOS ANGELES

Lab Hours
Sunday 11-5

er fort, indem er einen Parfumstreifen in eine Testerflasche der neuesten Kreation Santal 33 taucht, eine neue Interpretation des amerikanischen Westens, und damit leicht dramatisch in der Luft herumwedelt. Genauso wenig anbiedern will sich die Verpackung; klassisch halbrunde Flaschen, schlichte, wenn auch gewichtige Schraubdeckel, naturweiße Etiketten, die als schnörkelloser Hintergrund für alte Schreibmaschinenschrift dienen. Unspektakulärer geht es nicht. Auch das Konzept hinter der Namensgebung ist äußerst nüchtern – die Parfums werden einzig mit dem Hauptduft bezeichnet, gefolgt von einer Zahl, die alle Ingredienzen zusammenzählt. Von Fantasiegebilden, Traumwelten oder gar Romantik keine Spur. »Nichts soll vom Duft selbst ablenken«, sagt der »Le Labo«-Gründer.

Umso theatralischer wirken die Handlungen, die Store Manager Justin hinter der Duftbar vollbringt. Er hantiert in weißem Laborkittel und Latexhandschuhen mit Laborgläsern und Pipetten. Dann entnimmt er dem Kühlschrank aus Chrom und Glas ein Fläschchen hochkonzentrierter Parfumessenz Rose 31 und tröpfelt diese sorgfältig in ein Glas mit Alkohollösung, das auf einer Hochpräzisionswaage steht. Diesen Vorgang kommentiert Penot mit: »Das Mischverhältnis muss ganz genau stimmen.« Dann füllt Justin die Mischung sorgfältig in ein Parfumfläschchen. »Welcher Name darf aufs Etikett?«, will er vom Kunden wissen. Dann druckt er dieses, versehen mit dem persönlichen Namen des Duftträgers, dem Abfüllort und einem Haltbarkeitsdatum auf einem kleinen Heimbürodrucker aus und klebt es präzise auf den Flakon.

reinterpretation of the spirit of the American West – and then giving it a slightly theatrical wave in the air. The packaging for the perfumes equals the no-nonsense approach to doing business: a classic bottle with a simple, yet heavy cap and a plain white label imprinted with an old-style typewriter font. Not a frill in sight. And the concept behind naming the perfumes is equally unspectacular: each fragrance is named after the main scent note and followed by a number that indicates the amount of ingredients used for the concoction. Absolutely no fantasy creations, imaginary worlds or romantic gimmicks. "We don't want anything to distract from the actual fragrance itself," the Le Labo founder says. "We rarely launch a new perfume. And when we do, it has to be meaningful. It's about harmony in the construction and the performance of the perfume, even if it takes hundreds of modifications and years before we get it right."

By comparison, store manager Justin's manipulations behind the fragrance bar are positively dramatic. Wearing a white lab coat and surgical gloves he readies test tubes and pipettes. Then, from a chrome and glass refrigerator, he selects a small container of the highly concentrated essence "Rose 31" and carefully adds a few drops into a glass vessel containing an alcohol-based solution that rests on a set of high precision scales. While observing Justin, Penot explains that the compounding has to be done very precisely. After completing his task, Justin fills the resulting perfume into a flask. "Which name would you like me to print on the label?" he asks the client. Bearing the name provided by the customer as well as the location the perfume was compounded and the fragrance's best-before date, the label is printed off on the little office printer and affixed to the flask with the utmost precision.

NEUE PARFUMS LANCIEREN WIR NUR DANN, WENN WIRKLICH ALLES DRAN STIMMT – VON DER KOMPOSITION ÜBER HAFTBARKEIT UND DUFTENTWICKLUNG BIS ZUR AUSSTRAHLUNG. AUCH WENN DAS HUNDERTE VON MODIFIKATIONEN BEDEUTET UND DER PROZESS JAHRE DAUERT.

Le Labo ist das völlig ungeplante Resultat einer Ausbildung, die Penot bei Hermès-Chefparfumeur Jean-Claude Ellena in Grasse absolvierte. »In einer Atmosphäre wie im Labor von Ellena«, sinniert des Meisters Lehrling über sein zukünftiges Projekt, »würden die Kunden am Verkaufspunkt in die faszinierende Parfumherstellung einbezogen.« Die direkte sinnliche Erfahrung mit Düften ist auch der Grund, weshalb heute in jeder Le Labo Boutique und jedem Le Labo Corner eine Box mit vierzig natürlichen Parfumessenzen aufliegt. An den kleinen Fläschchen können die Kunden schnuppern, ihre olfaktorischen Kenntnisse erweitern und die Herkunft der Blumen oder Hölzer, die den Düften ihre besondere Note geben, erfahren. Am gleichen Lehrgang nahm auch Penots damaliger Arbeitskollege

Le Labo is the entirely unplanned result of a training course that Penot did with Hermès master perfumer Jean-Claude Ellena in Grasse. "In an environment similar to Ellena's laboratory," he remembers thinking, "clients would be involved in the compounding of perfumes directly at the sales point." The direct olfactory perception of the different scents on the part of the customer is also the reason why each Le Labo Boutique and every Le Labo Corner is equipped with an "olfactionary" – a type of dictionary for the nose containing forty different natural essences. Customers can breathe in the various scents to develop their olfactory palette and learn about the provenance of the flowers and woods that lend the fragrances their distinct notes. Edouard Roschi, a work colleague of Penot's at the time, attended the same

bei L'Oréal, Edouard Roschi, teil. Die beiden entwickelten im gleichen Team Marketingkampagnen für Armani Parfums und merkten dort sehr schnell, dass sie gleiche Wertvorstellungen hatten. »Wir lästerten ständig über die Branche. Seelenlose, nach Marketingkonzepten entwickelte Massenparfums waren einfach nicht unser Ding. Und für Corporate Culture waren wir beide nicht geschaffen«, blickt Penot auf die Zeit bei L'Oréal zurück. »Es gibt nichts Traurigeres als einen tollen Brand, der sich ausverkauft.« Also träumten die beiden im marketing-dominierten Großkonzern zusammengeschweißten Individualisten von Duftkreationen mit künstlerischem Ausdruck, die aus »Inspiration, Entdeckergeist und Kreativität« entstehen. Ähnlich wie die Nischen-Düfte der Editions de Parfums Frédéric Malle oder von Serge Lutens, aber noch kantiger, noch charaktervoller, noch fokussierter auf den Inhalt. Die Labor-Idee gab den zundenden Funken. Penot und Roschi schlossen noch in Grasse einen »Wir machen unser eigenes Ding«-Pakt. 2006 lancierten die beiden, mittlerweile in New York lebend, Le Labo. Ohne jegliche Fremdfinanzierung, wenn man von ein paar kleinen Zustüpfen von Freunden absieht. »Wahrscheinlich hätten wir mit unserer komischen Idee auch gar keine Kapitalgeber gefunden«, lächelt Penot. »Aber darum ging es ja nicht, sondern darum, unsere Unabhängigkeit bewahren zu können.« Es war auch schnell klar, dass die »Le Labo«-Düfte nur über eigene Vertriebskanäle verkauft würden. »Unsere Geschichte und die Geschichte hinter den Kreationen können wir nur so unseren Kunden näherbringen.«

course in Grasse. Both men worked in a team that developed marketing campaigns for Armani Parfums and they soon came to realize that they shared the same values. "We were always running down the branch. We both disliked the soulless, mass perfumes that are created according to marketing concepts. And corporate culture just isn't us," Penot remarks, looking back on the time that served as the inspiration for their present venture. And so, the two individualists thrown together by circumstance dreamed of fragrant creations with artistic merit that would be born of inspiration, a pioneering spirit and creativity. They want their final products to be comparable to niche fragrances such as the Editions de Parfums Frédéric Malle or scents by Serge Lutens, yet bolder, with more character and still more focused on content. The idea of the laboratory setting provided the initial spark, and, while still in Grasse, Penot and Roschi made a solemn vow that one day they would do things differently. In 2006, they launched Le Labo in New York, the city that in the meantime had become their new home. Remarkably enough, apart from some small contributions by a few friends, they did not even need a loan. "We probably wouldn't have gotten a loan with our funny idea anyway," Penot laughs. "And even more importantly, we wanted to remain independent." Soon it became clear that they would be selling the Le Labo fragrances exclusively through their own distribution channels. "That is the only way to really make our customers aware of what we're about."

LE LABO
GRASSE – NEW YORK
fragrance
lab

Aus einem kleinen Lokal an der Elizabeth Street in NoLita wurde die erste Le Labo Boutique. »Zunächst zogen wir einen Architekten bei«, blickt Penot zurück, »merkten aber bald, dass er nur viel kosten würde, ohne jemals zu begreifen, was unsere Vision ist.« Also packten die Gründer selbst an. Beim Umbau kam ganz unerwartet eine Blechwand mit Reliefornamenten zum Vorschein, die heute zusammen mit einem maskulin-industriellen Look die Identity der Boutique-Ausstattungen ausmacht. Die Vorliebe für industrielles Design hat Penot bereits in seiner Kindheit entwickelt: »Mein Vater arbeitete in einer Fabrik in einem kleinen Ort in Zentralfrankreich. Von der Fabrikästhetik – vor allem dem Gusseisen – war ich absolut fasziniert.«

A small shop on Elizabeth Street in NoLita provided the venue for the first Le Labo boutique. "First we hired an architect," Penot recalls, "but we soon realized that he would simply cost a lot of money without ever really understanding what our vision was." So the Le Labo founders decided to take things into their own hands. During the refurbishment, a metal wall with relief ornamentation unexpectedly surfaced which, together with a masculine-industrial touch, has become the trademark look for the boutiques. Penot says he developed a penchant for industrial design when he was a boy: "My dad was working in a factory in a small place in the center of France, and I have been impacted by industrial design very early on. I love cast iron, I cannot get this out of my system."

THERE'S NOTHING SADDER THAN A GREAT BRAND THAT SELLS OUT.

Dass Maskulinität sehr weiblich sein kann, wusste er von seiner Zeit bei Armani. Deshalb auch sind die »Le Labo«-Düfte unisex. Auch wenn manche mehr auf der weiblichen und andere mehr auf der männlichen Seite liegen. Trotz Improvisation und bescheidenem Startkapital: Völlig konzeptlos ins Abenteuer gestürzt hat sich Penot nicht. »Ganz im Gegenteil«, sagt er. »Wir haben ausgiebig über jedem Detail gebrütet. Schließlich ist Le Labo unser Leben und der Spiegel unserer Wertvorstellungen.« Er rechnete sich aus, dass sie mit solch einer egozentrischen Haltung vielleicht vier Parfums im Tag verkaufen würden, und verkalkulierte sich damit gewaltig. Bereits nach zwei Monaten erreichte Le Labo den Breakeven. Heute erzielt das junge Parfum-Unternehmen einen Jahresumsatz von über fünf Millionen Dollar und ist mit vier eigenen Boutiquen und 18 Store-Corners auf der ganzen Welt vertreten. Ohne dass ein einziger Dollar in PR und Marketing gesteckt wird, schreiben Lifestylemagazin-Journalisten und Blogger begeistert über die Düfte, reißen sich Hotels wie Ian Schragers »Gramercy Park« oder die Lifestyle-Kette Anthropologie darum, mit Le Labo zusammenzuarbeiten, damit etwas vom Kultstatus auf sie abfällt. Den Erfolg erklärt Penot ganz einfach: »Wir sprechen zwar nur eine kleine Minderheit an, doch wer unsere Düfte mag, geht eine sehr enge, persönliche Beziehung mit ihnen ein.« So eng, dass rund 85 Prozent der Kunden der Marke treu bleiben. Eine Zahl, von der Marketingmanager nur träumen können. Fabrice Penot guckt auf seine Uhr. »Ich muss los«, sagt er. In wenigen Stunden geht sein Flug zurück nach New York. »Ohne New York gäbe es Le Labo nicht«, sagt er beim Aufstehen. »In New York wird Neues und Innovatives mit offenen Armen aufgenommen. Träume kann man dort nicht nur träumen, sondern auch realisieren. Die Stadt gab mir jedenfalls das Selbstvertrauen.« Der Parfum-Unternehmer im coolen Casual Look dreht sich zur Türe und verschwindet mit in die Luft geblasenen Bisou-Bisous. —

And Fabrice Penot learned already during his days working for Armani that masculinity can have a very feminine allure. Which is why the Le Labo fragrances are created unisex, although some have a more masculine and others a more feminine note. All the improvisation and meager start-up capital does not mean they embarked on this adventure without a clear business concept. "Not at all," Penot says, "we considered every aspect long and hard. After all, Le Labo is our life and mirrors our core values." The fledgling entrepreneurs expected to sell about four perfumes a day with their uncompromising attitude, but soon found they had miscalculated badly. In just two months, Le Labo reached break even. Today, the young fragrance company's turnover exceeds five million US dollars, with four boutiques and 18 store corners located globally. Without having invested a single dollar in PR and marketing, lifestyle magazines and bloggers began writing enthusiastic articles about the fragrances, and big names such as Ian Schrager's Gramercy Park Hotel and the lifestyle chain "Anthropologie" were eager to cooperate with them and have a little of the Le Labo cult status rub off on them. Penot's succinct explanation for their success is "we may only address a small minority with our fragrances, but those that do like our scent bond with them very closely." So closely, that approximately 85 percent of the customers are brand loyal. A figure that most marketing managers can only dream of. Fabrice Penot checks his watch. "I have to run," he says. His flight back to New York leaves in a few hours. "Le Labo would not exist without New York," he remarks as he gets up. "In New York there is a lot of space for change and innovation. It's a great place to make dreams happen, and I got the self-confidence in New York that things are possible." And with that, the unconventional perfume entrepreneur turns to the door and, after tossing a few air kisses, disappears. —

19

Le Pain Quotidien
Alain Coumont

Text **Barbara Markert** Photos **Kai Jünemann**

Pain de blé au levain
Farine bise moulue sur pierre
1/1 (2 kg) 9.60
1/2 (1 kg) 4.80
1/4 (500 g) 2.40
Whole wheat sourdough
Stone ground wheat flour

Belegte Brote kann eigentlich jeder selbst schmieren. Doch der Belgier Alain Coumont schmiert nicht nur, er hat daraus ein Geschäft gemacht. Seine aus über hundert Filialen bestehende Restaurantkette Le Pain Quotidien (Das tägliche Brot) liefert den Beweis, dass Passion gepaart mit Zufallsglauben zum Erfolg führen kann.

Making a sandwich is something everyone knows how to do. But Belgian national Alain Coumont does not simply make sandwiches; he has made a business. And his chain of restaurants, Le Pain Quotidien, or "our daily bread," in over one hundred locations worldwide is proof that passion paired with providence can lead to success.

Die erste, frühe Kundschaft ist gegangen. Auf den Tischen bleiben leere Eierschalen, in den Brotkörben hier und da ein Croissant zurück. Im Bäckerei-Bistro Le Pain Quotidien am Pariser Marché St-Honoré schaut es um elf Uhr aus wie in der Küche einer Großfamilie, die eilig den Frühstückstisch verlassen hat. Die Mitarbeitenden nutzen die kurze Ruhe, um ihr Lokal wieder auf Vordermann zu bringen. Auch die Kaffeemaschine schweigt zum ersten Mal an diesem Tag. Statt ihrer beschallt leise klassische Flötenmusik den Raum. Mitten in den Frieden platzt mit wehendem Haar und Rollkoffer in der Hand Alain Coumont, der Gründer und Miteigentümer der inzwischen international über ein Franchisingsystem agierenden Restaurantkette. Er kommt direkt aus Brüssel, dem Stammsitz des Unternehmens. Am Abend fliegt er weiter nach Montpellier, seine Wahlheimat. Letzte Woche war er in Mumbai, nächste Woche muss er nach São Paulo, wo er über den Standort der ersten brasilianischen Filiale entscheiden soll. »Ich reise viel«, sagt Coumont und zieht die hohe Stirn in Falten. Obwohl der Fünfzigjährige nur noch eine Minderheitsbeteiligung an seinem 1990 gegründeten Unternehmen hält, ist er noch immer zu hundert Prozent ins Tagesgeschäft involviert. Die Auswahl der Lagen seiner Restaurants gehört wie die Kontrolle der Dekoration, des Service und der Lieferanten zu seinem Job als Chief Creative Officer. »Vor allem anderen kümmere ich mich um das Produkt. Das ist das Wichtigste – egal in welchem Business.« Das Produkt, um das es im Le Pain Quotidien geht,

The morning customers have left, leaving behind eggshells and a few lone croissants in the breadbaskets. At 11 o'clock, the bakery-restaurant Le Pain Quotidien on Marché St. Honoré in Paris looks like the kitchen of a large family that left the breakfast table in a big hurry. The servers use the short respite to make everything spick-and-span again. For the first time today, the coffee machine is silent, and classical flute music can be heard piping softly in the background. Then, abruptly, the peace is shattered as Alain Coumont bursts in, suitcase in tow. He is founder and co-owner of the restaurant chain that has become established as an international franchise. He has just arrived from Brussels where the company's headquarters are located. Tonight, he will fly on to his adopted French hometown of Montpellier. Last week he was in Mumbai, and next week he will be traveling to São Paulo to choose the locale for the first Brazilian restaurant. "I travel a lot," says Coumont, furrowing his brow. Although the fifty-year-old retains only a minority stake in the company he founded in 1990, he is still a hundred percent involved in the daily operation. As Chief Creative Officer he is in charge of choosing the locations, deciding on the decorations, selecting the tableware, and naming the suppliers. "But first and foremost I look after the products. That is of prime importance – in any business." The product around which Le Pain Quotidien revolves is – as the name indicates – bread; more precisely, traditional farmer's or sourdough bread that is baked without using additional yeast. Four different kinds are on offer: the classic bread is made of wheat, but loaves of spelt, rye and multi-grain bread are also available as is a delectable range of pastry and cakes.

LES PLATS DU JOUR
SOUPE MAISON
AUX LEGUMES BIOLOGIQUES
: Courgette
11,60
Saumon

La table
d'Alain
Coumont

ist, wie der Name verrät, Brot. Genauer gesagt ein traditionelles Bauern- oder Sauerteigbrot, das ohne Hefezusatz gebacken wird. Vier verschiedene Sorten sind im Angebot: Der Klassiker ist aus Weizen, es gibt aber auch Dinkel-, Roggen- und Mehrkornbrot mit Rosinen. Dazu kommen jede Menge Gebäck und Kuchen. Die Produktion ist lokal organisiert. In jeder Stadt gibt es eine Zentralbäckerei für alle Filialen. Paris ist eine Ausnahme. Das Brot wird hier um fünf Uhr morgens aus Brüssel angeliefert. Eine eigene Bäckerei an der Seine wäre zu teuer. Das Geld gibt Coumont lieber für die Zutaten aus. Rund neunzig Prozent aller Inhaltsstoffe der Pariser Backwaren stammen aus biologischem Anbau.

Production is organized locally, and every city has a central bakery to supply all the restaurants in the vicinity. Paris is the exception to the rule. Here the bread is delivered directly from Brussels at five o'clock in the morning. A separate bakery on the Seine would be too costly, and, in any case, Coumont prefers to spend money on the ingredients. Roughly ninety percent of the ingredients in the baked goods available in Paris are grown organically. To us, organic is not a marketing gag as it is for other businesses who only offer environment-friendly coffee and basically greenwash the rest. Our ingredients are expensive, and we invest a lot of time and effort in locating the right suppliers. Organic is a tough business."

BIO IST BEI UNS KEIN MARKETING-GAG WIE BEI ANDEREN, DIE NUR ÖKOLOGISCHEN KAFFEE ANBIETEN UND ANSONSTEN GREENWASHING BETREIBEN. UNSERE ZUTATEN SIND TEUER UND WIR INVESTIEREN VIEL MÜHE UND ZEIT IN DIE SUCHE NACH DEN RICHTIGEN LIEFERANTEN. BIO IST EIN HARTES BUSINESS.

Vor rund zehn Jahren hat Alain Coumont mit der Bio-Ausrichtung begonnen. »Ich lebte damals in New York, ernährte zehntausend Menschen pro Woche mit normalen Zutaten und kochte für mich selbst nur mit Bioprodukten. Ich war ein Monster.« Nach dieser Selbsterkenntnis stellte der Belgier in seinen Restaurants peu à peu die Zutaten auf ökologische Herkunft um. Heute sei kein anderer Konkurrent in der Branche so weit wie er, schätzt der drahtige Manager stolz und gestikuliert wild mit seinen schmalen Händen, denen man die Arbeit im eigenen Bio-Gemüsegarten und im eigenen Weinberg nicht ansieht. Rund 45 Kilometer von Montpellier hat sich der gelernte Koch, der aus einer Hotel- und Gaststättenfamilie stammt, zusammen mit Frau und Tochter in einem alten Bauernhaus angesiedelt. Restaurants gebe es dort auf dem Land nicht, deswegen koche er selbst – für seine Familie und Freunde. »Ich habe einen fünfeinhalb Meter langen Tisch mit 16 Stühlen darum herum bei mir in der Küche stehen.«

Der zuhause gelebte Gemeinschaftsgedanke ist auch im Konzept von Le Pain Quotidien fest verankert. In jedem Lokal steht ein großer, rustikaler Holztisch, um den sich die unterschiedlichsten Gäste zum Essen zusammenfinden. Der »Gemeinschaftstisch« existiert seit Bestehen der Firma. »Wenn es diesen Tisch nicht gäbe, wären wir heute nicht da, wo wir sind«, urteilt der Kreativchef, der die Liebe zum Kochen von seiner Großmutter geerbt hat und nach eigenen Aussagen im Alter von nur drei Jahren seinen ersten Apfelkuchen buk. Ein großer Tisch sei wie ein guter Film: Das Setting allein reiche nicht, wichtig seien auch die Schauspieler. Die Hauptakteure im Le Pain Quotidien sind, so der Gründer, die großen Brotlaibe, die Kaffeehaferl, der stimmige Service und das Fehlen von Coca-Cola auf der Speisekarte. All die

Alain Coumont started putting the focus on organic produce roughly ten years ago. "At the time, I lived in New York and catered to an average of ten thousand people a week using ordinary products, all the while using exclusively organic products to do my own cooking. I was a monster." After an epiphany, the Belgian began, step by step, to replace ingredients used in his restaurants with organically-grown produce. Today, they have left the competition far behind, the wiry manager reckons proudly, gesticulating busily the entire time. In the present surroundings, it is difficult to imagine him working his own organic vegetable plot and organic vineyards. Food, however, runs in Coumont's family, and the trained chef lives with his wife and daughter in an old farmhouse some 25 miles outside of Montpellier. Apparently there are no restaurants nearby, which is why he cooks himself – for friends and family. "I have a 17-foot long kitchen table standing in my kitchen with 16 chairs around it."

The community spirit that he celebrates in his private life is also firmly anchored in the concept of Le Pain Quotidien. A large, rustic wooden table is set up in every locale for its diverse guests to sit at and break bread communally. Indeed, the so-called "communal table" has been in existence since the company was founded. "Without this table we would not be where we are today," says the creative head of the company whose love for cooking was handed down to him by his grandmother, and who remembers baking his first apple pie at the tender age of three. A big table, he tells us, is like a good movie; the setting is not the only criteria – the actors are also important. According to Coumont, the main actors at Le Pain Quotidien are the large loaves of bread, the coffee pots, the attractive table settings and the absence of Coca-Cola on the menu. "Together, these little details result in a harmonious overall concept." Which

Pain de blé au levain
Farine bise moulue sur pierre
1/1 (2 kg) 9.60
1/2 (1 kg) 4.80
1/4 (500 g) 2.40
Whole wheat sourdou
Stone ground wheat flour
Pain de seigle paysan
Farine bise moulue sur pierre
1/1 (2 kg) 9.60
1/2 (1 kg) 4.80
1/4 (500 g) 2.40
Sourdough peasant rye
Pain cinq céréales et raisin
1/1 6.60
1/2 3.25

Sel Gris de l'Atlantique

kleinen Details ergeben ein stimmiges Gesamtkonzept. Dieses ist seit zwanzig Jahren unverändert und entstand aus reinem Zufall. Als Alain Coumont noch als Koch in Brüssel sein eigenes Feinkostrestaurant unterhielt, fand er nicht das richtige Brot. Also buk er es selbst. Um die Ausgaben für den teuren Ofen zu rechtfertigen, eröffnete er eine kleine Back-Boutique. Der Laden hatte einen knarzenden Eichenboden, einen großen Tisch vom Flohmarkt, dazu ein altes Küchenbuffet. Diese Dekoration findet man heute in jedem Le Pain Quotidien auf der Welt wieder. »Einen Businessplan habe ich nie erstellt. Ich weiß gar nicht, wie man einen macht«, sagt der Erfolgsmanager, der in seinem karierten Holzfällerhemd tatsächlich eher wie ein Ökobauer als wie ein Firmenchef aussieht. »Ich wollte mir damals nur ein günstiges Hobby zulegen. Das war eine Art Boyscout-Kantine, gegründet mit einem Non-Profit-Hintergrund. Dass daraus ein rentables Geschäft wurde, verstehe ich bis heute nicht.«

has remained unchanged in twenty years and – remarkably – succeeded by pure chance. Back when Alain Coumont worked in Brussels as chef in his own gourmet restaurant, he could not find the bread he needed anywhere. So he baked it himself. And to justify the expensive oven, he opened a small bakery outlet. The shop boasted a creaky oak floor, a large table from a flea market and an old kitchen buffet – the same decor that visitors will find in every branch of Le Pain Quotidien today. "I never made a business plan. I wouldn't even know how," says the successful entrepreneur who, with his checked logger's shirt, bears more resemblance to an organic farmer than a business manager.

AT THE TIME, I THOUGHT THIS WOULD BE A CHEAP HOBBY. IT WAS SORT OF A BOY SCOUT'S CANTEEN AND MAKING A PROFIT WAS NOT A CRITERIA. IN FACT, I'M STILL NOT SURE HOW IT TURNED INTO A PROFITABLE COMPANY.

Coumonts Verwunderung über den eigenen Erfolg ist nicht gespielt, sondern authentisch. Für ihn zählt nicht die Rendite, sondern andere Werte: »Die Mitarbeitenden sind unser Schlüsselelement, egal ob sie bei uns die Brote schmieren oder im Management arbeiten. Aber um gute Talente zu halten, muss man ihnen auch etwas bieten.« Wachstum sei deshalb wichtig. Aber bitte ohne dabei den Planeten zu verschmutzen. Alain Coumont schiebt spitzbübisch die Brille auf die Nasenspitze und zwinkert mit den blauen Augen: »Wissen Sie, was mein ganz persönlicher Traum ist? Ich möchte die Tomate im Winter von der Speisekarte verdammen. Doch leider sind unsere Gäste noch nicht so weit, Gemüse dann zu genießen, wenn es wächst. Dabei ist das doch das größte Vergnügen überhaupt.« —

Coumont's bemusement at his own success is not an act; he is genuinely surprised. To him, other values matter more than high profits: "Employees are the key, whether they butter rolls or work in management." But to attract and hold talented workers, an employer has to be able to offer something in return. "That's why growth is important. But only if that doesn't mean polluting the planet. In fact, would you like to know what my personal goal is?" asks Coumont with a mischievous twinkle in his blues eyes. "I want to ban tomatoes from our menu during winter. But, regrettably, our customers have yet to learn to value the use of seasonal vegetables. Though, surely, eating food in season is one of the purest pleasures of all." —

20

MUTTERLAND
JAN SCHAWE

Text **Karen Naundorf** Photos **Henning Bock**

... und natürlich auch für zu Hause!

SAFT

»Was ich bin? Designer und Delikatessenhändler.« Vielleicht sollte Jan Schawe besser sagen: geschickter Markenmacher und Geschäftsmann, charmanter Überzeugungstäter. Denn innerhalb kürzester Zeit hat der 38-Jährige den Feinkostladen und die Marke Mutterland etabliert. »Die deutsche Antwort auf Dean & Deluca«, lobte die Zeitschrift Elle in einem Hamburg-Cityguide.

"What I am? I'm a designer and a gourmet food dealer." And maybe Jan Schawe should add: a skillful brand creator and businessman as well as a charismatic persuader. In almost no time at all, the 38-year-old has established the delicatessen and the brand Mutterland. "Elle" magazine lauds it as "Germany's answer to Dean & Deluca" in their Hamburg city guide.

Mutterland liegt hinterm Hauptbahnhof. Nur wenige Meter vom U-Bahn-Schacht entfernt, von den regenbogenbeflaggten Cafés der Langen Reihe, vom Schauspielhaus und vom Hansaplatz, auf dem die Callgirls – trotz Verbots – auf Freier warten. Erhaben sieht es aus, das alte Kontorhaus, erbaut vor hundert Jahren, dessen Eckladen im Erdgeschoss Jan Schawe als Stammsitz für seinen Delikatessenladen auswählte. Das war 2007 und es war ein wagemutiges Experiment, fanden viele. Ein Feinkostladen in Bahnhofnähe? In einem heruntergekommenem Gebäude, in dem die meisten Läden leer standen? Doch schon zwei Jahre später wählte der deutsche Einzelhandelsverband das Geschäft zum »Store of the Year«. Schawe eröffnete bald zwei weitere Läden und verkauft längst auch online.

Mutterland is located behind the main train station in Hamburg, just a few meters away from the subway tunnel, the Langen Reihe with its flamboyant bars and their rainbow flags, the theater and the Hansaplatz where prostitutes – notwithstanding the ban – wait for clients. Despite the general scruffiness of the neighborhood, the historical Kontorhaus, an imposing traditional business edifice built some hundred years ago, has a venerable air to it – which is what led Schawe to choose the corner premises as the headquarters for his delicatessen in 2007. Many considered his decision a risky experiment. A fine foods shop in this part of town? In a derelict building with any number of empty spaces? Yet a mere two years later the German retail association voted his business "Store of the Year." Soon Schawe opened two further outlets and started making his goods available online as well.

Meine Mutter ist meine härteste Kritikerin. Und sie hat immer Recht.

Das Konzept: Regionalität, Qualität, Herzblut. Drei Jahre lang recherchierte Schawe, besuchte Manufakturen und Familienbetriebe, bis er genügend Produkte zusammenhatte, um einen Laden zu bestücken. »Unser Konzept ist Made in Germany. Wir haben keine Marmelade aus Neuseeland und kein Wasser von den Fidschi-Inseln.« Schawe ist ein guter Verkäufer, das wird schnell klar: Er lächelt. Er strahlt. Und er schwärmt von Mutterland, als sei der Laden nicht sein Arbeitsplatz, sondern ein gelebter Traum. »Mutterland, das steht für Heimat, für Regionales, für Kindheitserinnerungen, Qualität«, sagt er und zeichnet mit seinen Worten en passant das Profil der von ihm entworfenen Marke. »Eine Vorzeigemutter ist fürsorglich, kocht zuhause und nicht mit Maggi, bringt die Kinder nicht zu McDonald's.« Schawes eigene Mutter kommt immer wieder mal im Laden vorbei.

The concept? Local sources, quality products, lifeblood. Schawe spent three years researching and visiting manufacturers and family businesses before he had taken aboard enough products to stock his store. "Our concept is 'Made in Germany.' We don't feature preserves from New Zealand or mineral water from the Fiji islands." Schawe is obviously a natural salesman, that much is immediately apparent. He smiles. He beams. And enthuses about Mutterland as if it were his dream come true and not his place of work. "Mutterland stands for home, local produce, childhood memories, quality," he explains, sketching a profile of the brand he created. "The epitome of the perfect mother, a mother who is always there for you, cooks only homemade meals, doesn't stoop to convenience food and never, ever feeds her children fast food." Schawe's own mother looks into the store regularly. "My mother is my toughest critic. And she is always right."

An den hohen Wänden stapeln sich Holzkästen zu Regalen, darin stehen ordentlich aufgereiht die Produkte – und zu jedem eine kurze Beschreibung. »Jedes Produkt hat eine Geschichte«, sagt Schawe. Das Chili-Chutney kommt aus Schleswig-Holstein: »Der Sohn eines Baumschulbesitzers pflanzt alte Chili-Sorten an.« Gleich daneben stehen edle Senfsoßen, hausgemacht vom Ehepaar Sierks. Ein paar Holzkisten weiter liegen handgefertigte Bruchschokolade,

Wooden crates are stacked to form shelves along the high walls. They contain neatly arranged products – along with a short description of each item. "Each product has its own story," Schawe explains. The chili chutney is made in Schleswig-Holstein. "By a tree nursery owner's son who plants old chili varieties." Next to this, intriguing mustards are displayed, all homemade by the family Sierks. A few wooden crates farther we find homemade broken chocolate, an array of cards with clever sayings and licorice

Say Cheese
Saftiger Käsekuchen mit
einer frischen Zitronen-Note
Frei von: Nuss
Ganzer Kuchen €
€ 3,40
zum Mitnehmen

delicacao
berlin
SCHOKOLADE
AUS FEINSTEM
ROHKAKAO.
DELICACAO

NOT MANY PEOPLE ARE CRAZY ENOUGH TO GO THROUGH AS MUCH TROUBLE AS WE DO.

Lobkärtchen, Lakritzbonbons. Mit der Eigenmarke Mutterland sind nur Produkte gekennzeichnet, an deren Produktion Schawe beteiligt war. Und es gibt auch immer etwas fürs Auge: Geschenke werden liebevoll verpackt – in bedruckten Papierbeuteln. Darauf steht je nach Anlass »Gute Besserung«, »Gratulation«, »Verzeihung« oder »Es muss nicht immer Kaviar sein«. Die Mitarbeitenden nähen den Geschenkbeutel vor den Augen des Kunden mit einer Nähmaschine zu. Das ist mehr, als viele Mütter tun würden. Für den kleinen Hunger steht im Kühlregal natürlich »Muttis Pausenbrot« – ehrlich und simpel, Vollkorn mit Käse. Und zum Kaffee gibt es frisch Gebackenes, zum Beispiel jüdischen Apfelkuchen oder Kalten Hund (aus Schokolade und selbst gebackenen Keksen). Die cremefarbene Variante heißt »Bootsmann«, so wie Schawes ähnlichfarbiger Labrador. Im hinteren Ladenteil ist das Café. Die Tische sind schlicht, auf allen stehen Blumen und frisch gemahlener Pfeffer. In einem Regal: Kinderbücher. Pippi Langstrumpf, Hänsel und Gretel, »Mein Bärenbuch«. Klassisch eben. Die Bedienung trägt eine beige Schürze, weißes Hemd, schwarze Hose. Aus den Lautsprechern klingt

candy. Articles carrying the home brand label "Mutterland" are products in whose manufacturing Schawe has been involved personally. And there is so much more to see: Gifts are wrapped with loving care – in printed paper bags which, depending on the occasion, may state "Get Well," "Congratulations," "Forgive Me" or "It Doesn't Always Have to be Caviar." The gift bag is sewn up with a sewing machine before the eyes of the customer. More than many mothers would do. On one of the shelves in the cooler we find "Muttis Pausenbrot," a no-frills whole-wheat cheese sandwich. Other shelves display freshly baked pastry to enjoy with a cup of coffee like Jewish apple pie or "Kalter Hund" (literally "cold dog"), a delicious cake consisting of alternating layers of chocolate and homemade cookies. The vanilla-colored version is called "Bootsmann" after Schawe's yellow Labrador. A café is located at the back of the shop with plain tables that may well have stood in an old-fashioned kitchen at one time. Each one is set with flowers and a bowl of freshly ground pepper. Children's books can be found on a shelf: Pippi Longstocking, Hansel and Gretel, My Bear Book. Children's classics. The staff wear white shirts and black trousers, covered by a beige apron. Amy Winehouse,

BORGMANN
SAFT
ECKART
3.80

erst Amy Winehouse, dann Nouvelle Vague.

then Nouvelle Vague can be heard from the speakers.

Doch was ist es nun, das Geheimnis von Mutterland? »Wir bauen keine Schwellenangst auf«, sagt Schawe. »Die Mitarbeitenden sind nicht schicker gekleidet als die Gäste und gehen auf alle gleich freundlich zu.« Aber die Preise – das kann sich doch nicht jeder leisten? »Natürlich sind wir nicht der Markt für den Wochenendeinkauf. Aber wir haben auch kleine Produkte, den kleinen Luxus. Bei uns kann sich jeder etwas Gutes tun«, sagt Schawe. Und wenn ein Konkurrent sein Konzept kopiert? Er lacht: »Es gibt nicht viele Wahnsinnige, die sich so viel Mühe machen wie wir!« Schawe arbeitet nicht mit Großhändlern, hat die meisten der über zweihundert Lieferanten persönlich besucht. Die Manufakturen müssen keine Werbekostenpauschalen zahlen und auch nicht für die Platzierung der Produkte im Laden. »Wir begegnen den Lieferanten auf Augenhöhe und sind transparent in der Kalkulation«, sagt Schawe. Wenn das Etikett einer Marmelade nicht taugt, hilft der Designer schon mal nach. Aber nicht immer: »Kenner wissen: Wenn ich in einem Delikatessenladen ein Produkt mit einem schlechten Packaging sehe, kaufe ich es. Denn dann muss die Qualität wirklich exzellent sein!«

Schawe liebt sein Mutterland. Das wird klar, wenn er durch die Regalreihen führt und erzählt und erzählt, obwohl er eigentlich längst weg sein müsste, der Designer Schawe ist andernorts gefragt. Denn noch kann er von Mutterland nicht leben: »Jeder Euro wird reinvestiert.« Trotzdem lehnt er Franchise-Anfragen ab: »Wir sind keine Kette. Mutterland gehört zu Hamburg. Ich brauche ja auch kein Harrod's außerhalb von London.« —

So, what is the secret of Mutterland? "We keep the threshold low," says Schawe in an attempt to analyze their success. "The personnel are not dressed more elegantly than the guests. And they are equally friendly to everyone." But the prices – surely not everyone can afford those? "Of course, we're not the place to do your weekly shopping. But we also have more affordable products, little luxuries. Everyone can buy themselves a treat in our shop." And what if a competitor copies the concept? "Not many people are crazy enough to go through as much trouble as we do!" Schawe does not collaborate with large distributors, and has visited most of his two hundred suppliers personally. The manufacturers pay neither a fee for advertising nor for the placement of their products in the shop. "We prefer to deal with our suppliers on an equal footing and keep our calculations transparent," Schawe explains. And if the label of a product is not up to his high standards, Schawe the designer occasionally helps out. Though not always. "When connoisseurs see a product with an inferior label, they reason that the content must be exceptional if the shop is willing to compromise on the packaging – and so they buy it."

Schawe loves his Mutterland. This becomes more than obvious as he leads us along the shelves and relates one anecdote after another, though he should have left ages ago – his services as a designer are needed elsewhere. At present he cannot live off the proceeds of his delicatessen: "Every euro is reinvested." However, he rejects offers to start a franchise. "We're not a chain. Mutterland belongs in Hamburg. After all, I have no need for a Harrods outside of London either." —

21

Nectar & Pulse
Tanja Sieder & Carina Schichl

Text **Olivia El Sayed** Photos **Gian Marco Castelberg**

INNER CITY
1. District
STEPHANSPLATZ
SCHWEDENPLATZ
KARLSPLATZ
STUBENTOR
STADTPARK
LANDSTRASSE WIEN MITTE
VORDERE ZOLLAMTSSTRASSE
AM HEUMARKT
PANTONE 629 C
PANTONE 630 C
PANTONE 631 C
PANTONE 632 C

Carina Schichl und Tanja Sieder lernten sich 2004 während ihres Studiums in Salzburg kennen und teilten sich seither Wohnungen in Stockholm, London und New York. Derzeit haben sie ihre Zelte in München aufgeschlagen. Die beiden Designerinnen bereisten schon die halbe Welt und hatten dafür das Nötigste stets dabei: einen Koffer voller Träume und einander. Und doch fehlte etwas zum perfekten Glück, denn die gängigen Reiseführer bedienten ihre Bedürfnisse nie ganz. Während eines Praktikums in London kam ihnen deshalb die Idee, eigene Travel Guides zu produzieren, die all das anbieten, was sie bisher vermisst hatten. Sie sammelten fortan Tipps von Einheimischen aus aller Herren Länder und gelangten so an Empfehlungen, die Eiffelturm, Big Ben und Sachertorte alt aussehen lassen. Auf dieser Idee basierend gründeten sie 2010 ihr eigenes Unternehmen Nectar & Pulse.

Carina Schichl and Tanja Sieder met in 2004 when they were both studying design and product management in Salzburg. Since then, they have shared digs in Stockholm, London, New York, and are currently living in Munich. Together, they have traveled the globe with a suitcase full of dreams and each other – all they needed. And yet, over time they discovered that something was lacking – that something being a really good travel guide. The plethora of existent guides never quite seemed to fulfill their expectations. Then, during an internship in London, the idea arose to create their own travel guides – guides that would offer what they had missed in the existing ones. They began gathering insider tips from locals in cities all over the world, discovering attractions that put the Eiffel Tower, Big Ben and Sachertorte in the shade. Encouraged by their findings, they decided, in 2010, to establish their own enterprise, Nectar & Pulse.

Auf dem Küchentisch der Altbauwohnung im Münchner Quartier Giesing stehen leuchtend rote Erdbeeren, mütterlich in Stücke geschnittenes Gebäck und ein kleiner Strauß Tulpen, der in einer zur Vase umfunktionierten Keksdose steckt. Lifestyle-Magazine türmen sich in einer Ecke und verdecken fast die »Soziologie der Marke« von Kai Uwe Hellmann, das Fundament des kreativen Turms. Die Wohnung ist Büro und Heim in einem. Mit lackierten Fingernägeln und frisch tätowierten Handgelenken bereiten Carina und Tanja Kaffee zu, um sich für die nächste Runde fit zu machen. Schnell noch eine SMS getippt und eine neue Playlist angewählt, und dann geht es weiter mit der Arbeit ihres neuesten Reiseführers. Die beiden Globetrotter sind Tag und Nacht mit Verpackung, Versand und Vermarktung ihres Produkts beschäftigt. Trotz des zelebrierten Verzehrs von Koffeintabletten haben sie sich für diese intensive Zeit zur zusätzlichen Unterstützung eine Praktikantin ins Boot geholt.

Freshly washed strawberries, lovingly cut cake and a small bouquet of tulips placed in a converted cookie jar decorate the kitchen table in the pre-war apartment in the Giesing quarter of Munich. Lifestyle magazines are stacked in a tower in a corner, nearly obscuring Hellmann's magnus opus on the sociology of brands that forms the base of the creative construction. The apartment is both office and home in one. Fingernails brightly painted, and wrists displaying recent tattoos, designers Carina and Tanja are making yet another pot of coffee in order to prepare themselves for the next round. After quickly sending off the latest urgent text message and choosing a new playlist, they are ready to carry on with their most recent travel guide. Day and night, the two travel aficionados are busy packaging, sending and marketing their product. And, despite heavily indulging in caffeine abuse, they have found it necessary to hire temporary help for additional support during this hectic phase. "You only live once, and maybe not even very long at that. Who knows, right? So, why wait?"

"READY TO STROLL AWAY"

Man lebt nur einmal und das vielleicht auch nicht allzu lange, wer weiß das schon. Worauf also warten?

Dem Produkt der beiden Jungunternehmerinnen liegt ein simples, aber schönes Konzept zugrunde: in jeder Metropole den Nektar aufzuspüren und so den Puls der Stadt mit all ihren Subkulturen, Geheimtipps und versteckten Schätzen zu erleben. Dies gelingt am besten mit Insiderwissen, das die beiden Frauen durch Gespräche mit Einheimischen sammeln und dann in ästhetischer Form weitergeben.

The young entrepreneurs' product is based on a simple yet elegant premise: to find the nectar in every city, thereby uncovering the metropole's vibrant pulse with all its subcultures, its secret delights and hidden treasures. Because insider knowledge is necessary for this, both women gather information during numerous conversations with locals and then convert the gradually gleaned knowledge into an aesthetic package.

Every city has a special feel that is created by the people who live there.

»Wie sich eine Stadt anfühlt, ist immer von den Menschen abhängig, die sie bewohnen.« Und wann ist Reisen schöner, als wenn man dabei auf Leute trifft, die sich unverhofft als Seelenverwandte entpuppen? »Your local soulmates« ist deshalb der Claim von Nectar & Pulse und bezieht sich auch auf das eigentümliche Gefühl, eine Stadt zu kennen, obwohl man selbst noch nie da war. Der Kaffee schmeckt, wie man ihn gern mag, die Boutiquen bieten an, wonach man schon immer suchte, und die Clubs spielen die Musik, zu der man am liebsten bis in die frühen Morgenstunden tanzt. Kurz: Man fühlt sich unter Freunden, obwohl man Neuland betritt.

Und so funktioniert das Prinzip: Auf der Website von Nectar & Pulse sucht man nicht nach Restauranttipps oder Übernachtungsmöglichkeiten, sondern nach Seelenverwandten. In jeder Stadt präsentiert sich eine Galerie sogenannter »local soulmates«, die ihre Lieblingslabels und Leidenschaften verraten und in einem Interview Rede und Antwort stehen. Fühlt man sich jemandem ähnlich, wählt man diese Person aus, und erhält so ihre persönlichen Empfehlungen, zwischen zwanzig und dreißig an der Zahl, und kann diese dann seinem individuellen Reiseführer beifügen. »Die Tipps von nur einer Person übersteigen jeweils schon das Angebot eines einzelnen Wallpaper Guides.« Für die anvisierte Destination können beliebig viele Soulmates ausgewählt werden. Tummeln sich genug Seelenverwandte pro Stadt im Warenkorb, drückt man die Enter-Taste und Carina und Tanja stellen das personalisierte Ringbuch in München – oder wo auch immer sie gerade sind – entsprechend zusammen und versenden es an den Besteller. »Das Produkt ist wie wir selbst: sehr flexibel. In unserem Auto finden sich alle nötigen Utensilien, so dass wir auch von unterwegs arbeiten können.«

Traveling is at its best when you meet people who, quite unexpectedly, turn out to be soulmates. Nectar & Pulse claim to be able to supply your local soulmates on demand, thus literally allowing you to feel oddly at home despite never having set foot in a city before. The coffee tastes the way it should, the boutiques offer what you've always been looking for, and the clubs play your favorite music. In short, you feel you belong, even though this is your first visit.

And this is the concept: visitors to Nectar & Pulse's website do not look for recommendations for restaurants or accommodations; instead they look for soulmates. A gallery of local soulmates is presented for every city. In personal interviews, they talk about their passions, favorite labels and other interests in life. You choose the people whose tastes and views you feel are most similar to yours, and their twenty to thirty insider tips are added to your own loose-leaf binder, or collector, as Tanja and Carina call their personalized travel guides. "The tips from just a single person give more information than an entire Wallpaper city guide." A random number of locals can be selected for the chosen destination and, when you feel your shopping cart contains enough soulmates, you click on enter. Then, from Munich – or wherever they happen to be at that moment – Carina and Tanja create a personalized binder for you and send it to you. "The product is like us: very flexible. We always have the necessary tools in our car so that we can work away from home as well."

Being good friends does not necessarily translate into the ability to work well and productively together. Despite unsolicited, yet well-meant warnings, Tanja and Carina have chosen to follow this path together. They radiate the unwavering conviction that this is the right decision, not least because they believe they have an identical understanding of their brand. They want it to be honest and authentic, and embody what they themselves stand for.

Dulce
Nectar

STOCKHOLM
STOCKHOLM
STOCKHOLM
VIENNA
BREADLOVER
WRITER
BIRDWATCHER
SHOPOWNER
FASHIONLOVER
HARLEYRIDER
MUSICPRODUCER
HIPSTER
DESIGNER
COLLECTOR
PHOTOGRAPHER
LISTENER
SHOPAHOLIC
GLAMOURGIRL
PARTYQUEEN
JEWELLERYDESIGNER
DANCER
ACTIVIST
BEST FRIENDS
BATIKBOYS
ADVENTURERS

Wer gut befreundet ist, arbeitet nicht automatisch auch gut und gern zusammen. Trotz allen abratenden Mahnungen von außen haben sich Tanja und Carina dazu entschlossen, diesen Weg einzuschlagen. Die felsenfeste Überzeugung, dass das die richtige Entscheidung war, funkelt aus den zwei euphorischen Augenpaaren und gründet auf dem deckungsgleichen Verständnis ihrer Marke. Ehrlich und authentisch soll sie sein und das verkörpern, was sie beide sind. »Uns treibt dasselbe an: der Drang, einen Unterschied machen zu wollen.« Den Markenkern von Nectar & Pulse zu leben, fällt Carina und Tanja nicht schwer, denn er ist, was auch den Charakter der Gründerinnen definiert: Neugierde, Ambition und Lebensfreude. —

"We are both driven by the same urge: to make a difference." It is easy for Carina and Tanja to live the philosophy of the brand Nectar & Pulse. It is, after all, indistinguishable from the two entrepreneurs' key characteristics: curiosity, ambition and a zest for life. —

22

Pedrazzini
Claudio Pedrazzini

Text **Jürg Zbinden** Photos **Gian Marco Castelberg**

Gross
klein
Sitzbock

Der Großvater, Augusto Pedrazzini, gründete vor mehr als hundert Jahren die Firma mit den schnittigen, zusehends exklusiveren und längst international begehrten Holzbooten. 1928 gewann der Einwanderer die 1. Zürcher Outboard-Regatta. Zwei nachfolgende Generationen brausten in seinem Kielwasser über den Zürichsee und auch der Urenkel sieht seine Zukunft konsequent als Bootsbauer.

Over one hundred years ago, founder Augusto Pedrazzini established a boatyard on the shores of Lake Zurich, Switzerland, and started constructing sleek crafts that were to become increasingly renowned and internationally sought after. An Italian immigrant, it was Augusto's boat that won the first Zurich Outboard Regatta in 1928. The two following generations followed in his wake, and, next in line, Augusto's great-grandson, is also determined to become a boatbuilder.

Wenn bei Capri die rote Sonne im Meer versinkt, so bedeutet das nicht, dass andernorts nur graue Tristesse herrscht. Die Sonne scheint zum Glück auch auf weniger besungene Gewässer. Und wenn dann auch noch ein mit Mahagoni verkleidetes Boot seine Kurven durch die Bläue zieht, reckt selbst der stolze Schwan seinen Hals.

Wer über einiges an Vermögen verfügt – die Preise erreichen je nach Modell bis 650 000 Franken – und mit den anderen nicht im selben Boot sitzen möchte, ist bei der Yacht- und Bootswerft Pedrazzini im Schwyzer Dorf Bäch an der richtigen Adresse. Allein schon die Lage am oberen Zürichsee kommt einer malerischen Unique Selling Proposition gleich. Bäch war einmal überregional bekannt für einen mittlerweile fast ausgestorbenen Brauch, die Bächer Fastnacht. Während sich für das närrische Treiben von anno dazumal kaum noch Auswärtige interessieren, brauchen die schwimmenden Schmuckstücke aus der Werft niemals lange im Showroom auf ihre neuen Besitzer zu warten.

Das Chefbüro des aktuellen Patrons Claudio Pedrazzini ist klein, aber fein. Neben dem mit Intarsien geschmückten Tisch liegen einige Design-Magazine sowie ein Schinken mit Gadgets: »Toys for Boys« (Verlag teNeues). Ein erster leiser Verdacht drängt sich auf: Bootssport ist vorwiegend Männersache. Immerhin heißt die vielleicht berühmteste Privatyacht der Welt »Christina O«. An Bord des legendären Schiffes parlierten einst Winston Churchill, John F. Kennedy, Eva Perón und Maria Callas, und anlässlich der Hochzeitsfeierlichkeiten von Grace Kelly und Rainier III. floss Champagner in Strömen. Allein die Größe eines Schiffs ist es nicht, die das Glück an Deck verantwortet. Die Schicksale von Christina Onassis, John F. Kennedy, Grace Kelly oder der Diva assoluta Maria Callas sprechen eine deutliche Sprache. Es sind denn auch insbesondere Pedrazzinis kleine Sportboote, sogenannte »Runabouts«, die von der Kundschaft im In- und Ausland hoch geschätzt werden. Es sind vor allem Persönlichkeiten aus Wirtschaftskreisen, die den wassersportiven Glamour en miniature suchen. Von Runabouts spricht man ebenfalls bei Autos, vor allem bei Vintage-Vehikeln. Ob es auch bei Sportbooten einen Oldtimermarkt gibt? »Nach der Preisliste von 1965 kam ein Boot auf dreißig- bis fünfzigtausend Franken zu stehen. Wir haben eben eins überholt, das nun in den Verkauf gelangt, und rechnen, dass es um die hunderttausend Franken bringt«, verrät Pedrazzini.

Despite the name of their most famous model, the Capri Super Deluxe, you do not have to travel to Capri to behold the magnificent sight of a Pedrazzini craft skimming over the waves. The Capri, first produced in the mid-20th century, still inspires the design of contemporary motorboats today. Pedrazzini's exclusive vessels have their admirers everywhere; small wonder, we realize upon seeing one of these rare crafts cutting through the blue waters of Lake Zurich in consummate mahogany perfection on a sunny day. It is a truly uplifting sight that has even the elegant white swans turning their heads to take a second look.

For those who have cash to spare – depending on the model, prices can reach 650,000 Swiss francs – and seek something distinct, the Yacht- und Bootswerft Pedrazzini, Pedrazzini's yacht and boatyard, in the village of Bäch may have something to offer. The location alone constitutes an extremely picturesque unique selling proposition. Bäch was once famed in the region for its now all-but-forgotten Carnival celebrations, the Bächer Fastnacht. While the town no longer woos visitors from afar for this event, its boatbuilding yard does attract constant interest. The floating gems that are crafted here, each taking up to nine months to finish, never seem to grace the showroom for long.

Present-day padrone Claudio Pedrazzini's office is small, but exquisitely furnished. Next to a couple of design magazines displayed on an inlaid mahogany table lies a hefty publication featuring gadgets, "Toys for Boys" (from the publisher teNeues), that catches the eye. A hunch arises that boating must be more of a man thing, even though the all-time most famous private yacht was the "Christina O": The vessel that was the society venue of the mid-20th century. Where Winston Churchill and John F. Kennedy first met. Which carried the likes of Eva Perón and Maria Callas. And where it is reported champagne flowed in rivers on the event of Rainier III and Grace Kelly's wedding celebration. "The difference between a boat and a yacht is simply the size. Everything under 12 meters is a boat, the rest are yachts," Claudio Pedrazzini explains. But then size is not everything and is no guarantee for a happy ending. The fate of Christina Onassis, John F. Kennedy, Grace Kelly or La Divina Maria Callas speaks for itself. Pedrazzini's domestic and international clientele favor the boatbuilder's smaller sports crafts, so-called runabouts. Clients, themselves often extremely successful players in the business world, delight in engaging in water sports with these powerful and timelessly classy motorboats.

SZ 3738

Fehr 51

Pedrazzini

2x4t

Some people buy a Maserati and don't care about the engine, others buy one because, to them, it is the most powerful car and they love the sound of the engine. Our customers want smooth handling at all times.

Pedrazzinis Erfolgsgeschichte ist keine maritime, sondern eine, die ihren Anfang im Binnenland nahm. Anno 1906 wanderte der Großvater Augusto Pedrazzini vom Lago di Como her in die Schweiz ein. In einer hiesigen Werft fand er eine Stelle. 1914 machte er sich in Wollishofen selbständig, anfangs mit dem Bau von Fischer- und Ruderbooten, später folgten Segeljollen und Motoryachten. 1929 kam er nach Bäch und baute das Haus und die Werft. Augusto und sein ältester Sohn Ferruccio waren noch Italiener. Augustos Enkel, der heutige Chef, ließ sich mit siebzehn als Schweizer einbürgern. Wie schon sein Vater, bei dem er in die vierjährige Lehre ging, hat Claudio Pedrazzini den Beruf des Bootsbauers erlernt. Ganz ausgelernt wird on the job. Gewisse Fertigkeiten wie etwa das Verarbeiten von Messingbeschlägen eignet man sich später an. »In der Schweiz gibt es zwei Schulen für Bootsbauer, eine in Luzern für die Deutschschweiz und eine in Lausanne für das Welschland. In der deutschsprachige Schweiz fangen jährlich etwa fünfzehn neue Lehrlinge an«, erklärt Claudio Pedrazzini.

Beim Bootsdesign ist Pedrazzini seit Jahrzehnten strikt auf dem Holzweg – eine tragende Rolle spielt nämlich edles Mahagoni, nur eine Nebenrolle spielt Teak. In den Werkstatträumen der Werft ist Holz in verschiedenen Entstehungsstadien omnipräsent. Ein aufgebockter Schiffsrumpf, sich stapelnde Planken, große und kleinere Holzteile, deren Verwendungszweck sich dem unkundigen Betrachter entzieht, befinden sich in Gesellschaft mächtiger Schrauben aus Stahl. Doch hat alles seine Ordnung, die Männer arbeiten mit Ruhe und Bedacht. In der Ruhe liegt die Kraft. Mahagoni wächst gerade und in großen Baumstämmen, es ist nicht zu hart, nicht zu weich, überdies lässt es sich hervorragend von Hand verarbeiten. Und farblich ist es wohl am allerschönsten. Außerdem lässt es sich leicht lackieren. Wenn ein Teakholz lackiert werden soll, ist es schwieriger, weil Teak ölhaltig ist. Durch die Jahrzehnte hat Pedrazzini mit Mahagoni die besten Erfahrungen gemacht. Die Frage nach dem Herzstück eines Motors beantwortet Claudio Pedrazzini, indem er den Vergleich mit dem Käufer eines Rennwagens wagt: »Der eine kauft einen Maserati und interessiert sich nicht für den Motor, ein anderer, weil er ihn für den stärksten hält und den Motorsound liebt. Unser Kunde will, dass die Technik funktioniert.« Sei's drum, Claudio Pedrazzinis Herz schlägt in erster Linie fürs Wasser, salzig oder süß, und nicht für den Asphalt. Liebhaber schöner Boote sind ihm dafür dankbar. —

The term runabout, an expression also applied to cars, especially vintage automobiles, prompts us to ask whether an old-timer market exists for motorboats as well. "Back in 1965, our boats cost between 30,000 and 50,000 Swiss francs. We just overhauled one of these crafts to put back on the market and expect it to go for about 100,000", Claudio reveals.

The family's success story does not have a seafaring backdrop, but begins in inland Italy. In the year 1906, Augusto Pedrazzini, grandfather of the present director, came from Lago di Como, Italy, to Switzerland where he found employment in a boatyard in Zurich. He started his first boatbuilding yard in 1914 in Wollishofen, a district of Zurich, where he initially built fishing boats and rowboats, eventually going on to construct sailboats and yachts. In the year 1929, he moved to Bäch where he constructed a house and a boatbuilding yard. Augusto and his oldest son, Ferrucio, retained their Italian citizenship as by Italian law dual-citizenship was not eligible for Italian citizens until 1992. Augusto's grandson, the present director, is therefore the first Pedrazzini to take on Swiss nationality. Like his father, Claudio accomplished a four-year apprenticeship, a combination of vocational schooling and on-site training, to become a boatbuilder. The final tweaks are learnt on the job, and certain skills such as working the brass fittings take years to master: "In Switzerland there are two schools for boatbuilders. One in Lucerne for the German-speaking part of Switzerland and one in Lausanne for the French-speaking part. In Lucerne, which caters to our region, about 15 new apprentices begin to learn the trade each year."

After experimenting in the past with other materials, Pedrazzini has returned to using that traditional and supremely elegant natural resource – wood – for the past several decades. Mahogany is their prime material, with teak coming in a distant second. As it is used in every step of the boatbuilding process, an abundance of wood in all shapes and sizes can be found in the workshop. A hull on a trestle, stacks of planks, and a profusion of unfathomable bits and pieces of wood are piled next to mighty steel propellers. Yet calm reigns in the workshop, apparently everything has its proper order and the craftsmen work deftly in quiet concentration. Mahogany is a wood that grows in large, straight trunks. It is not too hard and not too soft, which makes it wonderful for handcrafting. Colorwise, is it probably the most beautiful of woods, and it varnishes easily. Teak wood, with a higher percentage of natural oils, is much harder to varnish. Over the years, Pedrazzini has consistently found mahogany to be the best wood for the job. When we asked which engine suits which boat best, Claudio Pedrazzini draws a comparison to a sports car aficionado. Quite clearly, Claudio is a tar at heart and not a fast-car buff. Around the globe, connoisseurs of beautiful boats thank him for this. —

23

Playmobil
Horst Brandstätter

Text **Karen Naundorf** Photos **Stephanie Füssenich**

Das Gespräch mit Horst Brandstätter war für unsere Autorin nicht irgendein Interview: Vor ihr saß der Mann, der ganze Jahre ihrer Kindheit geprägt hatte. Wenige Playmobilmännchen in der Hosentasche genügten und sie tauchte in Fantasiewelten ein, deren Dimensionen sie als Erwachsene nur noch erahnen kann.

Interviewing Horst Brandstätter is no ordinary assignment for this writer: I'm sitting across from the man whose creations had a very meaningful impact on my childhood. With just a couple of Playmobil figurines in my pocket I would enter a fantasy world, the dimensions of which today, as an adult, I cannot begin to recreate.

Das Kinderglück misst 7,5 Zentimeter. Es lächelt, hat keine Nase und ist ein bisschen steif in der Hüfte. 2,4 Milliarden dieser Männchen soll es auf der Welt geben. Playmobil – das klingt so amerikanisch wie Marshmallow oder Hollywood. Doch die kleinen Männchen mit der Zackenfrisur stammen aus Deutschland. Genauer gesagt aus dem fränkischen Zirndorf, keine zwanzig Minuten von Nürnberg entfernt. Der Mann, der für viele Kinder der Welt ein Held sein dürfte, heißt Horst Brandstätter. Der Playmobil-Chef sitzt an einem langen Schreibtisch im ersten Stock der Firmenzentrale, zu seinen Füßen döst ein Hund, die Augen halb geschlossen, das Geschehen im Raum immer im Blick. Brandstätter, Manager des Jahres 2009, Träger des Bundesverdienstkreuzes, Ehrenbürger der Stadt Zirndorf, ist 78 Jahre alt und Unternehmer durch und durch. Hinter ihm hängen gerahmte Leitsprüche an der Wand: »Der Weg zum Reichtum liegt hauptsächlich in zwei Worten: Arbeit und Sparsamkeit.« Oder: »You never get a second chance to make a first impression.« Doch Brandstätter verständigt sich nicht in der Sprache der Manager. Er wirkt freundlich, fast bodenständig, der fränkische Akzent trägt dazu bei. Er selbst habe als Kind ein Tretauto gehabt (»Des hab ich geliebt!«) und einen Stoffkasper (»Den hab ich auch geliebt, aber der war dann irgendwann zerlegt.«). Schon im Schulalter war klar, dass er einmal im Familienunternehmen, bei »geobra Brandstätter«, einsteigen würde. Doch seine Mutter bestand darauf, dass er zunächst einen Beruf erlernen sollte. Also wurde er Geselle in einem Unternehmen für Formenbau.

Als HOB – so nennen ihn die Mitarbeiter – dann 1954 bei geobra Brandstätter anfing, stellte das Unternehmen Kunststoffspielzeug her. Doch in der Ölkrise Anfang der Siebzigerjahre wurde Plastik teuer. Brandstätter beauftragte Entwickler Hans Beck, von Haus aus Möbeltischler und Tüftler, mit der Suche nach neuen Ideen. Er wünschte sich ein System, das weiterentwickelt werden konnte. Mit kleinen Teilen, die wenig Kunststoff brauchten. An anderen Spielzeugmarken wollte Beck sich nicht orientieren, erinnert sich Brandstätter: »Ich habe Autos und Lastwagen gekauft, als Anregung. Da hat der Herr Beck mich bös angeschaut und gesagt: ›Nehmen Sie das weg! Sie engen damit meine Entwicklungsfähigkeit für etwas Neues ein!‹« Als Beck die ersten Entwürfe für die Männchen vorstellte, war Horst Brandstätter skeptisch: »Der Herr Beck hat mir die Figur gezeigt und da war kein Auto, kein Häusle.« Doch dann verstand er: Playmobil, das waren nicht nur die Figuren. »In das System ist etwas eingebaut, das andere Spielzeuge nicht haben: die Anregung der

The key to my childhood fantasy world was three inches tall. It had a smile, but no nose, and was a little stiff around the hips. Today, there are some 2.4 billion Playmobil figures spread over the globe. "Playmobil" – the name sounds as American as apple pie or Hollywood, but in actual fact, these little figures with their spiky hair have their origins in Germany. To be precise, in Zirndorf, some twenty minutes outside of Nuremberg. The person responsible for providing innumerable children all over the world with uncounted happy hours is Horst Brandstätter, the managing director of Playmobil. He sits behind a long desk on the first floor of the headquarters, a dog dozing at his feet with half-closed eyes that reveal the occasional watchful glint. Brandstätter – voted Manager of the Year 2009, bearer of the German Federal Cross of Merit, honorary citizen of the city of Zirndorf – is 78 years old and an entrepreneur to the bone. Behind him on the wall hang the framed maxims: "The path to wealth can be summed up in two words: work and thrift." Or: "You never get a second chance to make a first impression." Yet Brandstätter does not communicate in business speak. Instead, speaking with a strong local accent, he makes a genial, almost down-to-earth impression. "As a child I had a pedal car which I loved and a 'Stoffkasper,' a Punch-like rag doll which I literally loved to bits," he replies to our query. From an early age on, it was clear that one day he would join the family business "geobra Brandstätter." His mother, however, insisted that he learned a trade first. So he became an apprentice in a mold and die manufacturing company.

When HOB – as his employees call him – joined geobra Brandstätter in 1954, the enterprise was already producing plastic toys. Then during the oil crisis in the early 1970s, plastic became increasingly expensive. Brandstätter commissioned developer Hans Beck, a cabinetmaker by trade and amateur inventor, to come up with some new ideas. Ideally they were looking for a concept that could be further developed, added on to. With little pieces that required only small quantities of plastic. Beck refused to take inspiration from products by other manufacturers, Brandstätter recalls. "I bought him cars and trucks to help him with his research. But Herr Beck just gave me an annoyed look and said: 'Take it away! You're narrowing my developmental potential to come up with something new!'" When Beck presented the first designs of the little figurines, Horst Brandstätter was doubtful: "Herr Beck showed me these little figures, with no cars, no houses, no nothing!" But then he understood: Playmobil is not just about the figurines. "The concept has a special element to it that other toys don't have. It sparks the fantasy." Brandstätter says he is frequently asked to demonstrate what is so special about Playmobil. "But I can't!" he explains. "The special

1974
1976
1981
1982
1989
1990 PLA
2001

36

09/06

33

Le mammouth

Fantasie.« Er werde immer wieder gebeten zu zeigen, was so besonders sei an Playmobil: »Das kann ich nicht«, meint er dazu. »Das Besondere findet im Kopf des Kindes statt. Es lässt sich inspirieren und entwickelt Vorstellungen, die es mit Playmobil nachstellt.« Der Soziologe Christian Haug drückt es anders aus: Playmobilmännchen seien soziale Chamäleons. Neutrale Figuren, die eine Projektionsfläche für die Fantasien der Kinder bieten, wenn sie ihnen Rollen zuweisen. »Man kann da viel drüber reden. Mir macht es einfach Spaß zu sehen, wie intensiv die Kinder mit Playmobil zusammenleben«, sagt Brandstätter weniger analytisch. Er habe sich immer wieder mit Markenentwicklung beschäftigt. »Ich glaube gelernt zu haben, dass eine Marke nicht zu viel über das Produkt aussagen darf, sie muss Neugierde wecken. Bei Playmobil haben wir uns unterhalten: Wie nennen wir das jetzt? Mit Spiel müsste es etwas zu tun haben, mobil ist es.«

ingredient is the process it triggers in the minds of children. It fires their imaginations and they use the Playmobil figurines to make the stories they conjure up come to life." Christian Haug, a sociologist, expresses it differently. Playmobil figures are social chameleons; they are neutral figures onto which children can project their fantasies by assigning a different role to each figurine. "The topic can be discussed endlessly. Basically, I simply enjoy seeing how children get so thoroughly caught up in their Playmobil worlds," Brandstätter concludes. Developing the brand has been a process to which he has given a great deal of thought over the years. "I have come to the conclusion that a brand name should not reveal too much about the product; instead, it should make people curious. When we were trying to come up with a good name for Playmobil, we thought it should indicate that it is something to play with, and that it is mobile, too."

Playmobil entsorgt man nicht, es wird vererbt.

Es ist selten, dass Kinder mit den gleichen Dingen spielen wie ihre Eltern. Doch Playmobil wird weitervererbt. Die ersten Figuren kamen 1974 auf den Markt, sie führten drei Themenwelten ein, die es auch heute noch gibt: Indianer (»andere Kulturen«), Bauarbeiter (»Jetztzeit«) und Ritter (»Historie«). Es war der Beginn einer Erfolgsgeschichte. 507 Millionen Euro setzte geobra Brandstätter 2010, im elften Wachstumsjahr in Folge, mit Playmobil um. Längst gibt es Playmobil nicht mehr nur in Klein: siebenhunderttausend Besucher kommen jedes Jahr nach Zirndorf, um den Playmobil-Themenpark, FunPark genannt, zu besuchen. Auf neunzigtausend Quadratmetern gibt es die Welt des Lächelns in Lebensgroß. In der Westernstadt suchen Kinder im Sand nach Edelsteinen, andere striegeln auf dem Bauernhof die Plastikpferde. Das Piratenschiff steht zum Entern bereit. Auf den Toiletten stehen Kleidertrockner – falls mal ein Kind in einen der Teiche fällt. Am Eingang der Playmobil-Firmenzentrale steht hinter der Glastüre ein überdimensionales Männchen. Es ist ein Gärtner, trägt die berühmte Zackenfrisur, und natürlich, es lächelt. Neben ihm steht ein Blumenkübel: Lechuza-Pflanzsysteme sind das zweite Standbein des Familienunternehmens, mit dem 2010 insgesamt 40,5 Millionen Euro umgesetzt wurden.

Brandstätter plant langfristig. Dass er seit 15 Jahren in Florida überwintert, dafür gibt es viele Gründe. Eins: »Im Winter auf Schnee und Eis golfen ist schwierig.« Zwei: »Der bedeutendste Markt für Spielzeug ist der amerikanische. Da kann ich die Konsumenten beobachten.« Drei: »Ich habe mir vorgenommen, die Firma nicht erst am Tag X zu verlassen, sondern vorher in Etappen. Damit die Leute lernen können, wie man ohne mich arbeitet.« Führungskräfte kauft Brandstätter nicht von außen ein: »Ich war immer dafür, eigene Leute aufzubauen, anstatt über Kopfgeldjäger Fremdlinge zu holen.« Das Wichtigste sei, dass die Mitarbeitenden »sich in die Familie einfügen«, erklärt

Children rarely play with the same things their parents played with, yet according to Brandstätter, Playmobil doesn't get thrown away – it is passed down to the next generation. The first figurines were introduced on the market in 1974 together with three theme worlds that are still going strong today – Construction Workers ("present time"), Native Americans ("other cultures") and Knights ("history"). It was the start of a success story: geobra Brandstätter's 2010 turnover for Playmobil marks the eleventh consecutive growth year and amounted to 507 million euros. And Playmobil is no longer only available pint-size, either. Every year, 700,000 people visit Zirndorf, the location of FunPark, the Playmobil theme park where children's fantasies come to life. In the Wild West town, children can hunt for jewels in the sand or lovingly groom plastic horses at the farm. The pirate ship stands ready for intrepid buccaneers to board. And restrooms feature clothes dryers – in case a young guest falls into one of the ponds. Behind the glass entrance doors of the Playmobil headquarters, an over-sized figure can be made out. It's a gardener with the well-known spiky hair and a friendly smile standing next to a flower planter. Lechuza plant systems are the second business mainstay of the family establishment, and achieved a turnover of 40.5 million euros in 2010.

Horst Brandstätter is a long-term planner. This accounts for why he has been spending his winters in Florida for the past 15 years, though he concedes that the fact that it is hard to play golf in the snow may have something to do with this choice. However, he adds, "The American market is also the most important market for toys. In Florida I can observe the consumers." And, he goes on to say: "I decided to leave the company in a series of steps rather than all at once. This way, the office can slowly get used to working without me." Brandstätter does like to not recruit executives from the outside. "I have always preferred promoting our own people over engaging headhunters to procure candidates."

Playmobil sparks the imagination. And that's how we want it to stay.

der Playmobil-Chef. »Die Leute sollten mir sympathisch sein und logisch denken können.« Sechzig Entwickler beschäftigt das Unternehmen heute. Doch egal ob Steinzeit, Top Agents oder Drachenland – »eins bleibt immer gleich«, sagt Brandstätter: »Es geht nicht nur um Spielbeschäftigung. Playmobil soll die Fantasie anregen. Und das wollen wir auch beibehalten.« —

Above all, the Playmobil CEO values employees who are in line with the company's guiding principles. "I appreciate people who are pleasant to work with and able to think logically." Today, the company employs sixty developers. But whether the theme at hand is the Stone Age, Top Agents or Dragon Land – one criteria remains the same: "It's not just about getting the kids to play. Playmobil sparks the imagination. And that's how we want it to stay." —

SCHMIDTTAKAHASHI
EUGENIE SCHMIDT & MARIKO TAKAHASHI

Text **Olivia El Sayed** Photos **Henning Bock**

Ob Proenza Schouler, Viktor & Rolf oder Dolce & Gabbana – dass Designer im Duo arbeiten, erwies sich schon seit jeher als erfolgreiches Konzept. Jüngst bestehen die gestalterischen Paarungen immer häufiger aus zwei Frauen. Gerade in Berlin gibt es viele dieser kreativen Gespanne, die derzeit das Fashionbild prägen: Mongrels in Common, Malaika Raiss, Kaviar Gauche, Perret Schaad und Augustin Teboul sind nur einige davon. Um in diesem Reigen hervorzustechen, braucht es nicht nur eine eigene Idee, sondern manchmal auch ein Quäntchen Glück. So kam es, dass der Zeitgeist Eugenie Schmidt und Mariko Takahashi, die sich vor zwei Jahren mit ihrem Label selbständig machten, gut gesinnt war. Mit dem simplen, aber klugen Konzept hinter ihrer Mode katapultierten sie sich selbst mitten in den Megatrend der Nachhaltigkeit, und das ohne Absicht.

Be it Proenza Schouler, Viktor & Rolf or Dolce & Gabbana – it's long proven that designers working together as partners are a successful business model. Recently, these design duos tend increasingly to consist of two women. Especially in Berlin, where a number of creative twosomes are influencing the current face of fashion: Mongrels in Common, Malaika Raiss, Kaviar Gauche, Perret Schaad and Augustin Teboul, to name but a few. Standing out among this sharp competition requires not just an original idea; sometimes it also calls for a smidgeon of luck. Which is what occurred when Eugenie Schmidt and Mariko Takahashi started their own label two years ago and met the zeitgeist head-on. The simple, yet ingenious idea behind their fashion concept catapulted them into the sustainability megatrend, and this more or less by accident.

Im Berliner Bezirk Kreuzberg verläuft das Paul-Lincke-Ufer, benannt nach einem Komponisten und Ehrenbürger der Stadt, entlang dem Landwehrkanal. Eine Reihe von Gartenlokalen, Cafés und Restaurants säumt die Straße, die aufgrund ihrer niedrigen Mieten nicht nur eine beliebte Wohngegend ist, sondern auch den einen oder anderen Hinterhof beherbergt, wo sich das kreative Potenzial der Hauptstadt ein weiteres Ventil sucht. Hier, an der Hausnummer 41, findet sich auch das Studio des Labels Schmidttakahashi, das Altkleidern neues Leben einhaucht. Die beiden Designerinnen kamen über verschiedene Stationen nach Berlin. Eugenie Schmidt wurde in Duschanbe in Tadschikistan geboren. Ihre Familie zog 1990 nach Ulm. Ihre Ausbildung absolvierte sie dann in Berlin. Mariko Takahashi wuchs in Hiroshima auf und wollte nach ihrem Studium der Produktgestaltung in Tokio »einmal etwas völlig anderes machen«. Dieser Wunsch führte sie nach Berlin. Ihr Studium brachte die beiden Frauen 2005 zusammen.

Ihr Arbeitsmaterial bekommen die Designerinnen sozusagen geschenkt. In eigens gebauten Containern sammeln sie gebrauchte Kleidung. Die Holzcontainer stehen aber nicht irgendwo auf der Straße, sondern wandern über ausgesuchte Boutiquen, Hochschulen oder Designstudios um die Welt. »Das garantiert eine gewisse Qualität der Ware«, sagt Eugenie, während sie den Deckel der Holztruhe hebt. Hier sind Stoffsäcke angebracht, die wiederum mit einem Etikett versehen sind, das man zur Hälfte abtrennt. »Der Kleiderspender behält die eine Hälfte des Etiketts mit einer Nummer, über welche er digital nachsehen kann, was aus seinem Kleidungsstück geworden ist.« Und umgekehrt funktioniert das Stillen der Neugierde genauso: Kauft man ein neu geschneidertes Objekt des Designerduos, ist dieses ebenfalls mit einer Nummer versehen, mit welcher sich der komplette Stammbaum eines Kleidungsstücks auf der Website von Schmidttakahashi nachverfolgen lässt. Bevor es zu einer Weiterverarbeitung kommt, wird die gebrauchte Ware gereinigt, fotografiert und nach Farbe und Art sortiert im Archiv, einem randvoll gefüllten Stahlregal, abgelegt. Kleinere Defekte werden beibehalten.

In the Berlin district of Kreuzberg, the Paul-Lincke-Ufer, named after the composer and honorary citizen of the capital, runs parallel to the Landwehrkanal, a street lined with beer gardens, cafés and restaurants. The low rents attract tenants, and some of the courtyards contain premises in which creative minds vent their energies. Here, at number 41, lies the studio of the clothes label Schmidttakahashi. Here, old clothes are given a new lease on life. Both designers arrived in Berlin by very different routes. Eugenie Schmidt was born in Duschanbe in Tajikistan, and her family moved to Ulm, in Germany, in 1990. She later moved to Berlin to study. Mariko Takahashi grew up in Hiroshima and decided she wanted to do "something totally different for once," after studying product design in Tokyo. This urge brought her to Berlin where she and Eugenie met during their studies in 2005.

It could be said that they obtain their resources free of charge: The two women collect used clothing in self-made containers – but, these are not just placed on any street corner. Instead, the wooden containers make their way around the globe along a route of pre-selected boutiques, art schools or design studios. "This assures us of a certain quality," Eugenie says while she lifts the lid of a container. In it there are a number of cloth bags, each with a label that can be torn in half. "The donators keep half of the numbered label. They use it to digitally track what is happening to their garments." This satiation of curiosity works in the other direction too: People who buy a newly tailored item created by the design duo also receive a number to allow them to check the pedigree of their garment on the Schmidttakahashi website.
A new T-shirt from a shop is just a piece of material. A worn shirt, however, contains stories that have been woven into it by time. Before the pieces of clothing are processed, the used goods are cleaned, photographed, sorted according to color and type, and then stored in their archive – an over-brimming steel rack. Small defects are intentionally left in. "Traces of usage such as stains and small holes turn a piece of clothing into a sort of database and transport moments from the life of its previous wearer," Eugenie explains. "That fires the imagination." At some point,

A NEW T-SHIRT FROM A SHOP IS JUST A PIECE OF MATERIAL. A WORN SHIRT, HOWEVER, CONTAINS STORIES THAT HAVE BEEN WOVEN INTO IT BY TIME.

»Gebrauchsspuren wie Flecken und Löcher machen ein Kleidungsstück zu einer Art Datenspeicher, der die Momente aus dem Leben des früheren Trägers mit sich bringt«, sagt Eugenie. »Ein neues T-Shirt aus dem Laden ist einfach ein Stück Stoff. Ein getragenes Shirt hingegen erzählt eine ganze Geschichte. Das weckt die Fantasie.« Später wird so aus einer alten Manchesterhose, einem Strickpulli und zwei gemusterten T-Shirts also vielleicht eine einzigartige Jacke. Nicht immer bestehen die neuen Kleidungsstücke nur aus gebrauchtem Material, ab und an werden sie auch um neu fabrizierte Strickbahnen, kleine Details wie Knöpfe und Reißverschlüsse oder um edle Stoffteile ergänzt, um der Kreation den letzten Schliff zu verpassen. Weder Eugenie noch Mariko haben Geschwister, deren Sachen sie austragen mussten. Aber Mariko meint: »Es tut mir weniger weh, etwas Altes wegzugeben, wenn ich es einem Bekannten schenken kann. Und im Teenageralter tauschten wir andauernd unsere Sachen. Ich finde, die Tradition

an old pair of corduroys, a knitted sweater and two patterned T-shirts might be transformed into a one-of-a-kind coat. But, not only used materials go in the making of the new garments. Sometimes, new knitted insets and small details such as buttons, zippers or pieces of precious materials are added to give the creation its final polish. Neither Eugenie nor Mariko had a sibling whose clothing was handed down to them. But Mariko says: "I find it much easier to give away something I can't use anymore if I'm giving it to someone I know rather than if I have to throw it away. As teenagers, we were always trading off clothes with each other. To me, the custom of passing things on holds a special attraction." Eugenie thinks back to her childhood. "We didn't have much in the Soviet Union, and I often wore hand-me-downs from my older cousin." Her grandmother and great-aunt were both seamstresses, and so the clothes she received were always in good condition and lovingly embroidered. "Getting something like that was always special." She briefly pauses and continues: "After me

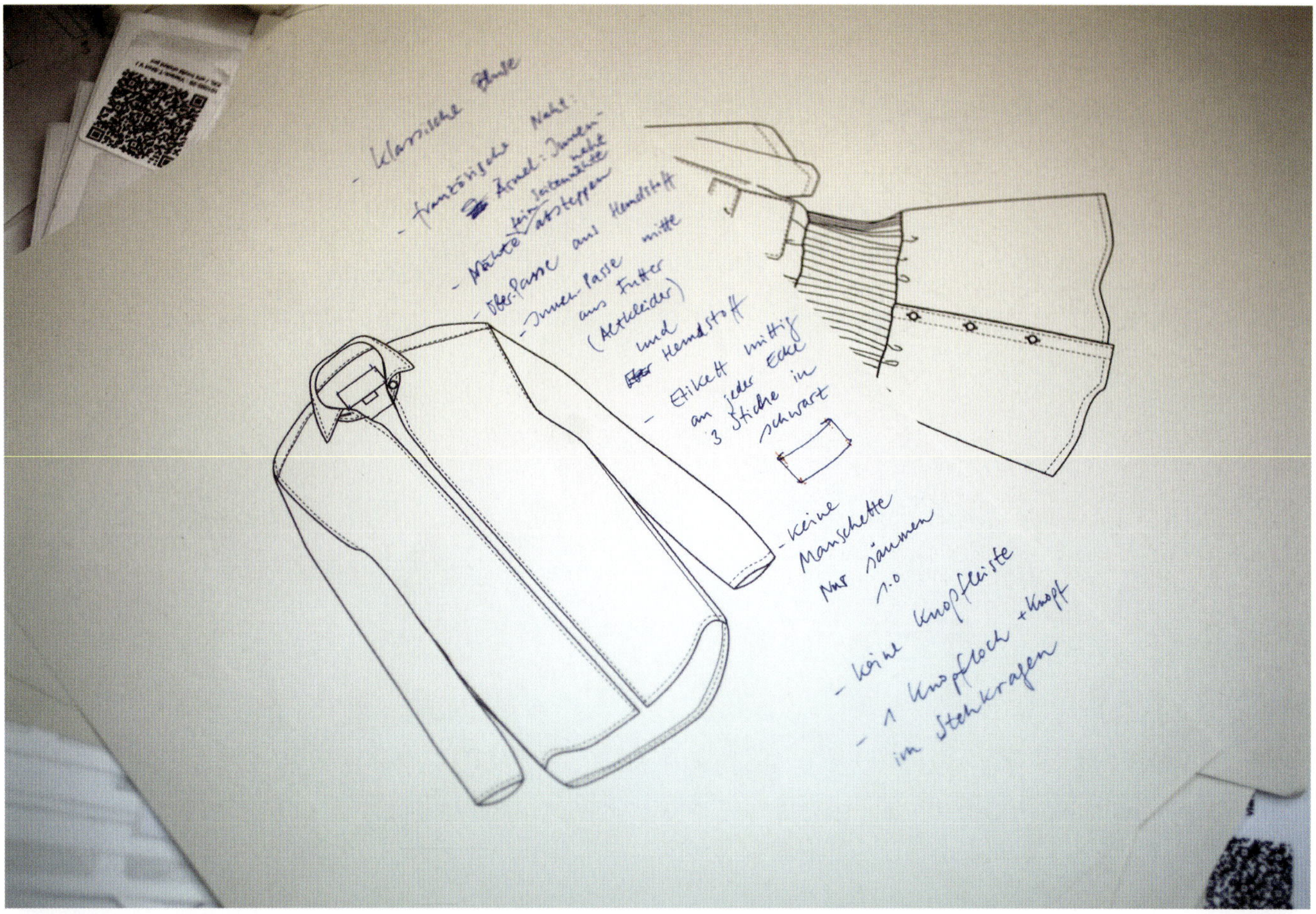

- klassische Bluse
- französische Naht
- Ärmel: Innennaht
  keine Seitennaht
- Nähte absteppen
- Ober-Passe aus Hemdstoff
- Innen-Passe mitte
  aus Futter
  (Altkleider)
  und
  Hemdstoff
- Etikett mittig
  an jeder Ecke
  3 Stiche in
  schwarz

- keine Manschette
  Nur säumen
  1.0

- keine Knopfleiste
- 1 Knopfloch + Knopf
  im Stehkragen

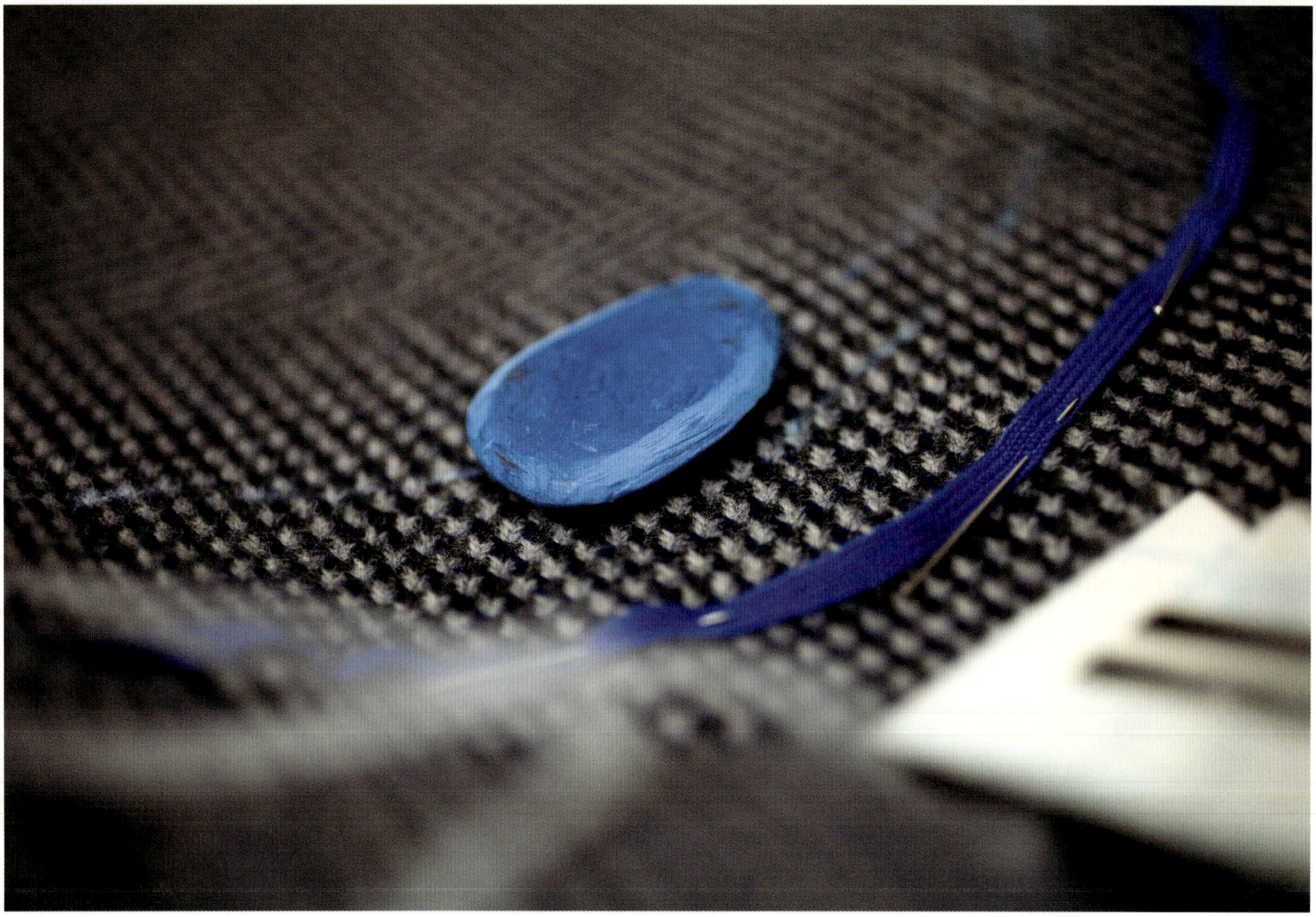

des Weitergebens hat etwas sehr Schönes an sich.« Eugenie erinnert sich an ihre Kindheit: »In der Sowjetunion hatten wir nicht viel und ich bekam oft die Sachen meiner älteren Cousine.« Ihre Großmutter und deren Schwester waren beide Schneiderinnen. Entsprechend liebevoll bestickt war die Kleidung, die sie als Kind erbte. »Es war etwas Besonderes, wenn man so etwas bekommen hat.« Sie überlegt kurz und fährt fort: »Nach mir gab es eine weitere Cousine, der ich meine Sachen weitergab. Und als diese aus den Kleidern herausgewachsen war, zeigte uns ihre Mutter zu einem viel späteren Zeitpunkt diese Sachen wieder und erzählte von den ›Erinnerungen an Annette‹. Da merkte ich, wie eine innere Stimme einen Besitzanspruch auf diese Erinnerungen erhob. Das ist doch aber eigentlich meine Erinnerung, dachte ich.« Das findet auch Mariko: »Geschichten und bestimmte Erlebnisse hängen oft an einem Kleidungsstück. Einen Pulli aus Paris wegzuwerfen fällt mir schwer, selbst wenn er nicht mehr passt. Einfach weil mit ihm eine gewisse Zeit verknüpft ist.« Dieser Gedanke faszinierte die zwei Kreativen schon während ihres gemeinsamen Studiums an der Kunsthochschule Berlin. Heute basiert ihre Marke darauf.

there was another cousin to whom my things were passed on. I remember that years after she had grown out of them, her mother showed us the garments and referred to them as 'memories of Annette.' And all of a sudden, something inside me laid a claim on those memories. 'These are really mine!' I thought indignantly." Mariko agrees. "Often stories and certain events are associated with a piece of clothing," she explains, "If I buy a sweater in Paris, it's hard to throw it away when it doesn't fit me anymore. Simply because I associate it with a certain period in time." It was during their time at the Berlin University of the Arts that both designers became fascinated by the notion of the stories behind clothes. It became the foundation upon which the two creative minds would later base their label. Clothes act as a storage device. "The longer a person wears them, the more they divulge about that person's lifestyle," Eugenie states.

Kleidungsstücke sind ein Speichermedium. Je länger ein Mensch sie trägt, umso mehr verraten sie über seinen Lebensstil.

Die Geschichten, die an der Kleidung haften, wollten Eugenie und Mariko erhalten, indem einzelne Teile wiederverwertet würden. ReClothing oder Upcycling wird das in Fachkreisen genannt. »Die Idee des Recyclings und des ökologischen Gedankens wurde aber mehr von außen an uns herangetragen. Es war eigentlich nicht etwas, das wir aktiv verfolgten und umsetzen wollten«, sagt Mariko. So kam es, dass sie etwas überrascht waren, als ihnen von der Senatsverwaltung für Wirtschaft, Technologie und Forschung der Green Fashion Award für Nachhaltigkeit verliehen wurde. »Unsere Grundidee war die Wiederbelebung der Kleidung und der Geschichten, die an ihr haften. Die Wiederverwertung ging damit einher und brachte das Etikett der Ökologie mit sich – Definitionen werden immer erst von außen an ein Objekt herangetragen.« Über den Preis haben sich beide sehr gefreut. »Es ist immer besser, etwas wiederzuverwerten, als es einfach achtlos wegzuwerfen. Und wir sind glücklich, mit unserer Arbeit ein solches Zeichen zu setzen«, fügt Eugenie an. Mit Stolz erfüllt die beiden auch das System, das sie sich für den Kreislauf der Kleidung ausgedacht haben.

»Die Hybride, die in dieser Welt entstehen, haben eine Art Familienstammbaum und das, als kreativer Moment, ist für uns sehr wertvoll», sagt Mariko. Künftig wollen sie den Aspekt der Geschichten noch mehr hervorheben und die Kleiderspender auffordern, zu den abgegebenen Teilen eine Anekdote dazuzuschreiben. Ob das für jemanden, der

Eugenie and Mariko decided they wanted to recycle the stories that linger in garments and keep both alive by reusing parts of the clothing: ReClothing, or Upcycling, as it is referred to in professional circles. "The fact that recycling is ecologically sustainable is entirely coincidental. It wasn't something we actively intended to include from the outset," says Mariko. "Definitions are always applied to an object from the outside first." And so it came as some surprise when they heard they were being awarded the Green Fashion Award for Sustainability by the Berlin Senate Department for Education, Science and Research. "Which is not to say that we don't support the idea of sustainability. It's always better to recycle something than to throw it away thoughtlessly," Eugenie interjects. "Our main intention, however, was to recycle and resuscitate the garments and the stories that they had accumulated over time. Ecology just sort of got included along the way." Fact is, the system they came up with to record the life cycle of a garment gives them noticeably more satisfaction.

"The hybrids that are conceived in this protected environment have a sort of pedigree and this, as a creative element, is very valuable to us," Mariko explains. In the future, they want to draw even more attention to the narrative aspect and are considering requesting that donors write a small anecdote about the garments they contribute. Do they really believe that anybody who simply wants to dispose of their old clothing meaningfully will want to go into that much trouble? They both seem to think it's not

Being able to track the history of a garment by its number in a way creates a little world, giving us the ability to work within a functioning and sustainable system.

einfach nur seine Altkleider sinnvoll entsorgen will, die Mühe wert ist? Sie sind sich beide einig, dass schon: »Oft kommen Leute direkt bei uns im Studio vorbei und erzählen uns ungefragt die Geschichte ihrer Kleidungsstücke.«

Die bewusste Auseinandersetzung mit dem Thema Marke geschieht bei Schmidttakahashi nicht in einem Konferenzraum oder mit Stift und Papier. »Das Bewusstsein dafür wächst kontinuierlich«, sagt Eugenie. »Wir machen Mode, aber auch Kunst«, ergänzt Mariko. »Es ist Mode mit weiterführenden Informationen, wenn man so will.« Der Entscheid zur Labelgründung kam, als die »New York Times« über die beiden berichtete. »In diesem Moment wurde uns klar: Jetzt oder nie. Und wir entschieden uns für jetzt.« Schmidttakahashis Stil, und damit ihre gesamte Marke, entwickelt sich von Kollektion zu Kollektion. »Es ist ein bisschen wie mit einem Kind«, sinniert Eugenie. »Man ist voller Erwartung, und wenn es dann da ist, ist man ersteinmal überrascht und staunt selbst. In welche Richtung es sich dann entwickelt, zeigt sich erst mit der Zeit.« —

an unreasonable request. "Often people drop by our studio and, without prompting, tell us the stories of their garments."

Conscious analysis of such questions as: label, yes or no, are not dealt with at a conference table or put down on paper by Schmidttakahashi. "Our awareness for the business aspects grows continually," Eugenie says. Mariko adds: "We are making fashion, but art as well. It's fashion with an additional dimension if you will." The decision to establish a label was made when "The New York Times" wrote an article about the two of them. "At that moment we realized it's now or never. And so we chose now."Schmidttakahashi's style – really their entire label – evolves from collection to collection. "It's a bit like having a child," Eugenie muses. "You have lots of plans and ideas, and then, when it arrives, you're simply surprised and amazed. The direction it develops in only reveals itself with time." —

STOCKMAN
STOCKMAN
STOCKMAN
PARIS
50497

25

Schumann's
Charles Schumann

Text **Olivia El Sayed** Photos **Gian Marco Castelberg**

BASIC BAR
SELECTION
by Charles Schumann
Schumann's
PORT
LATE BOTTLED VINTAGE
1996
RESERVIERT

Jeden Freitag ab 23:00 Uhr
JAZZ IM
CAMPARINO

Das »Schumann's« in München wird seit fast dreißig Jahren von seinem Namensgeber Charles Schumann geführt und geprägt – und das an jedem einzelnen Tag eines jeden Jahres seit 1982. Darin liegt der unangefochtene Erfolg: Charles Schumann ist immer im »Schumann's« anzutreffen, sei es in der Küche, hinter der Bar oder im Gespräch mit seinen Gästen, von denen viele zur High Society gehören. Sein markantes Gesicht wurde durch seine Nebentätigkeit als Model bekannt, seine Person und manche seiner Cocktails erreichten durch den Ruf des »Schumann's« als »deutschlandweit beste Bar« globalen Markenstatus. Besonders bekannt ist Schumanns Colada-Cocktail Swimming Pool, dessen Rezept man neben zahlreichen Ausführungen zur Arbeit eines guten Barkeepers in seinem beliebtesten Buch »American Bar« findet.

Charles Schumann has been running and putting his mark on Schumann's in Munich for nearly thirty years now – every single day of every single year since 1982. And therein lies its indisputable success: Schumann can always to be found in Schumann's, be it in the kitchen, behind the bar, or talking to his guests, many of whom belong to Munich's high society. His distinctive face seems familiar, probably due to Schumann's moonlighting as a model, and he and his cocktails have attained worldwide brand status thanks to the bar's reputation as "the best bar in all of Germany." A particularly in-demand drink is Schumann's colada cocktail "Swimming Pool," and the recipe can be found along with numerous reflections on what constitutes a good barkeeper in Schumann's favorite book "American Bar."

Die Einrichtung ist schlicht, das Licht gedimmt, illustre Gäste aus aller Welt sitzen an kleinen Tischen, Kellner in Schwarzweiß servieren Essen oder mixen Drinks und vom klappernden Geschirr und dem angeregten Wortaustausch fast übertönt klimpert im Hintergrund ein bisschen Jazzmusik. Mittendrin Charles Schumann: ein großer, schlanker Mann mit bergblauen Augen, das weißgraue Haar nach hinten frisiert. Hie und da klopft er jemandem auf die Schulter und ruft etwas Italienisches durch den Raum. Er wird begrüßt, es wird auf ihn gezeigt und er reagiert, immer darauf bedacht, eine Sekunde später schon wieder ganz woanders zu sein. Auch wenn er angezogen ist wie die übrigen Kellner und sich auch das Tellerabräumen nicht nehmen lässt; Man erkennt sofort, dass er es sein muss, der diesem Lokal seinen Namen gegeben hat. Er lebt tagtäglich vor, wie er es gern hätte: rücksichtsvoll, unaufdringlich, aufmerksam und immer respektvoll. Schumann bewegt sich schnell und wendig zwischen den gedeckten Tischen, ist überall und nirgends. Ein fahriger Typ, der schwer zu fassen scheint. Laut eigener Aussage war sein Problem immer dasselbe: zu lernen, mit anderen Menschen zusammenzuarbeiten. Als alleinerziehender Vater weiß Schumann jedoch nur zu gut, wie viel allein möglich ist, was es nicht leichter macht, sich das Arbeiten im Team schönzureden.

An interior bordering on the austere, dimmed lights, a prominent international clientele seated around small tables, and black-and-white clad waiters serving food or mixing drinks; in the background, almost drowned out by the clattering of cutlery and animated chit-chat, strains of jazz can be heard. In the middle of all this: Charles Schumann, a tall, lean man with sky-blue eyes and slicked back pewter-colored hair. Once in a while, he pats a passerby on the back and calls out something in what sounds like Italian across the room. If someone greets him, or points him out, he reacts immediately, all the while planning to be off again the next second. Although outfitted identically to the waiters, and not above clearing the tables personally, it is instantly clear that this is the person who lent the premises his name. "I always have a clear concept of how something should look, and I'm never entirely satisfied by how other people do things," he says. And so, day in, day out he demonstrates how he wants things to be handled. Considerately, unobtrusively, attentively, and, at all times, respectfully. Schumann's movements between the set tables are quick and agile, he is everywhere and nowhere. A restless person, not easy to pin down. By his own admission he has always struggled with the same problem: that of learning to work with other people. As a single father Schumann knows all too well how much you can accomplish on your own, and this does not make working in a team any more attractive to him.

Ich habe immer eine klare Vorstellung davon, wie etwas aussehen soll. Es passt mir eigentlich nie, wie es andere machen.

Karl Georg Schumann, den seit seinem Frankreichaufenthalt in jungen Jahren niemand mehr mit diesem Namen anspricht, war seit jeher ein Verfechter der klassischen amerikanischen Bartradition: schnörkellose Einrichtung, klassische Drinks und eine einheitliche Klientel von Kreativen und Intellektuellen. So

Karl Georg Schumann, a moniker that has not been in use since a sojourn to France in younger years, has always been a champion of the traditional American bar: no frills, classical drinks, and a regular clientele of artists and intellectuals. At least, that is how it should be. But times have changed, and with them a different

sollte es sein. Doch die Zeiten haben sich geändert und mit den Gästen veränderten sich auch die Ansprüche an die Servicemarke »Schumann's«. »Es gibt sie nicht mehr, die Männer, die Abende lang in einer Bar sitzen und sich betrinken. Und die Intellektuellen – sie allein halten den Barbetrieb auch nicht am Laufen.« Schumann steht dem Konzeptwechsel von klassischer amerikanischer Bar hin zu einem Lokal, das seit einiger Zeit nun auch Essen anbietet, nach wie vor etwas widerwillig gegenüber. Auf die Frage hin, wie das »Schumann's« seiner Meinung nach idealerweise definiert werden sollte, antwortet er eigensinnig: »Das ›Schumann's‹ in drei Worten? B,A,R.« Und das, obwohl bewusst ein Schritt weg von der klassischen Bar getan werden musste, um mit der Zeit Schritt halten zu können. »Die klassische Bar ist klein und führt Drinks. Das »Schumann's« ist dafür zu groß«, findet Schumann selbst, »die Leute wollen auch essen.« Hinzu kommt, dass die Leute weniger trinken. Man ernährt sich gesünder, trinkt selten schon mittags.

clientele with divergent expectations of the Schumann's service brand has emerged: "They've disappeared, those men that would sit at the bar night after night and slowly get drunk. And the intellectuals alone won't keep a bar afloat either." Schumann is still not entirely happy with his concept change that dates back several years now from a classical American bar into a bar that serves food as well. To our question on what the ideal definition of Schumann's would be to him, his unbending response is: "Schumann's in three words? B.A.R." Even so, it had become necessary to take a deliberate step away from a traditional bar in order to keep up with the times. "The classical bar is small and only stocks beverages. Schumann's is too big for that," Schumann himself says. "People want to eat, too." And people drink less nowadays. They tend to eat healthier and rarely start drinking at noon. "A bar should be a place where people feel at ease and enjoy coming to." If people's expectations change, then the experience they desire to encounter has to be taken into account.

SOME WOULD LIKE THIS PLACE TO BE COZIER. BUT THERE'S A LIMIT TO THE CHANGES I'M WILLING TO MAKE. I PREFER THINGS WITHOUT FRILLS.

»Eine Bar soll ein Ort sein, wo sich Menschen wohl fühlen und gern herkommen.« Wenn sich die Bedürfnisse dieser Menschen ändern, muss auch die gewünschte Erlebniswelt entsprechend angepasst werden. »Die Leute wollen's halt gern kuschlig haben. Aber auf alle Wünsche geh ich nicht ein. Ich mag es lieber schlicht«, sagt Schumann trocken. Das Konzept zu ändern fiel ihm nicht leicht, aber durch das erweiterte Angebot, das nun auch warme Speisen enthält, hat er einen für ihn vertretbaren Kompromiss gefunden. Seine Kundschaft dankt es ihm und der Umsatz wohl auch.

Schumann nippt an seinem Espresso und sinniert über die Zeit. Während beim Sprechen schwankt er zwischen verträumten Ideen (gern würde er die Wartung eines Sportplatzes übernehmen) und realitätsnahen Gedankenfetzen, die selten zu Ende gesprochen werden. Oft unterbricht er sich selbst und begrüßt lautstark einen Mitarbeiter oder einen neuen Gast: »Eh, toi! Qu'est-ce que tu fais ici, à cette heure-là, hein?« Dann ein Lachen und immer wieder die Frage: Wo waren wir noch gleich? Bei den Marken, stimmt.

Das Leben beeindruckt ihn nicht mehr so schnell und generell gilt: »Je schlichter, desto besser.« Kaum ein Tag vergeht, an dem Schumann nicht gern in seiner Bar arbeitet. »Es gibt aber auch Tage, da käme ich gern gar nicht mehr.« Mehr lesen würde er dann, häufiger Sport treiben (er läuft bereits mehrmals die Woche und surft gern) und privat mehr Musik machen, nicht nur ab und an spätnachts, wenn fast alle Gäste gegangen sind, dem Sinnbild eines Barkeepers gemäß auf dem Piano der Bar spielen. Aber dafür ist die Zeit noch nicht reif, denn solange kein würdiger Nachfolger gefunden ist, verlässt Schumann seinen Platz nicht. Und dies nicht

Schumann did not find it easy to change his concept, but by widening his services to now include warm meals, he has hit upon a compromise that he can live with. His clientele in any case reacted enthusiastically to the changes, and the turnover most likely also responded in kind.

Schumann sips his espresso and ruminates about time in general. During our conversation he vacillates between wishful thinking (he would like to be a caretaker at a sports complex) and more concrete thoughts that are mostly imparted in fragments. He is prone to interrupting himself and loudly greets staff and guests: "Eh, toi! Qu'est-ce que tu fais ici, à cette heure-là, hein?" Then with a laugh, he turns back to repeat the same question he asked five minutes earlier: "What were we talking about? Ah, brands, that's right." Schumann is not that easily impressed by what life has to offer anymore. "Once you reach a certain age, you don't need prestigious status symbols anymore. I don't need a fantastic car, I don't need a stunning woman – well maybe once in a while," says the man whos general motto is: "The simpler the better." Still, not a single day passes that he does not enjoy working in his bar. "But there are also days on which I'd prefer not to come back at all."

He would read more, do more sports (he runs a few times a week and enjoys surfing) and play more music. Not just from time to time, as he does now, playing on the bar's piano late at night when nearly all the guests have left, living up to the image of the piano-playing barkeep. But that day may still be a long way off, because Schumann will not be leaving his post until he has found a satisfactory successor – which may take some time. Although not, Schumann hastens to add, because he has exaggerated expectations. Why then? "Nobody can really be expected to do my job."

PRIMA CAREZZA
SALON MUSIC AT SCHUMANN'S BAR
Schumann's
FUMIO YASUDA
Schumann's
BAR MUSIC
FUMIO YASUDA & THEO BLECKMANN
Schumann's

TAGESBAR
Maffeistrasse 6
80333 München

Ab einem gewissen Alter braucht man keine namhaften Statussymbole mehr. Ich brauche kein super Auto, ich brauche keine tolle Frau – allerhöchstens ab und zu.

aus falschen Besitzansprüchen. Sondern? »Es ist eigentlich einfach niemandem zuzumuten, dass er meinen Job macht.« Schumann würde sich über einen Nachfolger freuen, wenn sich denn jemand finden ließe, der mit neuem Elan an die Aufgabe herantreten würde. Aber bitte nur jemand, der den Schumannschen Ansprüchen gerecht wird. Eine professionelle Ausbildung wäre dabei die Mindestvoraussetzung, und damit meint Schumann kein Studium, denn »ein Studium nützt hier nichts, ein Studium ist Bildung, aber keine Ausbildung«. Schumann weiß, wovon er spricht, denn er hat Philosophie studiert, wie sein Sohn auch, und Journalismus. Den Barbetrieb hat er sich selbst beigebracht. Nach dreißig Jahren weiß er auch, wie alles geht; nichtsdestotrotz glaubt er, es gebe noch viel mehr Fachwissen, das er gern hätte. Eine Person schwirrt am Tisch vorbei. Schumann streckt die Hand nach ihr aus und ruft: »Che ora è? Cinco minutos? Ti vale?« Er nickt. »Gut, gut, gleich.« Er räuspert sich und lächelt. Wäre Zeit eine Marke, sie wäre wohl Schumanns liebstes Luxusgut. Aber wo waren wir noch gleich? Fertig, stimmt. —

Schumann would be pleased to find someone to take on the enterprise with fresh vigor. Of course, it would have to be someone who satisfies all the Schumannian requirements. A professional qualification is an absolute must, and by this Schumann is not referring to a university degree. "Just holding a university title would be useless here. Studying is about gaining knowledge, but it is not a practical education." Schumann knows what he is talking about. He studied philosophy himself, as did his son after him, as well as journalism, and then taught himself how to run a bar. After thirty years he knows the ropes, but nevertheless believes there is much more expert knowledge out there that Schumann's could benefit from. Another person scurries by the table. Schumann stretches out a hand and calls: "Che ora è? Cinco minutos? Ti vale?" He nods. "Fine, I'll be there in a minute." Clearing his throat he chuckles; if time were a brand it would certainly be Schumann's favorite possession. What were we talking about? – Oh, we're finished, that's right. —

26

Stoned Cherrie
Nkhensani Nkosi

Text **Judith Reker** Photos **Graeme Williams**

In Südafrika ist Stoned Cherrie das wohl bekannteste Modelabel. Wenn die südafrikanische Tourismusbehörde seit Kurzem weltweit neben der wunderbaren Landschaft auch die Coolness der Städte anpreist, werden Models in Stoned Cherrie gezeigt. Heute existiert eine ganze Reihe von Modemarken im Land, doch im Jahr 2000, als Stoned Cherrie gegründet wurde, sah das noch ganz anders aus. Damals, sechs Jahre nach dem offiziellen Ende des rassistischen Apartheidregimes, machten die wenigen Designer noch immer Couture für die kleine weiße Minderheit. »Es gab keine afrourbanen Marken«, sagt Nkhensani Nkosi, »keine lokale Ästhetik.« Sie sah diese Lücke und füllte sie. Heute steht Stoned Cherrie für Damenmode, die weibliche Formenbetont, lokale Stoffe verwendet und mit universellen, zeitlosen geometrischen Formen arbeitet.

Stoned Cherrie is probably South Africa's best-known fashion label. Along with showing footage of the country's breathtaking nature, the latest South African worldwide tourist campaigns present models dressed by Stoned Cherrie in order to extol cool city vibes. Today there is a multitude of fashion labels throughout the land, yet in 2000, the founding year of Stoned Cherrie, matters were very different. In those days, just six years after the racist Apartheid regime had officially ended, there were only a handful of designers to be had, and these continued to cater to a small white minority. "There weren't any South African afro-urban brands," says Nkhensani Nkosi, "no local aesthetic." After becoming aware of this gap, she decided to do something about it. Today, Stoned Cherrie stands for women's fashion. A fashion that emphasizes the female figure and combines local materials with universal, timeless, geometrical patterns.

Der neue Showroom von Stoned Cherrie liegt in einem der teuren Vororte von Johannesburg, Südafrikas Wirtschaftsmetropole. Die Einrichtung ist funky und gleichzeitig gemütlich, mit Stoffen und Kissen von Stoned Cherrie sowie drei Kleiderpuppen, die unaufdringlich am Eingang zum Atelier der Näherinnen stehen und Abendkleider aus Seidenchiffon und Shweshwe-Stoffen tragen. Als Nkhensani Nkosi von draußen in ihren Showroom hereingeschneit kommt, fünf Minuten vor dem vereinbarten Treffen, weiß man es gleich: Die Gründerin von Stoned Cherrie ist zwar selbst mit hohen Keilabsätzen noch eine kleine Person, aber ihre Präsenz füllt das riesige Atelier mit den sieben Meter hohen Decken problemlos. Das Haar trägt sie an diesem Tag zu zwei dicken Zöpfen geflochten und die Nägel sonnengelb lackiert. Sie ist ungeschminkt und sieht kein bisschen aus wie 39.

Es überrascht im ersten Moment, dass Nkhensani den dänischen Industriedesigner Marcus Vagnby als eine ihrer

Stoned Cherrie's new showroom is located in one of more exclusive suburbs of Johannesburg, South Africa's economic hub. Inside it's funky and friendly at the same time, decorated with Stoned Cherrie materials and cushions. Three dressmaker's mannequins draped in evening dresses of silk chiffon and Shweshwe material stand unobtrusively by the door to the sewing workshop. The instant Nkhensani Nkosi enters the showroom, a full five minutes before we'd arranged to meet, we recognize her vibrant personality. Despite wearing high wedge heels, the founder of Stoned Cherrie remains petite, but her aura easily fills the enormous space with its high ceilings. Today, her hair is braided into two chunky plaits and her fingernails are painted a sunny yellow. Her face reveals no trace of makeup, and she doesn't look like she could possibly be 39.

Initially, we're a bit surprised when Nkhensani names Danish industrial designer Marcus Vagnby as one of her favorite brands. Yet the reason soon becomes clear when she explains that

Lieblingsmarken nennt. Doch hat das auch damit zu tun, dass Stoned Cherrie gerade im Übergang von einem reinen Modelabel zu einer breiter aufgestellten Marke steckt. Nkosi will neben ihren bereits produzierten Stoffen, Tapeten und Kissen nach und nach alles anbieten, was in ein schönes Zuhause passt. An Modedesignern fällt ihr als erstes Manish Arora ein, dessen »farbenfrohe, lebendige, ausdrucksstarke Ästhetik« Nkosi schätzt. »Er arbeitet mit der indischen Kultur, dem indischen Erbe, aber gibt ihnen eine moderne Wendung, einen revolutionären Blickwinkel«, sagt sie. »Genau darum geht es auch bei unserer Marke.«

Ihr eigenes historisches und kulturelles Erbe wurde durch das Aufwachsen in der Township Soweto unter dem Apartheidregime geprägt. »Ich komme aus einer Generation, die sehr bewusst wahrgenommen hat, was in unserem Land geschah.« Sie beschreibt ihre Angst als Kind vor nächtlichen Besuchen der Polizei, die Massenproteste, die Gewalt. Ihre Eltern, Akademiker, förderten ihr politisches Bewusstsein, eine Achtsamkeit für ihre Gesellschaft. Und sie nährten in ihr den Glauben, dass alles möglich ist. Das Ende der Apartheid und die Aufbruchstimmung mit der Wahl Nelson Mandelas zum Präsidenten festigten diesen Glauben. Mit ihrem Heimatort Soweto südwestlich von Johannesburg verbindet sie geradezu romantische Vorstellungen. Regelmäßig fährt sie am Wochenende mit ihrem Mann und den drei Kindern in die Township, obwohl sie längst in einem der feinen Johannesburger Stadtteile wohnen. »Wenn ich an Soweto denke, denke ich an Orange und Sepia und kräftige Farben und an Häuser mit türkisfarbenen Dächern«, sagt sie und bricht in Lachen aus. Wenn sie nicht in Johannesburg lebte, dann wäre es Amsterdam. »Ich finde die Stadt einfach großartig. Mit ihren Kanälen und wie die Leute überall mit dem Fahrrad fahren können, sogar mit Kindern, weil sie wissen, dass es einen gegenseitigen Respekt voreinander gibt.« Ihre Kinder, zwischen fünf und elf, ihre Ehe, die enge Bande zur ganzen erweiterten Familie betrachtet sie als ihren größten Erfolg. »Familie ist alles«, sagt sie, auch ihre stärkste Antriebskraft. Eine weitere Motivation zieht sie aus Vorbildern wie den Ikonen des südafrikanischen Befreiungskampfes, zum Beispiel dem von der Polizei ermordeten Steve Biko. »Dieser unglaubliche Mut, besonders wenn man Familie und Kinder hat – ich kann mir gar nicht ausmalen, was für Entscheidungen diese Menschen mit sich selbst ausmachten.« Aber das Leben im Apartheidstaat war nicht nur düster und grau. Es gab auch Orte wie Sophiatown, wo die schwarze Bevölkerung vor allem in den Vierziger- und Fünfzigerjahren mit Jazz, Tanz und eleganten Roben das Leben feierte. Es war Nkosis Geniestreich, kurz nach der Gründung von Stoned Cherrie mit einer Kampagne an diese Zeit zu erinnern. Sie erwarb das exklusive Recht, alte Titelfotos einer legendären südafrikanischen Zeitschrift auf ihre T-Shirts zu drucken. »Drum« heißt das Magazin und war so etwas wie das »Vanity Fair« der schwarzen Bevölkerung, eine Mischung aus Glamour und guten Reportagen. Die T-Shirts machten Stoned Cherrie mit einem Schlag über Südafrika hinaus bekannt.

Nkhensani Nkosi wird oft eingeladen, um andere mit ihrem Lebensweg zu motivieren. Von Firmen, Organisationen, Fernsehen und Radio. Dann erzählt sie ihren gar nicht so

Stoned Cherrie is at present in a transitory process, moving from being a pure fashion label to a more broadly positioned brand. Next to the materials, carpets and cushions they already produce, little by little Nkosi wants the brand to stand for everything a beautiful home requires. The first fashion designer who springs to her mind is Manish Arora whose "aesthetic is very colorful and vibrant and expressive and creative," Nkosi says with approval. "He has taken Indian culture and heritage, but given it a kind of modern twist and a revolutionary angle," she explains. "Obviously, I found a lot of kinship in that because that is what our brand is about."

Her own past and cultural background was influenced by growing up in the Soweto Township during the reign of Apartheid. "I was part of a generation that was very conscious of what was happening in our country." She describes her childhood fears of nighttime visits by the police and tells of the mass protests and the violence. Her parents, both with an academic background, nurtured her political awareness and mindfulness for their society. And they nurtured her belief that everything is possible. A belief that was fed by the end of Apartheid and the spirit of optimism generated by Nelson Mandela's election to the presidency. She relates almost romantic impressions of Soweto, which lies to the southwest of Johannesburg. On weekends, she and her husband regularly drive down to the township with their three children, although they have been living in one of the more upscale residential districts of Johannesburg for some time now. "I always feel that the sun shines differently in Soweto," she says and starts laughing. "My memories of it are very orange and sepia; with strong colors and houses with turquoise roofs." If she didn't live in Johannesburg she would choose to live in Amsterdam. "I just love it. With the little canals, and how people can ride their bikes, even take their kids, and there is an utter respect between people." She says her children, aged between five and eleven, her marriage and the close ties with the entire extended family are her greatest successes. "Family is everything," she says; it is also her strongest source of inspiration. She gleans further motivation from the heroes of the South African fight for liberation, including the iconic anti-Apartheid activist Steve Biko who was murdered while held in police custody. "I think it takes an incredible amount of courage, especially if you've got a family and children. I can't imagine the inner turmoil they must have gone through on account of their choices." But life in the 20th century was not just dismal and grey. Black South Africans also have a rich culture to cherish. An example of this is former freehold town, Sophiatown, a suburb in Johannesburg where the black population celebrated life with jazz, dance and elegant gowns in the 1940s and 1950s – before the town was crushed by Apartheid. Just after establishing Stoned Cherrie, Nkosi had the brilliant idea to revive this era to public awareness with a special campaign. She procured the exclusive rights to old cover photos from a legendary South African publication and printed these on T-shirts. The magazine, called "Drum," a sort of "Vanity Fair" for the black population, offered a mix of glamour and good journalism. Drawing lots of media attention, the T-shirts established the brand Stoned Cherrie far beyond the South African borders, and that practically overnight.

Mir kommt es immer so vor, als würde die Sonne in Soweto anders scheinen.

geradlinigen Weg: von ihrer ersten Liebe, der Schauspielerei und wie sie vom Studium der Psychologie ans Theater kam. Vom Theater ging es ins Fernsehen, mit einer eigenen Talkshow. Und seit nun zwölf Jahren: Stoned Cherrie. Vor allem aber spricht sie über die wichtigen Dinge. »Mir geht es um die moralischen Werte, die Dinge, die uns alle als Menschen vereinen.« Wenn es Stoned Cherrie nicht gäbe, würde Nkosi nur noch Reden halten, glaubt sie. »Ich liebe es, jungen Leuten Mut zu geben. Denn unser Bildungssystem war so gestaltet, um die Leute in einer Schachtel einzusperren, wie unsere Häuser.« Und noch längst hat die schwarze Bevölkerung keine Chancengleichheit erlangt. »Ich möchte am liebsten die Dächer von all dem runterpusten«, sagt Nkhensani Nkosi versonnen. —

Nkhensani Nkosi often receives invitations from companies, organizations, television and radio stations to give talks and encourage others with her story. She is happy to tell her audiences about her long and winding path: about her first love, acting, and how after studying psychology she ended up in the theater. From the theater, she moved on to television and hosted her own talk show. And now for the past 12 years: Stoned Cherrie. Whatever she talks about, however, it is always of importance: "It's really about the moral fiber, the things that unify us as human beings." If she didn't have Stoned Cherrie, Nkosi thinks, she would probably spend all her time giving speeches. "What I love to do is inspire young people. Our education system was designed to keep people in a box, everything was designed like that, even our houses." And there's a long way to go before it can truly be said that the black population has equal rights. "I would like to blow the roof off of all of that," Nkhensani Nkosi says with a thoughtful look. —

27

Studio Toogood
Faye Toogood

Text **Olivia El Sayed** Photos **Reto Caduff**

Mit einem kunsthistorischen und einem musischen Studium im Gepäck machte sich vor gut zehn Jahren eine eigenwillige junge Dame auf den Weg ins Berufsleben. Sie landete nicht wie als Kind erträumt im Weltall oder auf der Theaterbühne, sondern zunächst in einem Architekturbüro, wo sie vor allem lernte, was sie nie werden wollte (Architektin). Aus einem Impuls heraus bewarb sie sich daraufhin bei einem der renommiertesten Magazine der Welt: »The World of Interiors«. Nachdem sie anstelle einer Bewerbung einen Koffer voller gesammelter Sachen bei der Redaktion abgegeben hatte, bekam sie, zu ihrem eigenen Erstaunen, die ausgeschriebene Stelle als »Stylist«, ohne genau zu wissen, was fortan ihre Aufgabe sein würde. Um einen Mann, der inzwischen ihr Ehemann und Vater ihrer Tochter ist, und viele Erfahrungen reicher verließ sie die britische Designbibel nach acht erfolgreichen Jahren und machte sich mit ihrem kreativen Studio Toogood selbständig.

With an academic training in the theory and practice of fine art under her belt, some ten years ago an unconventional young lady with a pixie haircut and her signature flats entered the employment market. Despite childhood dreams of becoming an astronaut or acting on a stage, she ended up in an architect's office where she learned one thing in particular: that she didn't want to be an architect. On a whim, she applied for a job with one of the most renowned design and decorating magazines in the world, "The World of Interiors." In lieu of the usual job application, she dropped off a case full of collected items at the editorial department. It came as a somewhat unexpected surprise that she was offered the vacant position of stylist, especially since she wasn't quite sure what her tasks would include. After eight successful years, she left the British design bible – where she had also met the man she has meanwhile married and started a family with – to establish her own creative enterprise, the Studio Toogood.

Zwei Äpfel, ein Joghurt und ein Pappbecher mit Deckel und »Planet Organic«-Aufdruck stehen neben Faye Toogoods MacBook, das auf dem großen Gemeinschaftstisch in der Mitte des Raumes liegt. Sie trägt Ballerinas, sitzt auf einem roten Gummiball, rollt leicht vor und zurück und lauscht den Ausführungen zweier Mitarbeitender. Ebenfalls am Tisch sitzen zwei weitere Gestalter, die Skizzen besprechen. Aus dem einen oder anderen Computer dringt leise Musik, ab und an klingelt ein Telefon. Ein konstanter, aber sanfter Geräuschpegel erfüllt den offenen Arbeitsraum. Die eine Fensterfront, die einen Blick auf die typischen englischen Backsteingebäude, Bäume und die Kräne am Horizont gewährt, ist gesäumt von einer Reihe von Designern, die modisch kreativ verpackten Hinterteile auf von Toogood entworfenen Stühlen. Der Himmel draußen ist ein grob gewobener Teppich und die Ränder der grauen Wolkenstränge werden vom Kontrast des fordernden Sonnenlichts dahinter hervorgehoben.

Two apples, a yogurt and a paper cup with "Planet Organic" printed on the side are lined up next to Toogood's MacBook that rests on the large communal table in the middle of the workspace. Wearing ballet flats, she sits on a red rubber ball, rocking back and forth slightly while listening to briefings from her two co-workers. Two further designers discussing some sketches are also seated at the table. Quiet music issues from a computer somewhere in the room, and occasionally the phone rings; a constant, yet low-key sound backdrop to the open workspace of the studio. One of the large windows, which looks out on a typical British vista of brick buildings, trees and building cranes on the horizon, has a row of designers in front of it, busily working at their screens, their fashionably dressed derrières parked on chairs also designed by Toogood. The skies outside resemble a loosely woven carpet, with the linings of the thick, gray skeins of clouds highlighted by changeable sunlight.

ДОМАШНЕЕ ПЛАТЬЕ
из ГОЛОВНОГО
ПЛАТКА
to scatter
to arrange
to repair
to discard
to pair
to distribute
to surfeit
to complement
to enclose
to surround
to encircle
to hide
to cover
to wrap
to dig
to tie
to bind
to weave
to join
to match
to laminate
to bond
to hinge
to mark
to expand
to dilute
to light
to modulate
to distill
of waves
of electromagnetic
of inertia
of ionization
of polarization
of refraction
of simultaneity
of tides
of reflection
of equilibrium
of symmetry
of fluction
to stretch
to bounce
to erase
to spray
to systematize
to refer
to force
of mapping
of location
of context
of time
of carbonization
to continue
WEAVE
MAN

Mit ihrer beruflichen Selbständigkeit ist Faye Toogood (die übrigens tatsächlich so heißt) erwachsen geworden. Nicht so erwachsen, dass sie im Dunkeln keine Angst mehr hätte oder dass man sie nun in eine Schublade stecken könnte, sondern vielmehr im Sinne von selbstbewusst genug, all das zu tun, wonach ihr der Sinn steht. »Ich wurde schon als Möbeldesignerin, Stylistin, Künstlerin und Interior-Spezialistin beschrieben. Und das trifft wohl auch alles zu«, sagt sie, während ein Lächeln ihr apartes Gesicht krönt. »Aber ich bin an so, so vielen Dingen interessiert – ich würde mich nie auf etwas festlegen wollen! ›Gierige Designerin‹ träfe es wohl am besten, auch wenn das vermutlich keine adäquate Berufsbezeichnung ist«, scherzt sie. »Und ich mag es, wenn mich niemand ganz beschreiben kann, weil es bedeutet, dass meine Arbeit nicht stehenbleibt, sondern im steten Weiterentwicklungsprozess ist, und das ist gut. Sie soll immer mutig sein, außergewöhnlich und nicht in derselben Form schon vorhanden.«

Her step into professional autonomy has made Faye Toogood (her real name, in case anybody was wondering) grow up. Not so grown up that she's no longer afraid of the dark, or that she can be pigeon-holed, but more in the sense that she now feels confident enough to do all the things she wants to do. "I have been called a furniture designer, stylist, artist and interior specialist. And that is probably pretty accurate," she says, while a smile lights up her distinctive face. "There's a lot of things I'm interested in – I would never want to restrict myself to just one something. And probably I would describe myself as a greedy designer, although that's probably not a very good job title," she jokes. "I quite like that nobody can find the right word to describe me because it means that my work is moving, ever-changing, and that is good."

EVERYTHING I DO SHOULD BE BRAVE, AND IT SHOULD ALWAYS BE EXTRAORDINARY IN SOME WAY, AND I DON'T WANT IT TO LOOK LIKE ANYTHING ELSE THAT YOU'VE SEEN BEFORE.

Ihre wachen Augen, die je nach Lichteinfall den Anschein haben, nicht beide genau gleich blau zu sein, wandern den Holzbalken an der Decke entlang, bevor sie weiterspricht: »Im Design wird oft gelehrt, dass man sich spezialisieren sollte, um erfolgreich zu sein. Die meisten designorientierten Unternehmen machen ja auch so ihren Profit, indem sie sich auf einen Stil festlegen und sich in einer Disziplin möglichst viel Wissen und Können aneignen. Hier machen wir das anders und versuchen vielleicht manchmal beinahe zu viel abzudecken.« Und es ist wahrlich nicht leicht, ihre Arbeit zu kategorisieren. Für das britische Kaufhaus Liberty entwarf das Studio neue Fenster, für den Industriedesigner Tom Dixon wurden Ausstellungsstände konzipiert, für Kenzo eine Modenschau auf die Beine gestellt und für den 2010 verstorbenen Modeschöpfer Alexander McQueen kümmert sich das Studio unter anderem um die markengerechte Inszenierung der Produkte in aufwändigen Lookbooks. »Ich finde einfach, es gibt so viel, was man noch ausprobieren könnte«, sagt sie und lehnt sich etwas zurück.

Ihre Einstellung versucht sie auch im Team zu verbreiten. »Ich sage immer: Es geht nicht nur um Farben, Material und um das Kombinieren schöner Dinge.« Toogood legt viel mehr Wert darauf, was die Kompositionen aussagen. »Bevor wir ein Projekt beginnen, müssen wir uns die Frage stellen: Was wollen wir sagen und wie sollen sich die Leute fühlen? Alle Antworten darauf sollten in der Umgebung, die man kreiert, gegeben werden. Und das ist etwas sehr Kraftvolles, weil man die Gefühle einer Person mit einem Raum berühren

Her alert eyes, two distinct shades of blue depending on the fall of light, trace the wooden beams on the ceiling before she continues: "I think in design we are taught to specialize and stay really focused. Most design agencies make their money and commercial profit by specializing in a certain style or discipline. And here we probably try to cover too much." In truth it is not easy to categorize their work. For department store Liberty, the studio designed new windows; for industrial designer Tom Dixon, they planned exhibition stands; for Kenzo, a fashion show was organized; and for fashion designer Alexander McQueen, who died in 2010, they created elaborate lookbooks of McQueen's creations to embody the designer's brand – amongst other things. "I just find there's a lot out there left to try out," she says, leaning back.

She tries to spell out her views to her team. "I always say: It's not just about color and material and combining beautiful objects." Toogood places much more importance on what the compositions convey: "Before we start a project, we have to ask ourselves: What are we saying, how should it make people feel?" You can do all of these things with an environment. That's quite a powerful thing, to be able to influence or change someone's feelings or emotions with a space." "Essentially, I think, through space, you're trying to tell a story," Toogood explains. Using visual storytelling to provoke intense reactions is precisely what she finds most fascinating about her work. The fact that a three-dimensional space is better suited for visual storytelling than a two-dimensional image is not just the purely mathematical aspect of an extra dimension. Much more to the point is that

Ich glaube, unserem Geschmack wie auch unserem Stil wohnt eine gewisse Konsistenz inne. Aber es gibt keine Formel dafür und deshalb fürchte ich nicht, kopiert zu werden.

und verändern kann. Im Prinzip geht es darum, durch die Gestaltung eines Raumes eine Geschichte zu erzählen.« Nutzt man diese Kraft des visuellen Storytelling, bekommt man intensive Reaktionen und genau das ist es, was Faye an ihrer Arbeit am meisten fasziniert. Dass sich dreidimensionale Räume zum Geschichtenerzählen besser eignen als zweidimensionale Bilder, hat nicht nur damit zu tun, dass sie rein mathematisch schon um eine Dimension reicher sind, sondern vielmehr damit, dass Menschen involviert werden können und so einen Raum, oder eben die Geschichte, zum Leben erwecken und ihn durch ihr Erleben kontinuierlich verändern.

»Ein Stil, unser Design, entwickelt sich kontinuierlich und ist außerdem immer abhängig von vielen einzelnen Elementen: vom Auftraggeber, von der Zeit, von den Umständen ganz allgemein. Man mag ein einzelnes Objekt kopieren können, einen Stil nachahmen, aber das Gefühl, welches ein Objekt auslöst, die Geschichte, die es erzählt, ist nie dieselbe.« Faye freut sich darüber, dass ihr Stil »irgendwo da draußen« anderen Menschen zugänglich ist, ihnen sogar etwas bedeutet. Das Gefühl, dass sie ihre Ideen für sich behalten sollte, weil sie sonst kopiert werden könnten, kennt sie nicht. »Vielleicht liegt das daran, dass ich weiß, wie viel mehr da noch in meinem Kopf herumschwirrt, das nur darauf wartet, nach außen zu gelangen!«, lacht sie.

Für Faye Toogood scheint die Welt ein großes Bilderbuch zu sein. Wenn sie denkt, sieht sie Bilder. Stellt man ihr eine Frage, würde sie am liebsten mit einem Bild antworten. Wenn sie konzipiert, hat sie Visionen. Wie eine Übersetzerin muss sie ihre Bilder erst in Worte fassen, damit all diejenigen, die nicht in Bildern, sondern in Worten oder Zahlen denken, verstehen, was sie sagen will. Oder aber man lässt den verbalen Schritt aus, beruft sich ganz auf die Wahrnehmung und gibt sich dem wortlosen Erleben ihrer Arbeit hin. Diese Bereitschaft wird mit der Eintrittskarte in eine besondere Welt belohnt: Fayes Wunderland – das Bilderbuch in ihrem Kopf. —

people can enter into a space, thereby making it, or its story, come to life, and influence it while experiencing it.

"Our style and design evolves constantly and we are always dependent on a variety of factors: the client, the place, feeling, taste and smell. You can copy a single object, copy a style, but the sensation an object evokes, the story it tells is never the same. I believe," she adds, "that there is an inherent consistency in our taste and in our style. But there is no formula. I feel no one could copy it." Faye is happy that her style "is out there and available to other people and that it actually means something to them." She doesn't feel the need to keep her ideas to herself for fear they might be copied. "I just feel safe in the knowledge that there's more in my head. I don't need to hold on to it because I know there's more there, waiting to come out!" she laughs.

To Faye Toogood, the world is a large picture book. When she thinks, she thinks in pictures. If you ask her a question she finds it easiest to reply with a picture. She envisions the concepts she creates. "I see something and then I go on a journey with it," she explains. Like a translator, she first has to render her picture in words so that those who think in words and numbers, and not in pictures, understand what she wants to convey. Or, you can skip the verbal step altogether, trust your perception entirely and engage in a wordless exchange with Toogood's work. In the end, the reward is a pass to a very special world: Faye's Wonderland – the picture book in her head. —

28

Totem
Fred d'Orey

Text **Thomas Garms** Photos **Autumn Sonnichsen**

Kaum eine Modemarke verkörpert das unbeschwerte Lebensgefühl von Ipanema so bruchlos wie Totem Praia aus Rio de Janeiro. Gegründet wurde das brasilianische Label 1994 von Fred d'Orey, Globetrotter, Journalist, Radiomacher und Brasiliens Surfchampion von 1987. Farbenfrohe Drucke bilden das unverwechselbare, stilbildende Merkmal seiner Kleider, Shirts und Tops. Hautschmeichelnde, federleichte Stoffe und entsprechende Schnitte sorgen für perfekte Tragbarkeit. »Bei Mode geht es immer nur um Affirmation oder um Identität. Unsere DNA sind die Prints.«

Without a doubt, Totem Praia of Rio de Janeiro stands for the unencumbered beach lifestyle of Ipanema in a way no other fashion label does. It was established in 1994 by Fred d'Orey: globetrotter, journalist, radio producer and 1987 surf champion of Brazil. Bold, decorative prints are the unmistakable signature of his dresses, T-shirts and shorts. Skin-caressing, feather-light fabrics and effortless design combine seamlessly to ensure perfect wearability. "Fashion always comes down to either affirmation or identity. Our prints are our DNA."

Noch heute ist der Strand das zweite Wohnzimmer des Unternehmers. Sooft es ihm möglich ist, verbringt er seine Zeit im und auf dem Wasser. Dann schnappt sich der weißhaarige Hüne eines seiner Bretter, überquert die Straße zum Strand und paddelt bäuchlings hinaus durch die Brandung. »Das Meer ist Kraftquelle und Inspiration für mich. Ohne das Surfen hätte ich meine Mode nie so machen können, wie sie ist«, verrät er. Später, ein paar Autominuten entfernt, entert Fred d'Orey sein Büro im ersten Stock eines unscheinbaren Hauses in Rios Stadtteil Botafogo. Hier ist die Zentrale seiner Firma. Schöne junge Frauen mit sonnengebräunter Haut und leichten Kleidern warten schon auf ihn, den Boss von Totem, der inzwischen knapp zweihundert Mitarbeitende in Rio de Janeiro und auf Bali beschäftigt, wo sich seine wichtigste Produktionsstätte befindet.

The beach will always remain Fred d'Orey's first love, and he spends as much time as he can in and on the water. Grabbing one of his boards, the white-haired giant of a man only has to cross the street from his house to hit the beach and paddle through the surf. "The ocean is my source of strength and inspiration. Without surfing, I would never be able to create the kind of fashion I do," he reveals. Just a few minutes by car from the beach, Totem's headquarters are located on the first floor of an unassuming house in the Botafogo district of Rio. Several tan and young and lovely girls are already awaiting Fred's instructions to get started. All told, Totem employs a workforce of almost two hundred people both in Rio de Janeiro and in Bali, where its main manufacturing site is located.

EIGENTLICH FING ALLES DAMIT AN, DASS ICH GENÜGEND GELD IN DER TASCHE HABEN WOLLTE FÜR DEN SPORT UND DAS DAMIT VERBUNDENE REISEN.

Indonesien sei immer sein Traumziel gewesen – hin zu Wellen, die es so nirgendwo anders gibt. Für ihn kann die brechende Welle zum Ideal von Vollkommenheit werden, im Wissen, dass man diese niemals festhalten und besitzen kann. Wohl auch deswegen macht sich Fred d'Orey auch heute noch nicht viel aus Businessplänen und Excel-Tabellen. Freiheit sei ihm wichtiger als den ganzen Tag an die Firma zu denken und dem Geld hinterherzujagen. Die Idee mit dem Textildruck kam ihm auf Bali, wo er zum Surfen war. »Ich liebte schon immer kräftige, kontrastreiche Farben in starken Mustern«, erzählt er. Von einheimischen Handwerkern schaute er sich eine besondere Kunst des Stoffdrucks ab und produzierte auf diese Weise einige Mustershorts. Der Inhaber einer brasilianischen Boutiquenkette war so begeistert davon, dass Fred d'Orey unerwartet eine Bestellung über zehntausend Hosen in den Händen hielt, ohne die leiseste Ahnung, ob er diesen Auftrag jemals würde erfüllen können. Er flog wieder nach Bali, organisierte irgendwie die Produktion der bestellten

From the start, Indonesia had always been his dream destination on his quest to discover the perfect wave. To him, a breaking wave embodies the idea of perfection because it can never be held and possessed. "Everything began simply because I needed to earn money to pay for my surfer lifestyle and the traveling that goes with it," Fred d'Orey explains. And even today, he is not overly enamored by business plans and Excel spreadsheets – possibly because he continues to value his freedom far too much to spend the whole day thinking about the company and, as he puts it, chasing after money. The idea of making shorts with textile prints came to him one day while he was surfing in Bali. "I'd always loved bold patterns with vibrant and contrasting colors," he says. He learned a special local printing technique the native craftsmen employed and used it to manufacture a few pairs of sample shorts. Then he approached the owner of a Brazilian boutique chain who was so enthusiastic that he immediately placed an order for ten thousand shorts. Fred now had his first order although he was not at all sure how he was going to honor the contract. He flew back to Bali and

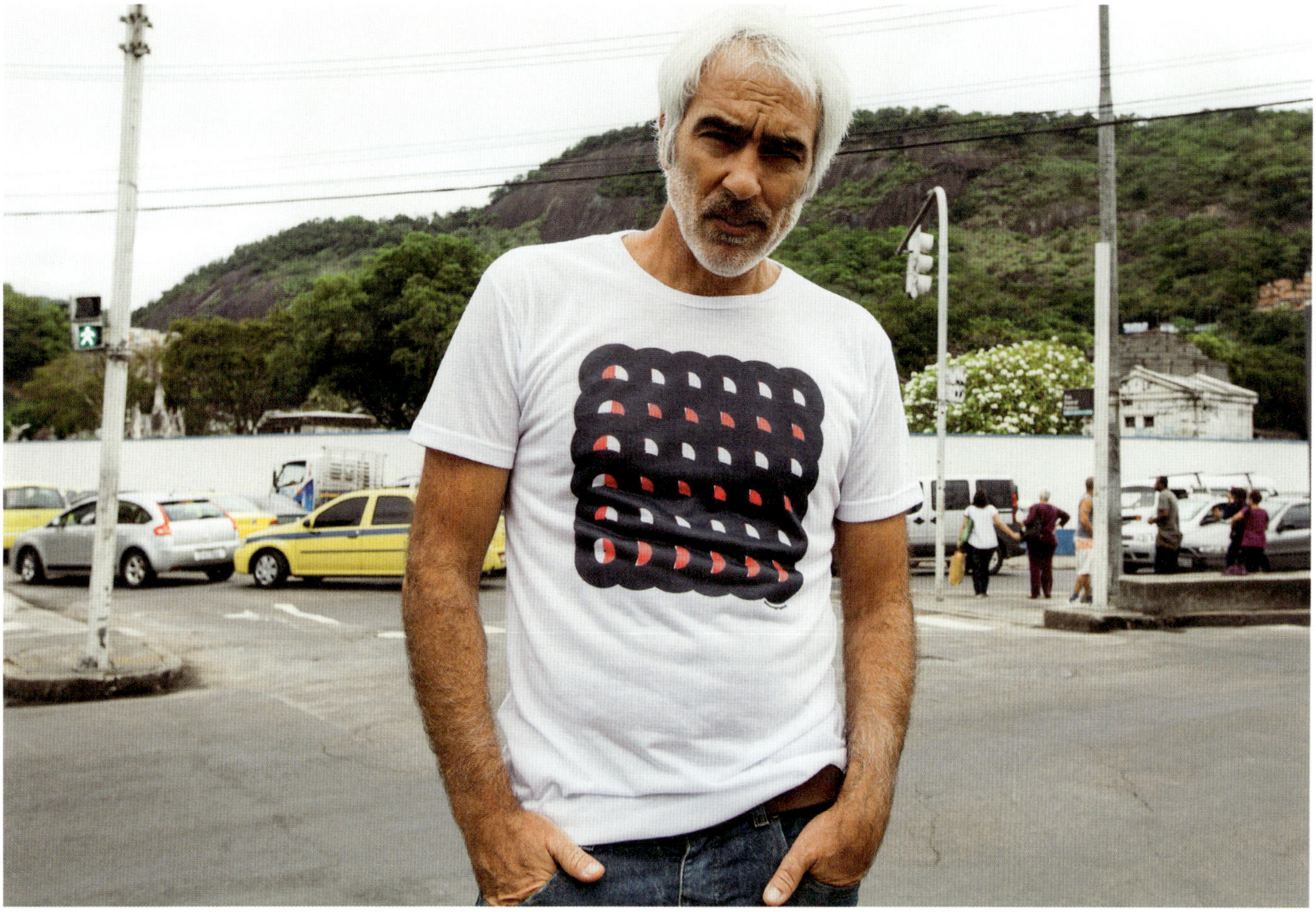

Shorts und von Bestelltermin zu Bestelltermin stiegen die Stückzahlen. 1994 gründete er in Ipanema den ersten eigenen Laden und bot dort unter dem Label Totem eine Beachwear-Kollektion für Männer an. Mit dem Erfolg der Marke entstand schnell auch eine Kollektion für Frauen, die bis heute sein Geschäft dominiert.

somehow managed to organize the production for the ordered shorts. After that, he began to receive ever-larger orders from delivery to delivery. In 1994, he opened his own store in Ipanema and offered a beachwear line for men under the label Totem. The brand became very popular and he soon started a collection for women as well which before long was to become their core revenue spinner.

BRAZIL IS A TROPICAL COUNTRY.
IT'S HOT HERE, AND THE SUN SHINES A LOT.
THERE IS NO POINT IN GEARING OUR FASHION
TO THE SOMBER, SEDATE EUROPEAN STYLE.
WE ARE CLOSER TO AFRICA THAN TO MILAN.

Das Wissen um die eigenen kulturellen Schätze seines Landes beflügelt Fred immer wieder. »Wir müssen in uns hineinschauen, sehen, dass wir als Einwandererland die unterschiedlichsten Wurzeln haben. Das ist eine Besonderheit, auf die Brasilien stolz sein kann. Und man darf eines nicht vergessen«, fügt er an, »Brasilien ist ein tropisches Land. Hier ist es heiß, hier scheint oft die Sonne. Es macht keinen Sinn, wenn wir uns bei der Mode am dunklen, gedeckten Stil der Europäer orientieren. Wir sind näher dran an Afrika als an Mailand.« 1998 begann Fred d'Orey damit, seine Kollektionen auf der Rio Fashion Show zu zeigen. Seither zählt er zu den stilbildenden Designern des Landes mit elf eigenen Geschäften. Alle kreativen Prozesse werden unmittelbar von ihm bestimmt, auch die Fotoshootings. Regelmäßig tauchen in den Aufnahmen für Werbung, Katalog und Internetauftritt Anspielungen aus der Welt der Rockmusik auf. »Musik und Kultur haben schon immer mein Handeln bestimmt«, sagt d'Orey. 1962 geboren, erlebte er in seiner Kindheit und Jugend den Einzug der Rockkultur in Brasilien und deren Vermischung mit dem Bossa Nova. Sein Podcast auf der Totem-Website ist Kult. Seit fünf Jahren initiiert er auch ein viel beachtetes Musikfilmfestival in Rio. Durch seine Prominenz und seine Glaubwürdigkeit steht Fred zudem an der Spitze der aktuellen Antikorruptionsbewegung im Bundesstaat Rio.

Fred sieht sich als politischen Menschen. Von der Schickimicki-Szene in Rio de Janeiro hält er sich bewusst fern. Als Sohn eines brasilianischen Formel-1-Piloten und einer schwedischen Diplomatentochter holte er sich schon in frühen Jahren sein Selbstbewusstsein durch das Surfen. Mit dieser Szene ist er noch heute verwachsen. John Seaton Callahan, der als Indiana Jones der Surf-Fotografen gilt, zählt zu seinen besten Freunden. Mit ihm und anderen Kumpels zieht Fred immer wieder zu den besten Surfspots der Welt. »Meine Aufgabe besteht darin, nein zu sagen«, erklärt Fred. Nein zu Entwürfen, die seiner Meinung nach den Stil seiner Mode verwässern, nein zur Vereinnahmung durch andere, um die Art von Frieden finden zu können, wie sie ihm das Meer schenkt. Wo Frauen ihre nackten Füße das ganze Jahr über eher notdürftig

Brazil's rich cultural treasures serve Fred as a continual source of inspiration. "We need to look at ourselves and see that we have great diversity thanks to our history as an immigration country. This is a feature that Brazil should be proud of." In 1998, Fred d'Orey started presenting his collections at the Rio Fashion Show. This established his reputation as an influential Brazilian designer and he has, in the meantime, expanded to 11 outlet stores. He personally manages all the creative processes himself – including the photo shoots. And a striking feature in his ads, catalogs and on his website are the recurring themes from rock culture and music. "Music and culture have always had a powerful influence on me," says d'Orey. Born in 1962, he grew up in a time when rock gained popularity in Brazil and started blending with the indigent bossa nova. His podcasts on the Totem website have attained cult status. And five years ago, he initiated a music and film festival in Rio that has meanwhile received a lot of favorable attention. Using his status and credibility, Fred also acts as a leading figure in the current anti-corruption movement in the province of Rio.

Fred sees himself as a political sort of person and has no desire to mingle with the rich and the beautiful in Rio. As the offspring of a Brazilian Formula One pilot and the daughter of a Swedish Ambassador to France, Fred soon discovered that surfing was the turf in which he excelled. Today, he is still closely connected with the surf scene and counts John Seaton Callahan – the "Indiana Jones" of surf photographers – among his best friends. Together with some other surf aficionados, they are always on the go to discover yet another excellent surf spot in the world. "Basically my main task in business is to say no," Fred explains. No to designs he thinks dilute the tone of his fashion, no to those who try to tie him down. The latter is crucial for him in order to maintain the sense of peace and inspiration the ocean gives him. In a land where women are accustomed to wearing flip-flops and sandals all year round, the clothes they wear should be geared to this casual lifestyle. As if they are made to be carelessly tugged out of a beach tote and pulled on over a body still glistening from the Atlantic waves. His most important employee is Design Director Yamê Reis, who maintains the continuous development of the Totem style. The mother of world-class surfer Maya Gabeira, she is in

*Totem
brazilian flavo
não dá pra parar

mit Flip Flops und Sandalen straßenfähig machen, soll und muss ein Kleid wirken wie schnell mal aus der Strandtasche befördert und über die feuchte, noch vom Salz des Atlantiks glitzernde Haut gezogen. Seine wichtigste Mitarbeiterin ist die Designdirektorin Yamê Reis. Sie hat die Aufgabe, den Totem-Stil weiterzuentwickeln. Als Mutter der Weltklasse-Surferin Maya Gabeira hat sie viel Gespür für die modischen Bedürfnisse der jungen Generation, gleichzeitig experimentiert sie mit für Totem ungewöhnlichen Materialien wie Seide oder gewebten Stoffen. »Eine Erfolgsformel kann irgendwann auch zu einer Falle werden, wenn man sich nicht weiterentwickelt. Wir haben eine herausragende Stellung durch unsere Prints, werden aber immer öfter kopiert. Deshalb müssen wir Nachahmern stets einen Schritt voraus sein. Wir wollen in Zukunft nicht nur das Strandfeeling abbilden, sondern auch den temporeichen urbanen Lebensstil des neuen Brasilien repräsentieren«, sagt Fred. »Absorbieren und Übersetzen heißt die Devise. Es wäre das Ende der Firma, wenn meine Neugier steckenbleiben würde.« —

touch with the fashion taste of the young generation and does not hesitate to experiment with fabrics that are new to the Totem line such as silk or woven textiles. "Even the most sure-fire formula for success can become a trap if it is not continually developed. Thanks to our prints we have achieved an excellent position, but we are being copied more and more. We need to stay one step ahead of our imitators. In the future, although we will continue with our beach experience lifestyle, we also intend to create fashion suited to the upbeat cosmopolitan lifestyle of the new Brazil," says Fred. "Soak up and interpret is our motto. It would be the end of the company if my sense of curiosity was to strand." —

29

Zai
Simon Jacomet

Text **Olivia El Sayed** Photos **Gian Marco Castelberg**

Die kleine Schweizer Skimanufaktur wurde nach ihren zwei Co-Brandings mit dem britischen Automobilhersteller Bentley und der Uhrenmarke Hublot dank ihrer außergewöhnlichen Geschichte 2011 zum ersten Mal offizieller Ausrüster der FIS Alpine Ski WM in Garmisch-Partenkirchen. Nun feiert die junge Marke Zai ihren neuesten Coup: Eine eigene, hochwertige Skibekleidungslinie in Zusammenarbeit mit Loro Piana.

After two prestigious co-brandings, one with British carmaker Bentley and the other with Swiss watchmaker Hublot, in 2011, the small Swiss ski manufacturer was chosen to be the official supplier for the FIS Alpine Ski world championship in Garmisch-Partenkirchen. Now the young brand Zai is celebrating its latest coup: an independent and high-quality skiwear range in cooperation with Loro Piana.

Bei den zahlreichen grellen Skiern, die uns in der Schlange vor dem Lift so oft über die eigenen Bretter scheppern, vergisst man schnell, dass unter all dem bunten Lack eigentlich nichts anderes liegt als zwei simple Holzlatten. Auch bei Zai ist dies nicht anders, nur dass diese Bretter ihren Ursprung nicht unter einer Schicht schreierischem Marketing verbergen, sondern ihn vielmehr unterstreichen: Je nach Modell ist das Holz am fertigen Produkt noch zu sehen, manchmal auch in unlackierter Form. Das Modell »spada«, das den Schnee in der Kurve schwertgleich unter sich teilt, verfügt sogar über einen Kern aus Granit.

Der typische Zai-Ski ist schlicht und elegant. Braun, schwarz oder grau. Jacomet vermutet als Grund für dieses – und damit auch sein eigenes – Designempfinden die Verwurzelung mit seiner Heimat. Ohne den fluffigen Schneemantel, der das Dorf im Winter umhüllt, ist Disentis ein ziemlich felsiger, rauer Ort. Die Farben von Stein, Erde und Holz dominieren und beeinflussen so seit jeher das ästhetische Empfinden des Skibauers, der nach seiner Zeit als Kunststudent in Florenz bei den Herstellern Völkl und Salomon in der Entwicklung tätig war, bevor er sich 2003 selbständig machte.

Garish and gaudy skis crossing our path on the slopes – or scraping over our own skis as we stand in line at the ski lift – have made us forget that, beneath all that bright varnish, a ski is essentially a wooden slat. Zai skis are no different, except that Zai chooses to not hide its prime material underneath a layer of flashy marketing, preferring instead to reveal it. Which is why on some models the wood is left bare, sometimes even unvarnished. Model "spada," which, true to its name, cleaves the snow beneath it like a sword, even features a granite core.

Typically a Zai ski is characterized by its understated elegance in brown, black or grey hues. Simon Jacomet, the ski-maker, suspects his alpine heritage is the reason underlying this – that is to say, his – choice in design. Underneath the fluffy white layer that coats his native Disentis in winter lies a stony, rugged mountain landscape. As far back as he can remember, the raw, natural colors of the rocks, soil and wood have dominated and influenced his aesthetic taste. Jacomet, who studied art in Florence, Italy, worked in the development department of ski manufacturers, Völkl and Salomon, before going independent in 2003.

OUR CREED IS THE REDUCTION TO THE ESSENTIAL
IN OUR QUEST FOR NATURAL BALANCE.
A ZAI SKI CONSISTS OF EVERYTHING A GOOD SKI
NEEDS – AND NOTHING MORE.

»Unser Ziel ist die Reduktion auf das Wesentliche und damit verbunden die Suche nach natürlicher Stimmigkeit. Ein Zai-Ski hat alles, was ein guter Ski braucht – und nichts mehr«, erklärt Jacomet. Die schlichte, naturbelassene Eleganz im Design findet inzwischen viel mehr Anklang, als Jacomet je erwartet hätte. Doch je größer die Nachfrage, umso wichtiger wird ihm zu betonen, dass nicht das Design, sondern die optimierte Fahrleistung den Zai-Ski definiert. Aber da der Mensch nun mal schneller schaut als auf besagtem Ski einen Hang bezwingt, hat Jacomet beim Pochen auf die inneren Werte einen ähnlich schweren Stand wie die Engel von Victoria's Secret. Ein Grund mehr, warum er sich so darüber

This concept, which translates into simple, natural elegance, has meanwhile created a much higher resonance than Simon Jacomet ever anticipated. The higher the demand, the more he feels compelled to emphasize that design is not the end to the means. What really counts is optimizing the ski's performance. But first impressions are generally formed in a brief glance, much faster than the time it actually takes to test the skis on a slope. And so, despite Jacomet's tireless repetition, he has a hard time getting his message about inner values across. Therefore, he was doubly delighted to be chosen as the official supplier for this year's FIS Alpine Ski world championship: "Our supplying the world championship is raising public awareness that underneath the

freut, Skiausrüster für die FIS Alpine Ski WM gewesen zu sein: »Durch diese Zusammenarbeit wurde offiziell bekannt, dass hinter der schönen Optik eine ausgeklügelte Technologie steckt – das Design allein hätte uns nicht so weit gebracht.« Für die Organisatoren der WM kamen nur Marken mit einer gewissen Philosophie als Ausrüster in Frage: Zai ist kein Großkonzern, der wie ein Sponsor Geld in die WM hätte investieren können. Es sind also vielmehr emotionale Werte, die Zai von der Konkurrenz differenzieren. Es ist die junge Geschichte dieser überschaubaren Manufaktur in Disentis, und es ist die technologische Innovation, die den Skihersteller auszeichnen. Während andere Hersteller sich in ihrer Arbeitsweise zu sehr gleichen, sich in manchen Fällen sogar die Investoren teilen, arbeitet Zai unabhängig. Der Drang, sich stetig zu verbessern und Neues auszuprobieren, spielt dabei eine bezeichnende Rolle. So führte das Co-Branding mit Hublot dazu, dass erstmals derselbe Kautschuk, wie er auch für die Hublot-Uhren verwendet wird, auf Skioberflächen angewandt wurde. Und in Zusammenarbeit mit den Bentley-Designern wurde ein gänzlich neuer Verbundstoff aus Karbonfasern erzeugt, der den geschützten Namen »Zaiïra« trägt. Dieser Verbundstoff erlaubt nicht nur eine Gewichtsreduktion des Skis, sondern trägt auch zu seiner Nachhaltigkeit bei. Die Oberflächen können dank der Verwendung des Verbundstoffs mit Karbonfasern nach Gebrauch mehrmals nachbearbeitet werden und bleiben so länger unversehrt. Das jüngste Modell der Manufaktur, der »nezza«, wird aus einem Rohling aus eben diesem Material gefräst. Die stetig angestrebte technologische Optimierung prägt die Markengeschichte und macht sie, so Jacomet, zu einem substanziellen Wert des Unternehmens. Es war nicht immer so, dass Simon Jacomet und sein Team den Anfragen fast nicht nachkommen konnten. Neben den Materialien brachten die Handarbeit und die oftmals limitierte Stückzahl der Zai-Ski für Käufer unerwartet hohe Preise mit sich, die sich erst etablieren mussten. Rückblickend meint Simon Jacomet, dass ihm seine Kompromisslosigkeit der letzten Jahre in dieser Sache viel geholfen habe. Den gerümpften Nasen um ihn herum erklärte er die Preise sachlich und unaufgeregt, denn er wusste stets um ihre Legitimität:» Qualität bedeutet für mich, dass ein Produkt mich nie langweilt und mir die Freude daran erhalten bleibt. Dafür muss es langlebig sein und das Material muss stimmen. Wenn diese Werte erfüllt sind, gehört der Preis dazu.«

attractive design lies sophisticated technology – the design alone would not have brought us this far. "Only companies with a clear philosophy are taken into consideration as potential suppliers. Zai is not a large manufacturer who could sponsor part of the event. It has, however, a distinctive appeal that sets it apart from its competitors. A relatively short history as a small-scale manufacturer in Disentis and its technological innovations make it attractive. Where other producers are nearly indistinguishable, sometimes even sharing the same investors, Zai works independently. The drive to continually improve and experiment with new materials and processes plays a crucial role. The co-branding with Hublot led to utilizing for the first time on a ski the same type of rubber that Hublot uses for their watches. And, during their cooperation with the Bentley designers, a new carbon fiber composite material was created that now carries the name "zaiïra." This material not only weighs less – it also contributes to the skis' longevity. Due to the use of carbon, the surfaces can be reworked several times, thereby significantly increasing the lifespan of the ski. The newest ski model in development, the "nezza," is shaped from a blank of the state-of-the-art material. Zai's continuous quest for technological improvement is an outstanding feature in the company's history and constitutes, says Jacomet, a significant asset to the brand. Today, Simon Jacomet and his team are hardly able to satisfy customer demand, but that was not always the case. The cost of choice materials and the handwork as well as the limited production numbers added up to an unusually high price tag that needed time to justify itself. Looking back, Jacomet muses that it was probably his refusal to compromise that helped them to overcome this hurdle. Knowing that prices were based on hard figures, he dealt with the raised eyebrows of skeptical clients by explaining the costs in a calm, businesslike manner: "Quality to me means that a product retains its thrill and continues to give satisfaction for a long time. The product has to have a long life span, and you need to use the right materials. Fulfilling these criteria comes with a certain price."

Each year, new models are developed with the aim to create the perfect equipment to dominate the slopes and to enable each skier to ratchet their skills up a notch. In order to achieve this, Jacomet takes each prototype and, after personally sanding and filing it down to his satisfaction, skis on them for days on end, honing the model until he is sure that he has created something that will stand up to his team's valued and crucial judgment.

Jedes nicht hundertprozentige Ja ist für mich ein definitives Nein.

Jedes Jahr entstehen neue Skimodelle mit dem Ziel, das optimale Instrument zu schaffen, um den Schnee zu beherrschen und es jedem Fahrer zu ermöglichen, seine persönlichen Grenzen auszuweiten. Um dies zu garantieren, schleift, feilt und fährt Jacomet einen Ski tagelang, bis er sicher ist, etwas geschaffen zu haben, das der geschätzten Kritik seiner Teamkollegen standhalten kann. Erst dann geht ein Modell in die

Only then does it go into production. "To me, every yes that is not a one-hundred-percent yes is simply a no," Jacomet says. This attitude is mirrored in the product's name. "Zai" is the word for tough and resilient in Rhaeto-Romanic, the tongue of the mountain folk in Jacomet's region. (The official fourth language of Switzerland, Rhaeto-Romanic is still spoken by some ten thousand people today.) The word "zai" also symbolizes a conviction: the